On Liberty

John Stuart Mill

On Liberty

John Stuart Mill

Edited by

Edward Alexander

broadview literary texts

Canadian Cataloguing in Publication Data

Mill, John Stuart, 1806–1873.
  On liberty

  (Broadview literary texts)
  Includes bibliographical references and index.
  ISBN 1-55111-199-3

  1. Liberty. I. Alexander, Edward, 1936– II. Title. III. Series.
JC585.M6 1999   323.44   C99-910132-3

Broadview Press
Post Office Box 1243, Peterborough, Ontario, Canada K9J 7H5

in the United States of America:
3576 California Road, Orchard Park, NY 14127

in the United Kingdom:
B.R.A.D. Book Representation & Distribution Ltd.,
244A, London Road, Hadleigh, Essex SS7 2DE

Broadview Press gratefully acknowledges the support of the Canada Council, the Ontario Arts Council, and the Ministry of Canadian Heritage.

Pre-Press Production:
Jeremy Drought, Last Impression Publishing Service, Calgary, Alberta

Cover:
Shad fishing in the Jesus Rapids, Back River (Rivière des Prairies), Montreal, c1865. William Notman.

PRINTED IN CANADA

Contents

Acknowledgements

I AM GRATEFUL to the University of Toronto Press, holder of the copyright, for permission to reproduce the text of *On Liberty* edited by the late Professor John M. Robson, and for permission to reproduce some of his notes. I would also like to thank Professor Jack Stillinger for permission to use some of the notes in his Riverside edition (1969) of *On Liberty*, published by Houghton Mifflin. For help and suggestions of various kinds, I am indebted to the following: Leon Bensadon, Courtney Chesser, Jennifer Holberg, Raymond Jonas, Hillel J. Kieval, Willis Konick, Kathy Mork, Bernard Saffran, Rob Weller, Helene Williams, and Ruth R. Wisse.

John Stuart Mill

John Stuart Mill:
A Brief Chronology

1806   Born 20 May in London, the eldest son of James and Harriet Mill. Eight sisters and brothers born between 1808 and 1825.

1809   Beginning of intensive education at home, which continues until his visit to France in 1820.

1820–21   Year in France, in the household of Sir Samuel Bentham.

1821   Studies the work of Bentham; the principle of utility becomes his "religion."

1822   Studies law with John Austin. First publication: two letters in a newspaper.

1823   Forms Utilitarian Society, lasting until 1826. Begins career with East India Company as a clerk in the office of the Examiner of India Correspondence. Arrested for distributing birth-control tracts.

1824   Founding of *Westminster Review*, for which he wrote until 1828.

1825   Begins editing Jeremy *Bentham's Rationale of Judicial Evidence*, published 1827. Helps found London Debating Society.

1826   Mental crisis.

1830   Meets and soon falls in love with Harriet Hardy Taylor, wife
        of John Taylor. Visits Paris during the Revolution, and starts
        to write extensively on French political affairs.

1831   Publishes a series of articles on "The Spirit of the Age" in
        the Examiner. Meets Carlyle.

1832   Death of Jeremy Bentham. Passage of first Reform Bill.

1835   Founds and edits the *London Review*, which continues (after
        first year) as *London and Westminster Review* until 1840.
        Accidentally destroys first volume of Carlyle's *French
        Revolution*.

1836   Death of father, James Mill. Several months of severe illness.

1838   Publishes "Bentham" in *London and Westminster Review*.

1840   Publishes "Coleridge" in *London and Westminster Review*.

1843   Publishes *A System of Logic* (eight editions in his lifetime).

1844   Publishes *Essays on Some Unsettled Questions of Political
        Economy*.

1848   Publishes *Principles of Political Economy* (seven editions in
        his lifetime).

1851   Marries Harriet Taylor, whose husband John had died in
        1849. Begins to sever links with his own family.

1854 From December until June 1855, on extended holiday for reasons of health in Italy and Greece.

1856 Becomes Chief Examiner of India Correspondence in East India Company, as his father had once been.

1858 Retires from East India Company when it is taken over by the Crown. Harriet Taylor Mill dies in Avignon, where Mill will subsequently spend half of each year.

1859 Publishes *On Liberty, Thoughts on Parliamentary Reform,* and *Dissertations and Discussions,* volumes I and II.

1861 Publishes *Considerations on Representative Government* and *Utilitarianism* (in *Fraser's Magazine,* and then as a book in 1863).

1862 Visits Greece with Helen Taylor.

1865 Elected as Member of Parliament for Westminster, and serves until defeat in 1868. Publishes *Auguste Comte and Positivism* and *An Examination of Sir William Hamilton's Philosophy.*

1866 Secures freedom of speech in Hyde Park.

1867 Publishes *Inaugural Address Delivered to the University of St. Andrew's* (Scotland), of which he had been elected Rector in 1866, and *Dissertations and Discussions,* volume III. Passage of second Reform Bill, which Mill had tried to amend to allow for women's suffrage and proportional representation. Tries to prosecute Governor Eyre of Jamaica for murder.

1868 Publishes *England and Ireland.*

1869   Publishes *The Subjection of Women* and a new edition of James Mill's *Analysis of the Phenomena of the Human Mind.*

1870   Publishes *Chapters and Speeches on the Irish Land Question* (reprinted from *Principles of Political Economy* and *Hansard's Parliamentary Debates*).

1873   Dies on 7 May in Avignon.

Posthumous publications, all edited by his stepdaughter, Helen Taylor:

1873   *Autobiography.*

1874   *Three Essays on Religion.*

1875   *Dissertations and Discussions,* volume IV.

1879   *Chapters on Socialism.*

Introduction

"How the sweet, ingenuous nature of the man has lived and thriven out of his father's cold and stringent atheism is wonderful to think, and most so to me, who during fifteen years have seen his gradual growth and ripening."

John Sterling (letter to Ralph Waldo Emerson, 7 October 1843)[1]

JOHN STUART MILL was one of the most ardent feminists of the Victorian era. Yet one searches his autobiography in vain for a single mention of his mother, Harriet Mill. She did appear in Mill's early draft of the book, but Mill—ever deferential to the instructions of his wife (also, as Freudians have noted with glee, Harriet Mill)—deleted all references to her. Among the cancelled passages, perhaps the one most revealing of the emotional tone that prevailed in the Mill family, of the predominance of fear over love, is the following: "I believe there is less personal affection in England than in any other country of which I know anything, & I give my father's family not as peculiar in this respect but only as a too faithful exemplification of the ordinary fact. That rarity in England, a really warm hearted mother, would in the first place have made the children grow up loving & being loved. But my mother with the very best intentions, only knew how to pass her life in drudging for them...but to make herself loved, looked up to, or even obeyed, required qualities which she unfortunately did not possess. I thus grew up in the absence of love & in the presence of fear: & many & indelible are the effects of this bringing-up, in the stunting of my moral growth."[2]

The dominant figure in Mill's childhood and early education was his father, James Mill, radical political reformer, historian of British India, associationist psychologist, theorist of education. The elder Mill presented his theory of education in an article that appeared in the supplement to the fifth edition of the *Encyclopedia Britannica*. In it he argued that education is essentially the skillful manipulation of sequences of thoughts or impressions. Since all differences between individuals and classes of men result from differences of education, education is the sovereign remedy for individual or class inferiority, and the means for raising the whole human race to the level of its noblest individuals. "What a field for exertion!" exclaimed Mill. "What a prize to be won!" To apply the science of education to the perfection of human life, one must decide what are the objects of human desire, select the morally best means of attaining them, and "accustom the mind to fill up the intermediate space between the present sensation and the ultimate object, with nothing but the idea of those beneficent means." Since sequences of impressions begin to occur as soon as a child is born, it becomes extremely important to begin the child's education while he is still in the cradle.[3]

James Mill decided to practice what he preached in the education of his first son, John Stuart, who was born on May 20, 1806, in London. He assumed exclusive charge of John's education from the beginning, and brought him up in isolation from other children and from adults who were not certified radicals, for sound education had to be in conflict with custom and communal traditions. Little John Stuart was also kept out of schools, which, his father believed, tended generally to reenforce the influence of a vicious and ignorant society. When opportunities arose in 1821 and 1823 for John to go to Cambridge, James Mill told the interested parties that his son already knew more than he could ever be taught at Cambridge. When John went abroad to France in 1820, he was put in custody of the brother of Jeremy Bentham, chief theorist of the radical movement; during the year there he became fluent in French.

It is no exaggeration to say that John Stuart Mill was brought up as the secret weapon (or, in Carlyle's jaundiced view, the "son of a demonstration") of the radical movement in England, a carefully nurtured prodigy from whom great things were expected (and from whom, after all, some great things did come). Just how closely the Benthamites guarded their special prodigy is suggested by a letter from Bentham to James Mill in 1812, when John was six. Hearing that James Mill was ill, Bentham, fearing the worst, offered his services in the education of the budding social reformer in case Mill did not live to complete the task:

> If you will appoint me guardian to Mr. John Stuart Mill, I will, in the event of his father's being disposed of elsewhere…by whipping or otherwise, do whatsoever may seem most necessary and proper, for teaching him to make all proper distinctions, as between the Devil and the Holy Ghost, and how to make Codes and Encyclopedias, and whatsoever else may be proper to be made, so long as I remain an inhabitant of this vale of tears.[4]

Mill claimed that he wrote his autobiography primarily to provide a record of "an education which was unusual and remarkable and which…has proved how much more than is commonly supposed may be taught, and well taught, in those early years which, in the common modes of what is called instruction, are little better than wasted." Although prior to 1819 (when he obtained an appointment in the India House) James Mill had no means of support except writing, he would always find time—perhaps more than any parent ever has—for the instruction of his son. "I have no remembrance of the time when I began to learn Greek. I have been told that it was when I was three years old. My earliest recollection on the subject, is that of committing to memory what my father termed Vocables, being lists of common Greek words, with their signification in English, which he wrote out for me on cards….I learnt no Latin until my eighth year. At that time I had read, under my father's tuition, a number of Greek prose authors, among whom I remember the whole of Herodotus, and of Xenophon's Cyropaedia and Memorials of Socrates; some of the lives of the philosophers by Diogenes Laertius; part of Lucian, and Isocrates ad Demonicum and ad Nicoclem. I also read, in 1813, the first six dialogues…of Plato, from the Euthyphron to the Theaetetus inclusive: which last dialogue, I venture to think, would have been better omitted, as it was totally impossible I should understand it." To this (somewhat humorless) recollection, Mill adds the highly revealing detail that since in those days Greek-English lexicons did not exist and, not having yet learned Latin, he could not make use of a Greek-Latin lexicon, he had to pester his father for the meaning of every single word he did not know. "This incessant interruption he, one of the most impatient of men, submitted to, and wrote under that interruption several volumes of his History and all else that he had to write during those years."[5]

Mill had no toys or children's books, apart from an occasional gift from a naive relative or acquaintance. Although his father did not consciously exclude such things from his son's childhood, it never occurred to him that they had any utility. This may explain why this highly unusual education has sometimes been thought the real-life model for Thomas Gradgrind's regimen of "fact" in Dickens' *Hard Times*, and for its disastrous effect on Gradgrind's daughter Louisa especially. Since *Hard Times* was published in 1854, Dickens could not have read Mill's autobiographical recollections before writing his novel, but he might have heard something of the extraordinary tale from Carlyle, the formidable gossip and onetime friend of Mill's to whom *Hard Times* is dedicated. In any case, the rigorous intellectual instruction that John Stuart received from his father was, whatever its shortcomings, very far from the anti-literary education of "fact" and cramming that Dickens contrives in his novel. Indeed, James Mill greatly preferred theory to fact; and his son read a great deal of poetry.

One aspect of Mill's unusual education worth keeping in mind when reading *On Liberty* is what his father taught him about religion. Although he had begun adult life as a Presbyterian clergyman, James Mill had long since rejected the doctrines of not only the Scottish, but of all churches. Indeed, he considered it his duty to inculcate in his son the conviction that Christianity was not merely false but was the epitome of wickedness. "Think (he used to say) of a being who would make a Hell—who would create the human race with the infallible foreknowledge, and therefore with the intention, that the great majority of them were to be consigned to horrible and everlasting torment." As a result of this training in anti-religion, John Mill became one of the very few Victorians who did not have the experience of losing, or of throwing off, religious belief because he never had it and was brought up in a wholly negative state with regard to it.

In 1823, when he was seventeen, Mill began his career with the East India Company as a clerk in the office of the Examiner of India Correspondence, where he wrote dispatches and made policy for the Princely States. When his father was promoted to second place in the Examiner's office of India House, his vacated post was conferred by the court of directors upon his son, "on a footing," wrote James Mill, "on which he will in all probability be in the receipt of a larger income at an early age than he would be in any profession."[6] The young Mill did not in fact receive a great deal of money (an annual gratuity of thirty pounds), but he had material security for life at a remarkably early age. True, he had to work under the eye and order of his father, but only for six hours a day, not very much by Millite standards of diligence and application.

In 1824 James Mill, having decided that England needed a third political party, a radical one, founded the *Westminster Review* to promote the radical program, and his son became an eager and prolific contributor. For the first eighteen numbers of the new quarterly, John Stuart supplied thirteen articles, more than any other contributor. He was a most able expounder of the principles of Benthamism, which was for him the secular substitute for the religious belief his father had denounced. Indeed, religious language permeates his account of how, after his first reading of Bentham's *magnum opus*, the *Traité de Législation*, the great principle of utility had unified all he had formerly thought and known, and given him "a creed, a doctrine, a philosophy; in one among the best senses of the word, a religion; the inculcation and diffusion of which could be made the principal outward purpose of a life."[7] (Later, when he departed from Benthamite orthodoxy, Mill had a strong sense of having apostatized. David Masson recalls how, in 1843, Mill, while discussing Bentham's remaining disciples, suddenly remarked: "And I am Peter, who denied his master."[8])

But Benthamism, like many another Victorian attempt to find a secular substitute for values that the religious tradition could no longer sustain, failed Mill in his time of crisis. This came in the autumn of 1826, when Mill, at age twenty, in "a dull state of nerves…one of those moods when what is pleasure at other times, becomes insipid or indifferent," awoke from the dream that dedication to the Benthamite goal of the greatest happiness for the greatest number would also make *him* happy. This crisis in his mental history was the defining moment of Mill's life; and his account of it in the fifth chapter of his autobiography affords a rare Victorian instance of a radical telling the truth about the personal failure of his political system:

> …[I]t occurred to me to put the question directly to myself, "Suppose that all your objects in life were realized; that all the changes in institutions and opinions which you are looking forward to, could be completely effected at this very instant: would this be a great joy and happiness to you?" And an irrepressible self-consciousness distinctly answered, "No!" At this my heart sank within me: the whole foundation on which my life was constructed fell down. All my happiness was to have been found in the continual pursuit of this end. The end had ceased to charm, and how could there ever again be any interest in the means? I seemed to have nothing left to live for.[9]

Mill goes on to affix blame for his crisis on the associationist psychology of his father's educational regimen: "My education, which was wholly his work, had been conducted without any regard to the possibility of its ending in this result." The rescue from suicidal despair came from Mill's accidental reading of Marmontel's Memoirs, in which the French writer relates his father's death, the distressed position of his family, "and the sudden inspiration by which he, then a mere boy, felt and made them feel that he would be everything to them—would supply the place of all that they had lost."[10] Mill was moved to tears by Marmontel's account; and from that moment forward his burden grew lighter. Mill does not comment on what nowadays would be called the "Freudian" implication of this episode, the suggestion that he harbored a death wish towards his own father. Freud himself did comment on Mill, but only on his (and his wife's) "inhuman" aversion to sensuality, as Freud had concluded on the basis of Mill's *Autobiography*.[11] Nor does he make explicit what surely is crucial in this contrast between Marmontel's youth and his own: namely, that it is suffering, not the pursuit of happiness, that is crucial in human experience.

Although Mill had several relapses after this recovery, he was never again so miserable as he had been before his experience of Marmontel. The crisis and its immediate aftermath led him to adopt a new theory of life, very similar to Carlyle's anti-self-consciousness theory: namely, that although happiness is indeed the test of all rules of conduct, as utilitarianism stipulated, "those only are happy...who have their minds fixed on some object other than their own happiness; on the happiness of others, on the improvement of mankind....Ask yourself whether you are happy, and you cease to be so."[12]

The second great change that resulted from Mill's crisis and recovery from it was that, for the first time, he assigned its rightful place among the necessary elements of human well-being to "the internal culture of the individual." He now understood that the passive susceptibilities needed to be cultivated as much as the active ones. He enlarged rather than rejected his old creed. Having discovered what may befall the mind through excess and distortion, the scanting of impulse and will, he still affirmed the idea of mind, which, properly used, is the sole means by which human beings can communicate with each other. "I never turned recreant to intellectual culture, or ceased to consider the power and practice of analysis as an essential condition both of individual and of social improvement. But I thought that it had consequences which required to be corrected, by joining other kinds of cultivation with it."[13]

By way of creating a due balance among his faculties, Mill now began to read poetry and listen to music with new seriousness. Crucial in his new idea of self-cultivation was the poetry of Wordsworth, whom he read for the first time (a remarkable admission!) in the autumn of 1828. Wordsworth's poems were "a medicine" for his state of mind, the very culture of the feelings which he was in quest of. The inward joy they conferred was independent of politics, had no connection with partisan struggle, and "could be shared in by all human beings."[14] At a time when Wordsworth had become a *bête noir* of radicals because of his growing conservatism, including support of capital punishment and of the established church, Mill—as if in defiance of his old teachers and his inherited creed—sought out Wordsworth's company. In July 1831, he made several pilgrimages to Grasmere in order to sit at the feet of the aging poet. Indeed, John Sterling told Mill that he had shared the widespread view of the utilitarians' prodigy as a manufactured man until he found that Wordsworth "belonged" to Mill just as much as to Sterling and his friends.

It should be remembered that our knowledge of the crisis in Mill's mental history derives largely from the account he gave of it in the early draft of the *Autobiography*, which he was working on in 1853–4, the very time that he had begun work on *On Liberty*, the work that concerns us in this volume. We should not therefore be surprised that the ideas about self-development and "many-sidedness" and the complexity of human character that are adumbrated in the fifth chapter of the *Autobiography* appear in a more socio-political form in *On Liberty*.

Almost as crucial in Mill's personal development as his mental crisis and recovery from it—a process extending almost three years and which he called the only actual revolution ever to take place in his way of thinking—was his meeting with Harriet Hardy Taylor (of Unitarian background) in 1830. Both of them were twenty-four years old; but Mill was single, and Harriet was very much married. She and her husband John, who was eleven years older than she, already had two children when Mill made their acquaintance; and he soon learned of her dissatisfaction both with her dull husband and with the messy experience of childbirth, which she would endure once more in 1832. By that time, encouraged by Mill, she was trying to become a writer like Harriet Martineau, contributing regularly to the *Monthly Repository* book reviews, poems, and articles.

A foreshadowing of the relation between illusion and reality in Mill's conception of Harriet's sublime genius, poetical and intellectual, may be found in an incident of July 1832. On a ramble in the Isle of Wight, Mill recalled an unsigned landscape description which he had read in the *Repository* and assumed to have been written by Harriet. He wrote in his journal: "To some it [Sandown Bay] might appear less interesting than many other parts of the southern coast; but to me it was consecrated by the touch of genius: it had been the subject of one of the most beautiful sketches in our recent literature, which, though it appeared in a fugitive publication (the *Monthly Repository*) will, I trust, some time or other be reprinted, and will hold a distinguished place among the works of its author."[14] Unfortunately, Mill learned (in November of the following year) that the author of the sketch was W. J. Fox, editor of the journal. But this did not lessen his confidence that Harriet could, and would, do something even better.

The question of Harriet Taylor's abilities and influence upon Mill has been debated for over a century. Not only Mill's fervent disciples such as Alexander Bain and John Morley, but later figures like Harold Laski took the view that Mill was "literally the only person who was in the least impressed by her"; and Diana Trilling acerbically remarked that the woman whom Mill considered the intellectual beacon of his life was really much closer to being a vest-pocket flashlight of a mind. But in the 1970s, with the resurgence of feminism, both her abilities and her influence began to be reassessed. Alice Rossi, for example, cast doubt on the accuracy of some of the scathing earlier judgments and questioned the motives behind them. Gertrude Himmelfarb argued, largely on the basis of a comparison of Mill's writing with the few sustained pieces of writing known to be by Taylor, that both *On Liberty* and *The Subjection of Women* were indeed much influenced by her; but Himmelfarb also went on to deplore that influence, finding that it made Mill a more dogmatic and less nuanced writer than he was in works not conceived jointly with her.[15]

Himmelfarb's thesis of "the two Mills" was itself called into question by both Phyllis Rose (*Parallel Lives: Five Victorian Marriages*, 1983) and C.L. Ten (*Mill on Liberty*, 1980). Rose argued that Taylor's strong sense of direction continued to exert influence on Mill's writing long after her death.

Ten criticized the "two Mills" thesis without arguing the question of Harriet Taylor's abilities or influence. The controversy is unlikely ever to be resolved, but the general view today is that although Taylor greatly influenced Mill in the conception and execution of *On Liberty*, the writing itself is his.[16]

What is entirely clear is that Mill was desperately in love with Mrs. Taylor, and she with him; nor, despite Carlyle's habit of referring to Harriet as "Mrs. (Platonica) Taylor," and Mill's tendency to speak of human sexuality as an "animal function," was their feeling for each other exclusively Platonic. Jane Welsh Carlyle was nearer the mark than her husband when she described Harriet as "a dangerous looking woman and engrossed with a dangerous passion."[17] There is, nevertheless, no reason to doubt Mill's claim (strongly supported by their correspondence) that their relation to each other prior to John Taylor's death was one of strong affection and confidential intimacy only. Carlyle might deride the relationship as "a verra foolish piece o' friendliness," and Alexander Bain might warn Helen Taylor, when she was editing the autobiography for publication in 1873, of the impropriety of "your printing those sentences where he declares her to be a greater poet than Carlyle...and a greater thinker than himself—and...a greater leader than his father"[18]; and that father himself might chastise his son (in a spectacular instance of "failure of communication" between the two) for forgetting that Mrs. Taylor was another man's property, and that utilitarians still believed in the sanctity of private property. But there is no denying that, for better or worse, Harriet exercised considerable influence on Mill, and nowhere more so than in the composition of *On Liberty*, as the dedication to it suggests.

After a great deal of disputation, frantic trips between London and Paris, attempts by Harriet to break off with Mill, the threesome finally worked out a friendly, if bizarre, arrangement in about 1834. For the next fifteen years, until John Taylor's death in 1849, John and Harriet took care never to be seen "in society" as a couple, but were allowed to go off on holidays together—one of the more peculiar examples of the Victorian "compromise."

Although the personal lives of some of the leading reformers were in turmoil—of the people he acidly referred to as "friends of the species," Carlyle said that "though this world is already blooming…in everlasting 'happiness of the greatest number,' these people's own *houses*…are little hells of improvidence, discord and unreason"[19]—the Age of Reform proceeded apace. The first Reform Bill was passed in 1832, but Mill and his fellow Radicals were quickly disappointed with the cautious spirit of the triumphant Whigs, whose leader John Russell announced in 1837 that no further reform of Parliament was necessary. In the Victorian period, as in modern times, Radicals, when frustrated, decided to start a magazine to promote their program. The idea of a new quarterly magazine had been in the mind of John Mill (who as an India House official was debarred from politics) ever since the passage of the bill; and in June of 1834 his wish was realized when a wealthy young baronet named William Molesworth guaranteed the money for the magazine on the sole condition that Mill should have total control over it.

As the *Autobiography* indicates, his editorship of what started in April 1835 as the *London Review* and then became the *London and Westminster Review* preoccupied Mill until 1840. Since he was now less firmly aligned with the old *Westminster Review* school of philosophic radicals than he once had been, he decided that every article in the new journal should carry an initial, or some other signature, indicating that it expressed the opinion solely of the individual writer, not of the editor or the magazine. While Mill was struggling with his new editorial responsibilities, he also had to face the decline in his father's health. Pulmonary consumption, a disease James Mill probably passed on to his son (who in turn probably infected Harriet with it, fatally) carried off James Mill on 23 June 1836.

In his conduct of the new review, Mill had two principal objects: one was "to free philosophic radicalism from the reproach of sectarian Benthamism"; the other was "to stir up the educated Radicals, in and out of Parliament, to exertion, and induce them to make themselves…a powerful party capable of taking the government of the country, or at least of dictating the terms on which they should share it with the Whigs."[20]

The latter attempt, Mill readily grants, proved chimerical. But the former resulted in two of his greatest essays, the paired philosophical estimates of the radical Bentham and the conservative Coleridge, the former published in the *London and Westminster* in 1838, the latter in the same journal in 1840.

These essays are important precursors to *On Liberty*, which they both foreshadow and contradict. Perhaps the wisest formulation of the complementary essays is the statement in "Coleridge" that "He has been, almost as truly as Bentham, 'the great questioner of things established'":

> for a questioner needs not necessarily be an enemy. By Bentham, beyond all others, men have been led to ask themselves in regard to any ancient or received opinion, Is it true? and by Coleridge, What is the meaning of it? The one took his stand *outside* the received opinion, and surveyed it as an entire stranger to it; the other looked at it from within, and endeavored to see it with the eyes of a believer in it....Bentham judged a proposition true or false as it accorded or not with the result of his own inquiries....With Coleridge, on the contrary, the very fact that any doctrine had been believed by thoughtful men, and received by whole nations or generations of mankind, was part of the problem to be solved, was one of the phenomena to be accounted for.

The fine evenhandedness of this comparison, shading slightly into a sympathy for the conservative idealist over the radical utilitarian, stands in contrast to the progressive Mill of *On Liberty*. So too does Mill's sympathetic rendition of Coleridge's insistence that one requisite of every civil society is the feeling of loyalty to "*something* which is settled, something permanent, and not to be called in question."[21]

But the essays also anticipate *On Liberty* in the theory of controversy that pervades them, the dialectical and synthetic method of seeking truth. Opposed thinkers like Bentham and Coleridge, Mill argues, may actually complement each other; each of them is so thoroughly the master of that portion of truth which he does see that he is blind to its incompleteness. It remains for the disinterested bystander (could he be J. S. Mill?) to synthesize into the whole truth the partial truths set forth by exponents of antithetical philosophical positions. What Mill in 1840 calls "the noisy conflict of half-truths" would much later, in *On Liberty*, supply one of his main justifications for freedom to challenge accepted opinions, which may be true or false, or only a part of the whole truth.

When the last hope for the formation of a Radical party disappeared, Mill decided it was time for him to stop the heavy expenditure of time and money which the *London and Westminster* cost him. After his Coleridge essay appeared, he turned the *Review* over to William Hickson and stipulated that the change be marked by its resuming the old name of the *Westminster Review*. As a writer, he preferred the greater circulation of the *Edinburgh Review*, and his inaugural contribution to it was his lengthy (and, for readers of *On Liberty*, very important) essay on Alexis de Tocqueville's *Democracy in America*. Even as he was composing his laudatory review, Mill told its author: "I do not think that anything more important than the publication of your book has happened even in this age of great events." Mill was especially pleased that Tocqueville had arrived at a conclusion exactly like the one that Mill had previously been "almost alone in standing up for here [in England]"—namely, that "the real danger in democracy, the real evil to be struggled against, and which all human resources employed while it is not yet too late are not more than sufficient to fence off—is not anarchy or love of change, but Chinese stagnation & immobility."[22] Nineteen years before the publication of *On Liberty*, Mill's reflections on Tocqueville's analysis of American democracy shadow forth not only a central theme of *On Liberty* but even its "Chinese" obsession.

From this time forth, says Mill at the beginning of Chapter VII of his autobiography, what is worth relating of his life can be contained within very small compass. In words that are eerily similar to those starting the fifth chapter of Newman's *Apologia pro Vita sua*—"From the time that I became a Catholic [1845], of course I have no further history of my religious opinions to narrate."—he declares that he has "no further mental changes to tell of, but only…a continued mental progress; which does not admit of a consecutive history, and the results of which…will be best found in my writings."[23]

The first use he made of his new leisure was to finish the *System of Logic*, a massive project that he had begun in 1830 and which would eventually be published in 1843. The book grew out of his (and his father's) conviction that everything rests on theory, that bad institutions and oppressive traditions derive from an unsound conception of the nature of the mind and of human knowledge: "The notion that truths external to the mind may be known by intuition or consciousness, independently of observation and experience is, I am persuaded, in these times, the great intellectual support of false doctrines and bad institutions."[24] His chief adversary was the German, or *à priori* view of human knowledge. As he told his German friend Theodor Gomperz, his great philosophical aim was to place "metaphysical and moral science on a basis of analysed experience, in opposition to the theory of innate principles so unfortunately patronized by the philosophers of your country.…I consider that school of philosophy as the greatest speculative hindrance to the regeneration so urgently required, of man and society."[25] The *Logic* would provide the philosophical underpinning for *On Liberty*'s belief in the possible improvement of mankind, and still more for *Subjection of Women*'s relentless assault on mistaking culture for biological destiny.

While he was laboring over the *System of Logic* Mill became involved with the work of Auguste Comte, at least with the first two volumes of the French philosopher's *Cours de Philosophie Positive*. Mill considered himself greatly indebted to Comte for insights into the theory of induction, and was for a time intensely respectful of his genius. But his disillusionment with Comte was perhaps as important a precursor of *On Liberty* as his unstinting devotion to Tocqueville. When Comte, in reaction against the Catholic Church, conceived a kind of Catholicism without Christianity, Mill became alarmed, and concluded that although they might be unified as logicians they were now sharply separated as sociologists. In the *Autobiography*, Mill observed that Comte, in his final work, the "Système de Politique Positive," had laid down "the completest system of spiritual and temporal despotism, which ever yet emanated from a human brain, unless possibly that of Ignatius Loyola."[26] In the first chapter of *On Liberty* Comte figures prominently as a frightening example of those modern reformers who, though they strongly opposed the religions of the past, asserted a right of spiritual domination at least equal to that of the churches or sects they had repudiated. The voice of Comte had been one of the clearest and most dangerous siren calls Mill ever heard; in 1859 he hoped to save others from the temptation that had nearly ensnared him.

In a cancelled passage of the original manuscript of his autobiography, Mill observed that the success of the *Logic* led to the publication in 1844 of the *Political Economy* essays. With these, he goes on, ended "what may be termed the second period of my writings; reckoning the old *Westminster Review* period as the first. The 'Principles of Political Economy' and all subsequent writings belong to a third and different stage of my mental progress, which was essentially characterized by the predominating influence of my wife's intellect and character."[27] In this third period, Mill turned back from what he thought to have been excessive in his reaction against Benthamism.

Mill's main intellectual preoccupations during the decade of the 1840s were the *Logic* and the *Principles of Political Economy*, which he worked on, with interruptions, from autumn 1845 until the end of 1847. The interruptions were occasioned mainly by Ireland's calamity—depopulation of that country occasioned by famine and continued by emigration. In the winter of 1846–7 Mill laid aside the *Principles* to urge (in a series of articles in the *Morning Chronicle*) the formation of peasant properties on the waste lands of Ireland in order both to relieve the immediate crisis and to effect the permanent improvement of the social and economic conditions of the Irish people.

Through these years Mill continued as a dutiful official of the British East India Company, albeit one who could complete his assigned tasks in half the hours he spent at India House and devote the remaining two or three to the *Logic* and the *Political Economy*, or to reading manuscripts—

he was very generous in this way—of neophyte writers. One of them described him as follows: "His tall slim figure, his youthful face and bald head, fair hair and ruddy complexion, and the twitching of his eyebrow when he spoke, first arrested the attention: then the vivacity of his manner, his thin voice approaching to sharpness, but with nothing shrill or painful about it, his comely features and sweet expression—would have remained in my memory though I had never seen him again."[28]

The *Principles of Political Economy* was published in April 1848. It would run into thirty-two editions in the next fifty years, and its peculiar evolution in its early years shows more strikingly (or shockingly) than anything else what Michael Packe calls "Harriet's astounding, almost hypnotic control of Mill's mind."[29] The book commenced its life as one of the classic expressions of *laissez-faire* economics and the desirability of a free market unfettered by monopoly: "wherever competition is not, monopoly is; and…monopoly, in all its forms, is the taxation of the industrious for the support of indolence, if not for plunder."[30] But Harriet was attached to communism, and instructed Mill to expunge from the second edition all his previous objections to socialism and communism. By the time Mill set to work on the third edition, Harriet had convinced him that the disabilities of women were the central issue of social philosophy. A newly inserted paragraph in the third edition asserted that once women "cease to be confined by custom to one physical function as their means of living and their source of influence,…they would have for the first time an equal voice with men in what concerns that function: and of all improvements in reserve for mankind which it is now possible to forsee, none might be expected to be so fertile as this in almost every kind of moral and social benefit."[31]

In July of 1849 John Taylor died, and after a decent interval of nearly two years Mill and Harriet married on Easter Monday 1851. The first year of marriage was a happy one, but by 1853 they began to be plagued by health problems, especially pulmonary consumption, diagnosed in Mill's case by March of 1854. The spectre of early death gave a sense of urgency to their work. In August 1853 Mill wrote this extraordinary (and dismaying) letter to Harriet:

We must finish the best we have got to say, & not only that, but publish it while we are alive—I do not see what living depositary [sic] there is likely to be of our thoughts, or who in this weak generation that is growing up will even be capable of thoroughly mastering & assimilating your ideas, much less of re-originating them—so we must write them & print them, & then they can wait till there are again thinkers.[32]

The emphasis now shifted from publication to writing everything of importance in draft. Five months later, repeating the slightly hysterical (and very arrogant) forecast of a dearth of future thinkers, Mill wrote: "Two years, well employed, would enable us I think to get most of it into a state fit for printing—if not in the best form for popular effect, yet in the state of concentrated thought—a sort of mental pemican, which thinkers, when there are any after us, may nourish themselves with & then dilute for other people."[33] And they did indeed plan together most of Mill's subsequent major works, including *On Liberty*, *Utilitarianism*, *Representative Government*, *Chapters on Socialism*, and *Three Essays on Religion*. In addition, the first draft of Mill's *Autobiography* was written between 1853 and 1856. *The Subjection of Women* (not published until 1869) grew out of the article Harriet wrote at this time called "The Enfranchisement of Women." Mill's biographer Packe argues convincingly that "every major work Mill published after the *Political Economy*, was drafted or at any rate planned during his first few years of married life."[34]

In 1858 Mill retired from the East India Company, with a pension of 1500 pounds, a considerable sum at that time. But the idyllic retirement he had hoped blissfully to share with Harriet was not to be: on November 3, 1858 she finally succumbed to her long-standing lung affliction. Six days later the bereaved Mill wrote to his friend W. T. Thornton: "It is doubtful if I shall ever be fit for anything public or private, again. The spring of my life is broken."[35] On November 25 he wrote in a slightly more hopeful vein to Herbert Spencer: "I have now next to nothing left to care for in life, except to use such power as I have of helping forward my opinions."[36]

He carried out this intention a few days later by submitting *On Liberty*, which had in fact been ready since spring of 1857, to the publishers. The book's seminal idea had been in Mill's mind still earlier. In January 1855, as he was climbing the steps of the Capitol in Rome, Mill had an intuition that a short essay he had written the year before, on the subject of liberty, should be made into a book: "So many things might be brought into it & nothing seems more to be needed—it is a growing need too, for opinion tends to encroach more & more on liberty, & almost all the projects of social reformers in these days are really *liberticide*."[37] Nor was his concern over what might be called the illiberal tendencies of many Victorian liberals and moral reformers in an age when morality seemed to be advancing, like a juggernaut, on a broad and invincible front confined to this (rarely mentioned) letter. It appears in the aforementioned remarks on Auguste Comte in the introductory chapter of the book and again in Chapter III. Here Mill remarks that "spontaneity forms no part of the ideal of the majority of moral and social reformers, but is rather looked on with jealousy, as a troublesome and perhaps rebellious obstruction to the general acceptance of what these reformers, in their own judgment, think would be best for mankind." Still later, in this discussion of individuality, Mill warns that "the spirit of improvement is not always a spirit of liberty, for it may aim at forcing improvements on an unwilling people; and the spirit of liberty, in so far as it resists such attempts, may ally itself locally and temporarily with the opponents of improvement."

Up until now, we have been viewing *On Liberty* against the background of Mill's life and developing ideas. But it also needs to be seen against the historical and intellectual background of Victorian England. Like many of his contemporaries, Mill was a critic of the new democratic dispensation. But, as Mill frequently pointed out, a critic need not necessarily be an enemy. Since boyhood he had been involved in the struggle to extend the franchise—to the middle classes in 1832 and to the working classes (with the notable and, for Mill, egregious exception of women) in 1867. For outright opponents of democracy like Carlyle, the Second Reform Bill of 1867 was a leap into the bottomless pit of anarchy and atheism. His apoplectic essay of that year, entitled "Shooting Niagara: And After?," described the new measure as follows: "Complete 'liberty' to all persons; Count of Heads to be the Divine Court of Appeal on every question and interest of mankind....The calling in of new supplies of blockheadism, gullibility, amenability to beer and balderdash, by way of amending the woes we have had from our previous supplies of that bad article." Matthew Arnold was closer to Mill than to Carlyle in his sense of unease about the new democracy, but he too saw the threat of anarchy, as the title of his great book of 1869, *Culture and Anarchy*, clearly indicated. Where Arnold thought that anarchy would ensue if democracy did not have the sanction of a strong central state to control unruly individuals and selfish classes in the interests of the nation as a whole, Mill was convinced, as we have seen, that the real threat of democracy lay not in anarchy at all but in "Chinese" stagnation, immobility, and conformity.

Also in the background of *On Liberty* is what the eminent Canadian critic Northrop Frye called the Victorian search for the source of spiritual authority.[38] Carlyle, having little interest in spiritual authority distinct from temporal authority, wanted to identify the two, if possible, by reactivating the principle of aristocracy and relocating it in the "Captains of Industry." Newman located the source of spiritual authority in the Church Catholic, and then had to decide whether that principle was embodied in the Anglican or the Roman Church. Arnold tried to locate the principle of spiritual authority in the State, but only in a State based on the "best self" rather than the "ordinary self" of each of its constituent classes and all of its citizens. Mill, in *On Liberty*, recognizes that the progress of democracy, in which he had played a great role, involved making the will of the majority of people the source of *temporal* authority; yet he believed that because the majority of people lived in a morass of habit and prejudice they could not be the source of *spiritual* authority. This, he was convinced, derived from individuals, especially liberal individuals, who initiated all wise and noble things. *On Liberty* may usefully be viewed as an attempt to find truth in the paradox that the majority is always right because, in a democratic society, it is the source of temporal authority, and that the majority is always wrong because it cannot be the source of spiritual authority, which resides in "the counsels and guidance" of the gifted and highly instructed One or Few.

Mill sometimes spoke of *On Liberty* as if it were less a critique of existing evils than a warning against impending dangers. Like other Victorians, he saw his own period as one of transition, in which, because old doctrines and institutions were unsettled and new ones not yet established, there was still a relatively fair and open field accorded to new opinions. But democracy, which Mill had long and strenuously supported, was soon to establish itself, and Mill (as noted above) had been frightened by Tocqueville's picture of the tyranny of the majority which had been one of the less happy results of democracy in America.

Nearly every contention of Mill's in *On Liberty* is contradicted or at least critically analyzed in the selection of contemporary critical essays included in this volume. (The great majority of the essays, naturally enough for a work which in Mill's view applied exclusively to the English situation, are English, but samples of French, Russian, and American reaction are also included.) It would be improper for the editor of this volume to prejudge the lively and numerous disputes engendered by *On Liberty*, whether over Mill's initial assumption that it is possible to distinguish between actions that affect only oneself and actions that affect other people, or his critique of Calvinist (and indeed all Christian) morality, or his insistence that individuality withers (rather than flourishes) under social pressures, or his declaration that all silencing of opinion is an assumption of infallibility, or his assertion that Western nations merit dominance over "the East" because they are more progressive.

Nevertheless, a few cautionary notes to modern readers inclined to transfer their assumptions about what constitutes liberalism to the Victorian period may be in order. Mill did not think of free speech and individuality as "rights" or things intrinsically and invariably good.[39] He believed that liberty, like everything else, had to be judged according to the principle of utility; but, as he states in the opening chapter, "it must be utility in the largest sense, grounded on the permanent interests of a man as a progressive being." *On Liberty* therefore defends freedom of expression not because the collision of antithetical opinions is always salutary. Indeed, Mill acknowledges in Chapter II that "the tendency of all opinions to become sectarian is not cured by the freest discussion, but is often heightened and exacerbated thereby" and that "it is not on the impassioned partisan, it is on the calmer and more disinterested bystander, that this collision of opinions works its salutary effect." Rather, he argues that freedom is essential to the full and harmonious development of society and human nature.[40]

Unlike many modern defenders of freedom of thought and discussion and unfettered individuality, Mill believed that truth and perfection, elusive and complex though they are, do exist and may one day be discovered. He did not suppose it illiberal or intolerant to believe and assert that one view of a question is more true than another. Moreover, he believed, as he wrote in his autobiography, that one day his own era of criticism and negation would be supplanted by one which had not only complete liberty of thought and unbounded freedom of individual action in ways not hurtful to others, but also "convictions as to what is right and wrong, useful and pernicious, deeply engraven on the feelings by early education and general sentiment, and so firmly grounded in reason and the true exigencies of life, that they shall not, like all former and present creeds, religious, ethical, and political, require to be periodically thrown off and replaced by others."[41]

Inevitably the political concerns which had been the original spring of his life drew Mill back into the public arena. His long-standing desire to dilute the absolute power of the numerical majority in a democratic polity led him first to propose a scheme of plural voting and then (more sensibly) Thomas Hare's doctrine of proportional representation. In 1861 he wrote *The Subjection of Women*, but withheld it from publication until 1869. In March 1865 he was urged to stand as radical Parliamentary candidate for Westminster in the General Election. He had declined a similar offer in 1851; this time he agreed, though only after his very stringent (perhaps priggish) conditions had been accepted. These were as follows: 1. if elected he would not support any special local interest; 2. since his only reason to be in Parliament was to promote the ideas expressed in his writings, he would tell his constituents how he intended to vote but would give no pledge of party loyalty; 3. he would not campaign for office; 4. he would not pay a penny towards the cost of his election. The Westminster electors nevertheless chose Mill as their candidate. Despite his adhering fairly strictly to his conditions—he even held out for some time against having his photograph taken for display—he was elected on 12 July 1865 to one of the two Westminster seats (the other going to the Liberal Party candidate).

Mill was slow to work himself into the rhythm of Parliamentary speechifying. His friend Kate Amberley wrote of his earliest performances that he "seems to bore the house, they say he has spoken too often—much, and cannot be heard."[42] Leslie Stephen described him as "a slight frail figure, trembling with nervous irritability. He poured out a series of perfectly formed sentences with an extraordinary rapidity suggestive of learning by heart; and when he lost the thread of his discourse closed his eyes for two or three minutes till…he could again take up his parable."[43] The sharp-tongued Disraeli, after seeing Mill in the House of Commons for the first time, said: "Ah, I see, the finishing governess."[44]

But with time Mill became much more adroit in the give and take of Parliamentary debate, and was even called upon to give "keynote" addresses at grand political occasions. Perhaps his most memorable and nimble retort in the House came when he was taunted by a Conservative member about his assertion in *Representative Government* that Conservatives are always the stupidest party in the state. Mill defended this (often insufferable) piety of radicals and liberals as follows: "I never meant to say that the Conservatives are generally stupid. I meant to say that stupid people are generally Conservative….Suppose any party, in addition to whatever share it may possess of the ability of the community, has nearly the whole of its stupidity, that party must, by the law of its constitution, be the stupidest party; and I do not see why honourable gentlemen should see that position as at all offensive to them, for it ensures their being always an extremely powerful party."[45]

Mill acquired the reputation of a conscientious member of Parliament, dutifully attending dull debates and accepting his share of committee work. He continued to work for the furtherance of proportional representation and voting rights for women. He even became something of a public figure in connection with three major political controversies. The Hyde Park riots incited by the Reform League in 1866, in large part thanks to Mill's intervention, led to the establishment of that place as a corner of London where anyone has a right to say what he likes on virtually any subject. The Governor Eyre affair of the same year saw Mill lead a campaign to bring the British governor of Jamaica to the gallows for wanton killing of rebels in that colony. After the Fenian Brotherhood rebellion of 1867, Mill persuaded Disraeli's government to forego capital punishment for the leaders of the uprising.

Mill stood for Westminster once more, in the election of November 1868, and was defeated. Among the reasons for his ouster were the superiority of the Tory party machine to his own, his refusal to pay anything towards election expenses, his history of meddling in other elections to support reformist candidates against incumbents, and—perhaps fatally— his contribution (of ten pounds) to the campaign of the militant atheist Charles Bradlaugh for a seat in Northampton. But Mill was more than content to "return to the only occupations which agree with my tastes and habits," that is to say, his writing.[46] Returning to unfinished work of earlier years, he published in 1869 a revised edition of James Mill's *Analysis of the Human Mind*, amplified by his own notes and introduction. In 1869–70 he completed the essay, "Theism," the last of the *Three Essays on Religion*, which would not, however, be published until 1874. Also revised for posthumous publication was the *Autobiography*. By now Mill had also become something of a national institution and even an ancient sage. He was besieged by correspondence, much of it from people seeking his wisdom on every conceivable subject, ranging from corporal punishment of schoolboys to pacifism and universal military conscription. (He was for the first and third, against the second.)

But the major political interest of his last years was the suffragette movement to obtain for women the right to vote. While still in Parliament he had proposed, during debate on the Reform Bill in May 1867, to replace the word "man" with the word "person," and his eloquence garnered a third of the votes of those (few) present. In 1869 he published *The Subjection of Women*, thinking the time was now right for a work that had been ready for publication for eight years. His name would henceforth be firmly attached to the most radical of Victorian causes, one opposed not only by conservatives like Fitzjames Stephen, but by sometime comrades of Mill like Alexander Bain and Herbert Spencer, to say nothing of such prominent women as George Eliot, Elizabeth Gaskell (biographer of yet another opponent of female suffrage, Charlotte Brontë), Elizabeth Barrett Browning, and Christina Rossetti.

Whatever may have been the general virtue of Mill's feminist position, it brought him into a kind of subservience to his overbearing step-daughter Helen Taylor that reflects badly on his personal character and, more crucially here, on the disinterestedness of his devotion to liberty. She persuaded him to work for the elimination of "dissident" members of the London Committee for Women's Suffrage and to make sure that new members should be on her side of disputes over feminist politics. In one letter of November 1871 to George Croom Robertson, for example, Mill writes: "It would be madness to add any more members to the Committee of whom you are not *absolutely* certain."[47] The tone and moral style of this and similar letters to Robertson are an unnerving reminder of Mill's warning that "almost all the projects of social reformers in these days are really *liberticide.*" Professors Mineka and Lindley, the editors of Mill's letters, justifiably remark that "this series of letters...is the only one in all his correspondence that reflects discredit upon Mill the advocate of freedom of opinion"; and they quote Charles Eliot Norton's letter expressing doubt as to "whether Mill's interest in the cause of woman is serviceable to him as a thinker. It has a tendency to develop the sentimental part of his intelligence, which is of immense force."[48]

Although she exacted a price for it, Helen Taylor's solicitousness for Mill was genuine. She remained loyally by his side throughout his last years and was present at his end, which came on the morning of 7 May 1873, in his beloved Avignon. His last words, uttered to her, were: "You know that I have done my work."[49]

Notes to Introduction

[1] E.W. Emerson, ed., *A Correspondence between John Sterling and Ralph Waldo Emerson* (Boston, 1897), 71–2.

[2] Jack Stillinger, ed., *The Early Draft of John Stuart Mill's "Autobiography"* (Urbana: University of Illinois Press, 1961), 184. (Hereafter cited as *Early Draft*).

[3] F.A. Cavenagh, ed., *James & John Stuart Mill on Education* (Cambridge: Cambridge University Press, 1931), 8, 11–12, 17, 20.

[4] Hugh S.R. Elliott, ed., *Letters of John Stuart Mill* (London, 1910) I, xv–xvi.

[5] Jack Stillinger, ed., *Autobiography and Other Writings* (Boston: Houghton Mifflin, 1969) 3, 5–6. (Hereafter cited as *Autobiography*).

[6] Alexander Bain, *James Mill: A Biography* (London, 1882), 207.

[7] *Autobiography*, 42.

[8] David Masson, *Memories of London in the Forties* (London, 1908) 35.

[9] *Autobiography*, 80, 81.

[10] *Autobiography*, 85.

[11] See the *Letters of Sigmund Freud*, ed., Ernst Freud (New York: McGraw Hill, 1964) 75–76; also quoted in Phyllis Rose's *Parallel Lives: Five Victorian Marriages* (New York: Knopf, 1983), 125.

[12] *Autobiography*, 86.

[13] *Autobiography*, 89.

[14] Quoted in Michael St. John Packe, *The Life of John Stuart Mill* (New York: Macmillan, 1954), 132. (Hereafter cited as Packe).

[15] Mark De Wolfe Howe, ed., *Holmes-Laski Letters* (Cambridge, Mass: Harvard University Press, 1953) I, 471, 668, 675–6; Diana Trilling, "Mill's Intellectual Beacon," *Partisan Review* 19 (1952), 116; Alice S. Rossi, "Sentiment and Intellect," Introduction to *Essays on Sex Equality by John Stuart Mill and Harriet Taylor* (Chicago: University of Chicago Press, 1970); Gertrude Himmelfarb, *On Liberty and Liberalism: The Case of John Stuart Mill* (New York: Knopf, 1974), especially chapter X, "A 'Joint Production.'"

[16] Himmelfarb continued her debate with Rose in the first essay of Himmelfarb's *Marriage and Morals Among the Victorians* (New York: Vintage, 1987).

[17] F.A. Hayek, *John Stuart Mill and Harriet Taylor: Their Friendship and Subsequent Marriage* (Chicago: University of Chicago Press, 1951) 82. (Hereafter cited as Hayek).

[18] Quoted in *Early Draft*, 23.

[19] Hayek, 82.

[20] *Autobiography*, 128.

[21] "Coleridge," *Autobiography and Other Writings*, 260, 276.

[22] Letter of 11 May 1840, in *Earlier Letters of John Stuart Mill: 1812–1848*, ed., F.E. Mineka (Toronto: University of Toronto Press, 1963) II, 434.

[23] *Autobiography*, 132.

[24] *Autobiography*, 134.

[25] Letter of 19 August 1854, in *Later Letters of John Stuart Mill: 1849–1873*, ed., Francis E. Mineka and Dwight N. Lindley (Toronto: University of Toronto Press, 1972) I, 239.

[26] *Autobiography*, 127.

[27] *Early Draft*, 169n.

[28] Alexander Bain, *John Stuart Mill* (London, 1882), 64–5.

[29] Packe, 315.

[30] *Principles of Political Economy* (Toronto: University of Toronto Press, 1965), 794.

[31] Quoted in Packe, 315.

[32] *Later Letters* I, 112.

[33] *Later Letters* I, 141–2.

[34] Packe, 370.

[35] *Later Letters* II, 574.

[36] *Later Letters* II, 576.

[37] *Later Letters* I, 294.

[38] Northrop Frye, "The Problem of Spiritual Authority in the Nineteenth Century," *Backgrounds to Victorian Literature*, ed., Richard A. Levine (San Francisco: Chandler Publishing Company, 1967), 129–30.

[39] As Wendy Donner puts it in her *The Liberal Self: John Stuart Mill's Moral and Political Philosophy* (Ithaca: Cornell University Press, 1991), "in Mill's moral philosophy the principle of the good is logically prior to the principle of right" (2). The essays collected in David Lyon's *Rights, Welfare, and Mill's Moral Theory* (New York: Oxford University Press, 1994) represent the most substantial and influential recent discussion of the extent to which rights may be incorporated into a utilitarian framework.

[40] As Alan Ryan puts it in his *The Philosophy of John Stuart Mill* (New York, 2nd. ed., 1990), "Mill's concern with self-development and moral progress is a strand in his philosophy to which almost everything else is subordinate" (255).

[41] *Autobiography*, 100.

[42] Bertrand Russell and Patricia Russell, eds., *The Amberley Papers* (New York: W.W. Norton, 1937) I, 470.

[43] Quoted in Packe, 452.

[44] W.F. Monypenny and G.W. Buckle, *The Life of Benjamin Disraeli*, 6 vols. (New York: Macmillan, 1910–20) V, 501.

[45] W.L. Courtney, *Life of John Stuart Mill* (London, 1889), 147.

[46] *Later Letters* III, 1506.

[47] *Later Letters* IV, 1852.

[48] *Later Letters* I, xxxvi.

[49] Packe, 507.

A Note on the Text

THE text of *On Liberty* used here is from the University of Toronto edition of Mill's *Collected Works*, published in 1977. The Toronto editor, the late Professor John M. Robson, based his text on that of the fourth edition of the book, the last to appear in Mill's lifetime, and collated it with the texts of the third, second, first, and People's Editions. Mill declared (in a passage printed in Appendix B of this volume) that after his wife died he "made no alteration or addition to [*On Liberty*] nor shall I ever." Nevertheless, Robson notes, "as is the case in all of Mill's major works, there was some revision, though in this instance very slight, and not of much consequence....In short, Mill's statement is not strictly accurate...but *On Liberty* is, by a significant margin, the least revised of his works."[1]

---

[1] John M. Robson, "Textual Introduction," *Essays on Politics and Society, Collected Works of John Stuart Mill* (Toronto: University of Toronto Press, 1977) XVIII, lxxxiv.

On Liberty

John Stuart Mill

On Liberty

"The grand, leading principle, towards which every argument unfolded in these pages directly converges, is the absolute and essential importance of human development in its richest diversity."

Wilhelm von Humboldt, *Sphere and Duties of Government.*
[Trans. Joseph Coulthard (London: Chapman, 1854), p. 65.]

To the beloved and deplored memory of her who was the inspirer, and in part the author, of all that is best in my writings—the friend and wife whose exalted sense of truth and right was my strongest incitement, and whose approbation was my chief reward—I dedicate this volume. Like all that I have written for many years, it belongs as much to her as to me; but the work as it stands has had, in a very insufficient degree, the inestimable advantage of her revision; some of the most important portions having been reserved for a more careful re-examination, which they are now never destined to receive. Were I but capable of interpreting to the world one half the great thoughts and noble feelings which are buried in her grave, I should be the medium of a greater benefit to it, than is ever likely to arise from anything that I can write, unprompted and unassisted by her all but unequalled wisdom.

Chapter 1: Introductory

THE SUBJECT of this Essay is not the so-called Liberty of the Will, so unfortunately opposed to the misnamed doctrine of Philosophical Necessity; but Civil, or Social Liberty: the nature and limits of the power which can be legitimately exercised by society over the individual. A question seldom stated, and hardly ever discussed, in general terms, but which profoundly influences the practical controversies of the age by its latent presence, and is likely soon to make itself recognised as the vital question of the future. It is so far from being new, that, in a certain sense, it has divided mankind, almost from the remotest ages; but in the stage of progress into which the more civilized portions of the species have now entered, it presents itself under new conditions, and requires a different and more fundamental treatment.

The struggle between Liberty and Authority is the most conspicuous feature in the portions of history with which we are earliest familiar, particularly in that of Greece, Rome, and England. But in old times this contest was between subjects, or some classes of subjects, and the Government. By liberty, was meant protection against the tyranny of the political rulers. The rulers were conceived (except in some of the popular governments of Greece) as in a necessarily antagonistic position to the people whom they ruled. They consisted of a governing One, or a governing tribe or caste, who derived their authority from inheritance or conquest, who, at all events, did not hold it at the pleasure of the governed, and whose supremacy men did not venture, perhaps did not desire, to contest, whatever precautions might be taken against its oppressive exercise. Their power was regarded as necessary, but also as highly dangerous; as a weapon which they would attempt to use against their subjects, no less than against external enemies. To prevent the weaker members of the community from being preyed upon by innumerable vultures, it was needful that there should be an animal of prey stronger than the rest, commissioned to keep them down. But as the king of the vultures would be no less bent upon preying on the flock than any of the minor harpies, it was indispensable to be in a perpetual attitude of defence against his beak and claws. The aim, therefore, of patriots was to set limits to the power which the ruler should be suffered to exercise over the community; and this limitation was what they meant by liberty. It was attempted in two ways. First, by obtaining a recognition of certain immunities, called political liberties or rights, which it was to be regarded as a breach of duty in the ruler to infringe, and which, if he did infringe, specific resistance, or rebellion, was held to be justifiable. A second, and generally a later expedient, was the establishment of constitutional checks, by which the consent of the community, or of a body of some sort, supposed to represent its interests, was made a necessary condition to some of the more important acts of the governing power. To the first of these modes of limitation, the ruling power, in most European countries, was compelled, more or less, to submit. It was not so with the second; and, to attain this, or when already in some degree possessed, to attain it more completely, became everywhere the principal object of the lovers of liberty. And so long as mankind were content to combat one enemy by another, and to be ruled by a master, on condition of being guaranteed more or less efficaciously against his tyranny, they did not carry their aspirations beyond this point.

A time, however, came, in the progress of human affairs, when men ceased to think it a necessity of nature that their governors should be an independent power, opposed in interest to themselves. It appeared to them much better that the various magistrates of the State should be their tenants or delegates, revocable at their pleasure. In that way alone, it seemed, could they have complete security that the powers of government would never be abused to their disadvantage. By degrees this new demand for elective and temporary rulers became the prominent object of the exertions of the popular party, wherever any such party existed; and superseded, to a considerable extent, the previous efforts to limit the power of rulers. As the struggle proceeded for making the ruling power emanate from the periodical choice of the ruled, some persons began to think that too much importance had been attached to the limitation of the power itself. *That* (it might seem) was a resource against rulers whose interests were habitually opposed to those of the people. What was now wanted was, that the rulers should be identified with the people; that their interest and will should be the interest and will of the nation. The nation did not need to be protected against its own will. There was no fear of its tyrannizing over itself. Let the rulers be effectually responsible to it, promptly removable by it, and it could afford to trust them with power of which it could itself dictate the use to be made. Their power was but the nation's own power, concentrated, and in a form convenient for exercise. This mode of thought, or rather perhaps of feeling, was common among the last generation of European liberalism, in the Continental section of which it still apparently predominates. Those who admit any limit to what a government may do, except in the case of such governments as they think ought not to exist, stand out as brilliant exceptions among the political thinkers of the Continent. A similar tone of sentiment might by this time have been prevalent in our own country, if the circumstances which for a time encouraged it, had continued unaltered.

But, in political and philosophical theories, as well as in persons, success discloses faults and infirmities which failure might have concealed from observation. The notion, that the people have no need to limit their power over themselves, might seem axiomatic, when popular government was a thing only dreamed about, or read of as having existed at some distant period of the past. Neither was that notion necessarily disturbed by such temporary aberrations as those of the French Revolution, the worst of which were the work of an usurping few, and which, in any case, belonged, not to the permanent working of popular institutions, but to a sudden and convulsive outbreak against monarchical and aristocratic despotism. In time, however, a democratic republic came to occupy a large portion of the earth's surface, and made itself felt as one of the most powerful members of the community of nations; and elective and responsible government became subject to the observations and criticisms which wait upon a great existing fact. It was now perceived that such phrases as "self-government," and "the power of the people over themselves," do not express the true state of the case. The "people" who exercise the power are not always the same people with those over whom it is exercised; and the "self-government" spoken of is not the government of each by himself, but of each by all the rest. The will of the people, moreover, practically means the will of the most numerous or the most active *part* of the people; the majority, or those who succeed in making themselves accepted as the majority; the people, consequently, *may* desire to oppress a part of their number; and precautions are as much needed against this as against any other abuse of power. The limitation, therefore, of the power of government over individuals loses none of its importance when the holders of power are regularly accountable to the community, that is, to the strongest party therein. This view of things, recommending itself equally to the intelligence of thinkers and to the inclination of those important classes in European society to whose real or supposed interests democracy is adverse, has had no difficulty in establishing itself; and in political speculations "the tyranny of the majority" is now generally included among the evils against which society requires to be on its guard.

Like other tyrannies, the tyranny of the majority was at first, and is still vulgarly, held in dread, chiefly as operating through the acts of the public authorities. But reflecting persons perceived that when society is itself the tyrant—society collectively, over the separate individuals who compose it—its means of tyrannizing are not restricted to the acts which it may do by the hands of its political functionaries. Society can and does execute its own mandates: and if it issues wrong mandates instead of right, or any mandates at all in things with which it ought not to meddle, it practices a social tyranny more formidable than many kinds of political oppression, since, though not usually upheld by such extreme penalties, it leaves fewer means of escape, penetrating much more deeply into the details of life, and enslaves the soul itself. Protection, therefore, against the tyranny of the magistrate is not enough: there needs protection also against the tyranny of the prevailing opinion and feeling; against the tendency of society to impose, by other means than civil penalties, its own ideas and practices as rules of conduct on those who dissent from them; to fetter the development, and, if possible, prevent the formation, of any individuality not in harmony with its ways, and compel all characters to fashion themselves upon the model of its own. There is a limit to the legitimate interference of collective opinion with individual independence: and to find that limit, and maintain it against encroachment, is as indispensable to a good condition of human affairs, as protection against political despotism.

But though this proposition is not likely to be contested in general terms, the practical question, where to place the limit—how to make the fitting adjustment between individual independence and social control—is a subject on which nearly everything remains to be done. All that makes existence valuable to any one, depends on the enforcement of restraints upon the actions of other people. Some rules of conduct, therefore, must be imposed, by law in the first place, and by opinion on many things which are not fit subjects for the operation of law. What these rules should be, is the principal question in human affairs; but if we except a few of the most obvious cases, it is one of those which least progress has been made in resolving. No two ages, and scarcely any two countries, have decided it alike; and the decision of one age or country is a wonder to another. Yet the people of any given age and country no more suspect any difficulty in it, than if it were a subject on which mankind had always been agreed. The rules which obtain among themselves appear to them self-evident and self-justifying. This all but universal illusion is one of the examples of the magical influence of custom, which is not only, as the proverb says, a second nature, but is continually mistaken for the first. The effect of custom, in preventing any misgiving respecting the rules of conduct which mankind impose on one another, is all the more complete because the subject is one on which it is not generally considered necessary that reasons should be given, either by one person to others, or by each to himself. People are accustomed to believe, and have been encouraged in the belief by some who aspire to the character of philosophers, that their feelings, on subjects of this nature, are better than reasons, and render reasons unnecessary. The practical principle which guides them to their opinions on the regulation of human conduct, is the feeling in each person's mind that everybody should be required to act as he, and those with whom he sympathizes, would like them to act. No one, indeed, acknowledges to himself that his standard of judgment is his own liking; but an opinion on a point of conduct, not supported by reasons, can only count as one person's preference; and if the reasons, when given, are a mere appeal to a similar preference felt by other people, it is still only many people's liking instead of one. To an ordinary man, however, his own preference, thus supported, is not only a perfectly satisfactory reason, but the only one he generally has for any of his notions of morality, taste, or propriety, which are not expressly written in his religious creed; and his chief guide in the interpretation even of that. Men's opinions, accordingly, on what is laudable or blameable, are affected by all the multifarious causes which influence their wishes in regard to the conduct of others, and which are as numerous as those which determine their wishes on any other subject. Sometimes their reason—at other times their prejudices or superstitions: often their social affections, not seldom their antisocial ones, their envy or jealousy, their arrogance or contemptuousness: but most commonly, their desires or fears for themselves—their legitimate or illegitimate self-interest. Wherever there is an ascendant class, a large portion of the morality of the country emanates from its class interests, and its feelings of class superiority. The morality between Spartans and Helots, between planters and negroes, between princes and subjects, between nobles and roturiers[1], between men and women, has been for the most part the creation of these class interests and feelings: and the sentiments thus generated, react in turn upon the moral feelings of the members of the ascendant class, in their relations among themselves. Where, on the other hand, a class, formerly ascendant,

---

[1] Sparta was a Dorian city-state in ancient Greece renowned for military prowess, political rigidity, and cultural austerity; Helots were a class of serfs in Sparta; roturiers are commoners, persons of plebeian rank.

has lost its ascendancy, or where its ascendancy is unpopular, the prevailing moral sentiments frequently bear the impress of an impatient dislike of superiority. Another grand determining principle of the rules of conduct, both in act and forbearance, which have been enforced by law or opinion, has been the servility of mankind towards the supposed preferences or aversions of their temporal masters, or of their gods. This servility, though essentially selfish, is not hypocrisy; it gives rise to perfectly genuine sentiments of abhorrence; it made men burn magicians and heretics. Among so many baser influences, the general and obvious interests of society have of course had a share, and a large one, in the direction of the moral sentiments: less, however, as a matter of reason, and on their own account, than as a consequence of the sympathies and antipathies which grew out of them: and sympathies and antipathies which had little or nothing to do with the interests of society, have made themselves felt in the establishment of moralities with quite as great force.

The likings and dislikings of society, or of some powerful portion of it, are thus the main thing which has practically determined the rules laid down for general observance, under the penalties of law or opinion. And in general, those who have been in advance of society in thought and feeling, have left this condition of things unassailed in principle, however they may have come into conflict with it in some of its details. They have occupied themselves rather in inquiring what things society ought to like or dislike, than in questioning whether its likings or dislikings should be a law to individuals. They preferred endeavouring to alter the feelings of mankind on the particular points on which they were themselves heretical, rather than make common cause in defence of freedom, with heretics generally. The only case in which the higher ground has been taken on principle and maintained with consistency, by any but an individual here and there, is that of religious belief: a case instructive in many ways, and not least so as forming a most striking instance of the fallibility of what is called the moral sense: for the *odium theologicum*[2], in a sincere bigot, is

---

[2] [*odium theologicum*] animosity characteristic of religious controversy.

one of the most unequivocal cases of moral feeling. Those who first broke the yoke of what called itself the Universal Church, were in general as little willing to permit difference of religious opinion as that church itself. But when the heat of the conflict was over, without giving a complete victory to any party, and each church or sect was reduced to limit its hopes to retaining possession of the ground it already occupied; minorities, seeing that they had no chance of becoming majorities, were under the necessity of pleading to those whom they could not convert, for permission to differ. It is accordingly on this battle field, almost solely, that the rights of the individual against society have been asserted on broad grounds of principle, and the claim of society to exercise authority over dissentients, openly controverted. The great writers to whom the world owes what religious liberty it possesses, have mostly asserted freedom of conscience as an indefeasible right, and denied absolutely that a human being is accountable to others for his religious belief. Yet so natural to mankind is intolerance in whatever they really care about, that religious freedom has hardly anywhere been practically realized, except where religious indifference, which dislikes to have its peace disturbed by theological quarrels, has added its weight to the scale. In the minds of almost all religious persons, even in the most tolerant countries, the duty of toleration is admitted with tacit reserves. One person will bear with dissent in matters of church government, but not of dogma; another can tolerate everybody, short of a Papist or an Unitarian; another, every one who believes in revealed religion; a few extend their charity a little further, but stop at the belief in a God and in a future state. Wherever the sentiment of the majority is still genuine and intense, it is found to have abated little of its claim to be obeyed.

In England, from the peculiar circumstances of our political history, though the yoke of opinion is perhaps heavier, that of law is lighter, than in most other countries of Europe; and there is considerable jealousy of direct interference, by the legislative or the executive power, with private conduct; not so much from any just regard for the independence of the individual, as from the still subsisting habit of looking on the government as representing an opposite interest to the public. The majority have not yet learnt to feel the power of the government their power, or its opinions their opinions. When they do so, individual liberty will probably be as much exposed to invasion from the government, as it already is from public opinion. But, as yet, there is a considerable amount of feeling ready to be called forth against any attempt of the law to control individuals in things in which they have not hitherto been accustomed to be controlled by it; and this with very little discrimination as to whether the matter is, or is not, within the legitimate sphere of legal control; insomuch that the feeling, highly salutary on the whole, is perhaps quite as often misplaced as well grounded in the particular instances of its application. There is, in fact, no recognised principle by which the propriety or impropriety of government interference is customarily tested. People decide according to their personal preferences. Some, whenever they see any good to be done, or evil to be remedied, would willingly instigate the government to undertake the business; while others prefer to bear almost any amount of social evil, rather than add one to the departments of human interests amenable to governmental control. And men range themselves on one or the other side in any particular case, according to this general direction of their sentiments; or according to the degree of interest which they feel in the particular thing which it is proposed that the government should do, or according to the belief they entertain that the government would, or would not, do it in the manner they prefer; but very rarely on account of any opinion to which they consistently adhere, as to what things are fit to be done by a government. And it seems to me that in consequence of this absence of rule or principle, one side is at present as often wrong as the other; the interference of government is, with about equal frequency, improperly invoked and improperly condemned.

The object of this Essay is to assert one very simple principle, as entitled to govern absolutely the dealings of society with the individual in the way of compulsion and control, whether the means used be physical force in the form of legal penalties, or the moral coercion of public opinion. That principle is, that the sole end for which mankind are warranted, individually or collectively, in interfering with the liberty of action of any of their number, is self-protection. That the only purpose for which power can be rightfully exercised over any member of a civilized community, against his will, is to prevent harm to others. His own good, either physical or moral, is not a sufficient warrant. He cannot rightfully be compelled to do or forbear because it will be better for him to do so, because it will make him happier, because, in the opinions of others, to do so would be wise, or even right. These are good reasons for remonstrating with him, or reasoning with him, or persuading him, or entreating him, but not for compelling him, or visiting him with any evil in case he do otherwise. To justify that, the conduct from which it is desired to deter him, must be calculated to produce evil to some one else. The only part of the conduct of any one, for which he is amenable to society, is that which concerns others. In the part which merely concerns himself, his independence is, of right, absolute. Over himself, over his own body and mind, the individual is sovereign.

It is, perhaps, hardly necessary to say that this doctrine is meant to apply only to human beings in the maturity of their faculties. We are not speaking of children, or of young persons below the age which the law may fix as manhood or womanhood. Those who are still in a state to require being taken care of by others, must be protected against their own actions as well as against external injury. For the same reason, we may leave out of consideration those backward states of society in which the race itself may be considered as in its nonage. The early difficulties in the way of spontaneous progress are so great, that there is seldom any choice of means for overcoming them; and a ruler full of the spirit of improvement is warranted in the use of any expedients that will attain an end, perhaps otherwise unattainable. Despotism is a legitimate mode of government in dealing with barbarians, provided the end be their improvement, and the means justified by actually effecting that end. Liberty, as a principle, has no application to any state of things anterior to the time when mankind have become capable of being improved by free and equal discussion. Until then, there is nothing for them but implicit obedience to an Akbar or a Charlemagne,[3] if they are so fortunate as to find one. But as soon as mankind have attained the capacity of being guided to their own improvement by conviction or persuasion (a period long since reached in all nations with whom we need here concern ourselves), compulsion, either in the direct form or in that of pains and penalties for non-compliance, is no longer admissible as to their own good, and justifiable only for the security of others.

It is proper to state that I forego any advantage which could be derived to my argument from the idea of abstract right, as a thing independent of utility. I regard utility as the ultimate appeal on all ethical questions; but it must be utility in the largest sense, grounded on the permanent interests of man as a progressive being. Those interests, I contend, authorize the subjection of individual spontaneity to external control, only in respect to those actions which concern the interest of other people. If any one does an act hurtful to others, there is a *prima facie* case for punishing him, by law, or, where legal penalties are not safely applicable, by general disapprobation. There are also many positive acts for the benefit of others, which he may rightfully be compelled to perform; such as, to give evidence in a court of justice; to bear his fair share in the common defence, or in any other joint work necessary to the interest of the society of which he enjoys the protection; and to perform certain acts of individual beneficence, such as saving a fellow-creature's life, or interposing to protect the defenceless against ill-usage, things which whenever it is obviously a man's duty to do, he may rightfully be made responsible to society for not doing. A person may cause evil to others not only by his actions but by his inaction, and in either case he is justly accountable to them for the injury. The latter case, it is true, requires a much more cautious exercise of compulsion than the former. To make any one answerable for doing evil to others, is the rule; to make him answerable for not preventing evil, is, comparatively speaking, the exception. Yet there are many cases clear enough and grave enough to justify that exception. In all things which regard the external relations of the individual, he is *de jure* amenable to those whose interests

[3] Akbar the Great was Mogul emperor of India from 1556–1605; Charlemagne, known as "Charles the Great," was King of the Franks from 768–814 and was crowned emperor of the Romans in 800.

are concerned, and if need be, to society as their protector. There are often good reasons for not holding him to the responsibility; but these reasons must arise from the special expediencies of the case: either because it is a kind of case in which he is on the whole likely to act better, when left to his own discretion, than when controlled in any way in which society have it in their power to control him; or because the attempt to exercise control would produce other evils, greater than those which it would prevent. When such reasons as these preclude the enforcement of responsibility, the conscience of the agent himself should step into the vacant judgment seat, and protect those interests of others which have no external protection; judging himself all the more rigidly, because the case does not admit of his being made accountable to the judgment of his fellow-creatures.

But there is a sphere of action in which society, as distinguished from the individual, has, if any, only an indirect interest; comprehending all that portion of a person's life and conduct which affects only himself, or if it also affects others, only with their free, voluntary, and undeceived consent and participation. When I say only himself, I mean directly, and in the first instance: for whatever affects himself, may affect others through himself; and the objection which may be grounded on this contingency, will receive consideration in the sequel. This, then, is the appropriate region of human liberty. It comprises, first, the inward domain of consciousness; demanding liberty of conscience, in the most comprehensive sense; liberty of thought and feeling; absolute freedom of opinion and sentiment on all subjects, practical or speculative, scientific, moral, or theological. The liberty of expressing and publishing opinions may seem to fall under a different principle, since it belongs to that part of the conduct of an individual which concerns other people; but, being almost of as much importance as the liberty of thought itself, and resting in great part on the same reasons, is practically inseparable from it. Secondly, the principle requires liberty of tastes and pursuits; of framing the plan of our life to suit our own character; of doing as we like, subject to such consequences as may follow: without impediment from our fellow-creatures, so long as what we do does not harm them, even though they should think our conduct foolish, perverse, or wrong. Thirdly, from this liberty of each individual, follows the liberty, within the same limits, of combination among individuals; freedom to unite, for any purpose not involving harm to others: the persons combining being supposed to be of full age, and not forced or deceived.

No society in which these liberties are not, on the whole, respected, is free, whatever may be its form of government; and none is completely free in which they do not exist absolute and unqualified. The only freedom which deserves the name, is that of pursuing our own good in our own way, so long as we do not attempt to deprive others of theirs, or impede their efforts to obtain it. Each is the proper guardian of his own health, whether bodily, or mental and spiritual. Mankind are greater gainers by suffering each other to live as seems good to themselves, than by compelling each to live as seems good to the rest.

Though this doctrine is anything but new, and, to some persons, may have the air of a truism, there is no doctrine which stands more directly opposed to the general tendency of existing opinion and practice. Society has expended fully as much effort in the attempt (according to its lights) to compel people to conform to its notions of personal, as of social excellence. The ancient commonwealths thought themselves entitled to practice, and the ancient philosophers countenanced, the regulation of every part of private conduct by public authority, on the ground that the State had a deep interest in the whole bodily and mental discipline of every one of its citizens; a mode of thinking which may have been admissible in small republics surrounded by powerful enemies, in constant peril of being subverted by foreign attack or internal commotion, and to which even a short interval of relaxed energy and self-command might so easily be fatal, that they could not afford to wait for the salutary permanent effects of freedom. In the modern world, the greater size of political communities, and above all, the separation between spiritual and temporal authority (which placed the direction of men's consciences in other hands than those which controlled their worldly affairs), prevented so great an interference by law in the details of private life; but the engines of moral repression have been wielded more strenuously against divergence from the reigning opinion in self-regarding, than even in social matters; religion, the most powerful of the elements which have entered into the formation of moral feeling, having almost always been governed either by the ambition of a hierarchy, seeking control over every department of human conduct, or by the spirit of Puritanism. And some of those modern reformers who have placed themselves in strongest opposition to the religions of the past, have been noway behind either churches or sects in their assertion of the right of spiritual domination: M. Comte, in particular, whose social system, as unfolded in his *Système de Politique Positive*,[4] aims at establishing (though by moral more than by legal appliances) a despotism of society over the individual, surpassing anything contemplated in the political ideal of the most rigid disciplinarian among the ancient philosophers.

Apart from the peculiar tenets of individual thinkers, there is also in the world at large an increasing inclination to stretch unduly the powers of society over the individual, both by the force of opinion and even by that of legislation: and as the tendency of all the changes taking place in the world is to strengthen society, and diminish the power of the individual, this encroachment is not one of the evils which tend spontaneously to disappear, but, on the contrary, to grow more and more formidable. The disposition of mankind, whether as rulers or as fellow-citizens, to impose their own opinions and inclinations as a rule of conduct on others, is so energetically supported by some of the best and by some of the worst feelings incident to human nature, that it is hardly ever kept under restraint by anything but want of power; and as the power is not declining, but growing, unless a strong barrier of moral conviction can be raised against the mischief, we must expect, in the present circumstances of the world, to see it increase.

It will be convenient for the argument, if, instead of at once entering upon the general thesis, we confine ourselves in the first instance to a

---

[4] Auguste Comte (1798–1857) published *Système de politique positive* in Paris in 1851–54. See Mill's book of 1865, *Auguste Comte and Positivism*, on the French philosopher and founder of Positivism.

single branch of it, on which the principle here stated is, if not fully, yet to a certain point, recognised by the current opinions. This one branch is the Liberty of Thought: from which it is impossible to separate the cognate liberty of speaking and of writing. Although these liberties, to some considerable amount, form part of the political morality of all countries which profess religious toleration and free institutions, the grounds, both philosophical and practical, on which they rest, are perhaps not so familiar to the general mind, nor so thoroughly appreciated by many even of the leaders of opinion, as might have been expected. Those grounds, when rightly understood, are of much wider application than to only one division of the subject, and a thorough consideration of this part of the question will be found the best introduction to the remainder. Those to whom nothing which I am about to say will be new, may therefore, I hope, excuse me, if on a subject which for now three centuries has been so often discussed, I venture on one discussion more.

Chapter II:
Of the Liberty of Thought
and Discussion

THE TIME, it is to be hoped, is gone by, when any defence would be necessary of the "liberty of the press" as one of the securities against corrupt or tyrannical government. No argument, we may suppose, can now be needed, against permitting a legislature or an executive, not identified in interest with the people, to prescribe opinions to them, and determine what doctrines or what arguments they shall be allowed to hear. This aspect of the question, besides, has been so often and so triumphantly enforced by preceding writers, that it needs not be specially insisted on in this place. Though the law of England, on the subject of the press, is as servile to this day as it was in the time of the Tudors, there is little danger of its being actually put in force against political discussion, except during some temporary panic, when fear of insurrrection drives ministers and judges from their propriety;[1] and, speaking generally, it is not, in constitutional countries, to be apprehended, that the government, whether completely responsible to the people or not, will often attempt to control the expression of opinion, except when in doing so it makes itself the organ of the general intolerance of the public. Let us suppose, therefore, that the government is entirely at one with the people, and never thinks of exerting any power of coercion unless in agreement with what it conceives to be their voice. But I deny the right of the people to exercise such coercion, either by themselves or by their government. The power itself is illegitimate. The best government has no more title to it than the worst. It is as noxious, or more noxious, when exerted in accordance with public opinion, than when in opposition to it. If all mankind minus one, were of one opinion, and only one person were of the contrary opinion, mankind would be no more justified in silencing that one person, than he, if he had the power, would be justified in silencing mankind. Were an opinion a personal possession of no value except to the owner; if to be obstructed in the enjoyment of it were simply a private injury, it would make some difference whether the injury was inflicted only on a few persons or on many. But the peculiar evil of silencing the expression of an opinion is, that it is robbing the human race; posterity as well as the existing generation; those who dissent from the opinion, still more than those who hold it. If the opinion is right, they are deprived of the opportunity of exchanging error for truth: if wrong, they lose, what is almost as great a benefit, the clearer

---

[1] These words had scarcely been written, when, as if to give them an emphatic contradiction, occurred the Government Press Prosecutions of 1858. That ill-judged interference with the liberty of public discussion has not, however, induced me to alter a single word in the text, nor has it at all weakened my conviction that, moments of panic excepted, the era of pains and penalties for political discussion has, in our own country, passed away. For, in the first place, the prosecutions were not persisted in; and, in the second, they were never, properly speaking, political prosecutions. The offence charged was not that of criticising institutions, or the acts or persons of rulers, but of circulating what was deemed an immoral doctrine, the lawfulness of Tyrannicide.

If the arguments of the present chapter are of any validity, there ought to exist the fullest liberty of professing and discussing, as a matter of ethical conviction, any doctrine, however immoral it may be considered. It would, therefore, be irrelevant and out of place to examine here, whether the doctrine of Tyrannicide deserves that title. I shall content myself with saying that the subject has been at all times one of the open questions of morals; that the act of a private citizen in striking down a criminal, who, by raising himself above the law, has placed himself beyond the reach of legal punishment or control, has been accounted by whole nations, and by some of the best and wisest of men, not a crime, but an act of exalted virtue; and that, right or wrong, it is not of the nature of assassination, but of civil war. As such, I hold that the instigation to it, in a specific case, may be a proper subject of punishment, but only if an overt act has followed, and at least a probable connexion can be established between the act and the instigation. Even then, it is not a foreign government, but the very government assailed, which alone, in the exercise of self-defence, can legitimately punish attacks directed against its own existence. (Mill's note.)

perception and livelier impression of truth, produced by its collision with error.

It is necessary to consider separately these two hypotheses, each of which has a distinct branch of the argument corresponding to it. We can never be sure that the opinion we are endeavouring to stifle is a false opinion; and if we were sure, stifling it would be an evil still.

First: the opinion which it is attempted to suppress by authority may possibly be true. Those who desire to suppress it, of course deny its truth; but they are not infallible. They have no authority to decide the question for all mankind, and exclude every other person from the means of judging. To refuse a hearing to an opinion, because they are sure that it is false, is to assume that *their* certainty is the same thing as *absolute* certainty. All silencing of discussion is an assumption of infallibility. Its condemnation may be allowed to rest on this common argument, not the worse for being common.

Unfortunately for the good sense of mankind, the fact of their fallibility is far from carrying the weight in their practical judgment, which is always allowed to it in theory; for while every one well knows himself to be fallible, few think it necessary to take any precautions against their own fallibility, or admit the supposition that any opinion, of which they feel very certain, may be one of the examples of the error to which they acknowledge themselves to be liable. Absolute princes, or others who are accustomed to unlimited deference, usually feel this complete confidence in their own opinions on nearly all subjects. People more happily situated, who sometimes hear their opinions disputed, and are not wholly unused to be set right when they are wrong, place the same unbounded reliance only on such of their opinions as are shared by all who surround them, or to whom they habitually defer: for in proportion to a man's want of confidence in his own solitary judgment, does he usually repose, with implicit trust, on the infallibility of "the world" in general. And the world, to each individual, means the part of it with which he comes in contact; his party, his sect, his church, his class of society: the man may be called, by comparison, almost liberal and large-minded to whom it means anything so comprehensive as his own country or his own age. Nor is his faith in this collective authority at all shaken by his being aware that other ages, countries, sects, churches, classes, and parties have thought, and even now think, the exact reverse. He devolves upon his own world the responsibility of being in the right against the dissentient worlds of other people; and it never troubles him that mere accident has decided which of these numerous worlds is the object of his reliance, and that the same causes which make him a Churchman in London, would have made him a Buddhist or a Confucian in Pekin. Yet it is as evident in itself, as any amount of argument can make it, that ages are no more infallible than individuals; every age having held many opinions which subsequent ages have deemed not only false but absurd; and it is as certain that many opinions, now general, will be rejected by future ages, as it is that many, once general, are rejected by the present.

The objection likely to be made to this argument, would probably take such form as the following. There is no greater assumption of infallibility in forbidding the propagation of error, than in any other thing which is done by public authority on its own judgment and responsibility. Judgment is given to men that they may use it. Because it may be used erroneously, are men to be told that they ought not to use it at all? To prohibit what they think pernicious, is not claiming exemption from error, but fulfilling the duty incumbent on them, although fallible, of acting on conscientious conviction. If we were never to act on our opinions, because those opinions may be wrong, we should leave all our interests uncared for, and all our duties unperformed. An objection which applies to all conduct, can be no valid objection to any conduct in particular. It is the duty of governments, and of individuals, to form the truest opinions they can; to form them carefully, and never impose them upon others unless they are quite sure of being right. But when they are sure (such reasoners may say), it is not conscientiousness but cowardice to shrink from acting on their opinions, and allow doctrines which they honestly think dangerous to the welfare of mankind, either in this life or in another, to be scattered abroad without restraint, because other people, in less enlightened times, have persecuted opinions now believed to be true. Let us take care, it may be said, not to make the same mistake: but governments and nations have made mistakes in other things, which are not denied to be fit subjects for the exercise of authority: they have laid on bad taxes, made unjust wars. Ought we therefore to lay on no taxes, and, under whatever provocation, make no wars? Men, and governments, must act to the best of their ability. There is no such thing as absolute certainty, but there is assurance sufficient for the purposes of human life. We may, and must, assume our opinion to be true for the guidance of our own conduct: and it is assuming no more when we forbid bad men to pervert society by the propagation of opinions which we regard as false and pernicious.

I answer, that it is assuming very much more. There is the greatest difference between presuming an opinion to be true, because, with every opportunity for contesting it, it has not been refuted, and assuming its truth for the purpose of not permitting its refutation. Complete liberty of contradicting and disproving our opinion, is the very condition which justifies us in assuming its truth for purposes of action; and on no other terms can a being with human faculties have any rational assurance of being right.

When we consider either the history of opinion, or the ordinary conduct of human life, to what is it to be ascribed that the one and the other are no worse than they are? Not certainly to the inherent force of the human understanding; for, on any matter not self-evident, there are ninety-nine persons totally incapable of judging of it, for one who is capable; and the capacity of the hundredth person is only comparative; for the majority of the eminent men of every past generation held many opinions now known to be erroneous, and did or approved numerous things which no one will now justify. Why is it, then, that there is on the whole a preponderance among mankind of rational opinions and rational conduct? If there really is this preponderance—which there must be unless human affairs are, and have always been, in an almost desperate state—it is owing to a quality of the human mind, the source of everything respectable in man either as an intellectual or as a moral being, namely, that his errors are corrigible. He is capable of rectifying his mistakes, by discussion and experience. Not by experience alone. There must be discussion, to show how experience is to be interpreted. Wrong opinions and practices gradually yield to fact and argument: but facts and arguments, to produce any effect on the mind, must be brought before it. Very few facts are able to tell their own story, without comments to bring out their meaning. The whole strength and value, then, of human judgment, depending on the one property, that it can be set right when it is wrong, reliance can be placed on it only when the means of setting it right are kept constantly at hand. In the case of any person whose judgment is really deserving of confidence, how has it become so? Because it has kept his mind open to criticism of his opinions and conduct. Because it has been his practice to listen to all that could be said against him; to profit by as much of it as was just, and expound to himself, and upon occasion to others, the fallacy of what was fallacious. Because he has felt, that the only way in which a human being can make some approach to knowing the whole of a subject, is by hearing what can be said about it by persons of every variety of opinion, and studying all modes in which it can be looked at by every character of mind. No wise man ever acquired his wisdom in any mode but this; nor is it in the nature of human intellect to become wise in any other manner. The steady habit of correcting and completing his own opinion by collating it with those of others, so far from causing doubt and hesitation in carrying it into practice, is the only stable foundation for a just reliance on it: for, being cognisant of all that can, at least obviously, be said against him, and having taken up his position against all gainsayers—knowing that he has sought for objections and difficulties, instead of avoiding them, and has shut out no light which can be thrown upon the subject from any quarter—he has a right to think his judgment better than that of any person, or any multitude, who have not gone through a similar process.

It is not too much to require that what the wisest of mankind, those who are best entitled to trust their own judgment, find necessary to warrant their relying on it, should be submitted to by that miscellaneous collection of a few and many foolish individuals, called the public. The most intolerant of churches, the Roman Catholic Church, even at the canonization of a saint, admits, and listens patiently to, a "devil's advocate." The holiest of men, it appears, cannot be admitted to posthumous honours, until all that the devil could say against him is known and weighed. If even the Newtonian philosophy were not permitted to be questioned, mankind could not feel as complete assurance of its truth as they now do. The beliefs which we have most warrant for, have no safeguard to rest on, but a standing invitation to the whole world to prove them unfounded. If the challenge is not accepted, or is accepted and the attempt fails, we are far enough from certainty still; but we have done the best that the existing state of human affairs admits of; we have neglected nothing that could give the truth a chance of reaching us: if the lists are kept open, we may hope that if there be a better truth, it will be found when the human mind is capable of receiving it; and in the meantime we may rely on having attained such approach to truth, as is possible in our own day. This is the amount of certainty attainable by a fallible being, and this the sole way of attaining it.

Strange it is, that men should admit the validity of the arguments for free discussion, but object to their being "pushed to an extreme"; not seeing that unless the reasons are good for an extreme case, they are not good for any case. Strange that they should imagine that they are not assuming infallibility, when they acknowledge that there should be free discussion on all subjects which can possibly be doubtful, but think that some particular principle or doctrine should be forbidden to be questioned because it is so *certain*, that is, because *they are certain* that it is certain. To call any proposition certain, while there is any one who would deny its certainty if permitted, but who is not permitted, is to assume that we ourselves, and those who agree with us, are the judges of certainty, and judges without hearing the other side.

In the present age—which has been described as "destitute of faith, but terrified at scepticism"[2]—in which people feel sure, not so much that their opinions are true, as that they should not know what to do without them—the claims of an opinion to be protected from public attack are

---

[2] Quoted from Thomas Carlyle, "Memoirs of the Life of Scott," *London and Westminster Review* VI & XXVIII (January 1838): 315.

rested not so much on its truth, as on its importance to society. There are, it is alleged, certain beliefs, so useful, not to say indispensable to well-being, that it is as much the duty of governments to uphold those beliefs, as to protect any other of the interests of society. In a case of such necessity, and so directly in the line of their duty, something less than infallibility may, it is maintained, warrant, and even bind, governments, to act on their own opinion, confirmed by the general opinion of mankind. It is also often argued, and still oftener thought, that none but bad men would desire to weaken these salutary beliefs; and there can be nothing wrong, it is thought, in restraining bad men, and prohibiting what only such men would wish to practice. This mode of thinking makes the justification of restraints on discussion not a question of the truth of doctrines, but of their usefulness; and flatters itself by that means to escape the responsibility of claiming to be an infallible judge of opinions. But those who thus satisfy themselves, do not perceive that the assumption of infallibility is merely shifted from one point to another. The usefulness of an opinion is itself matter of opinion: as disputable, as open to discussion, and requiring discussion as much, as the opinion itself. There is the same need of an infallible judge of opinions to decide an opinion to be noxious, as to decide it to be false, unless the opinion condemned has full opportunity of defending itself. And it will not do to say that the heretic may be allowed to maintain the utility or harmlessness of his opinion, though forbidden to maintain its truth. The truth of an opinion is part of its utility. If we would know whether or not it is desirable that a proposition should be believed, is it possible to exclude the consideration of whether or not it is true? In the opinion, not of bad men, but of the best men, no belief which is contrary to truth can be really useful: and can you prevent such men from urging that plea, when they are charged with culpability for denying some doctrine which they are told is useful, but which they believe to be false? Those who are on the side of received opinions, never fail to take all possible advantage of this plea; you do not find *them* handling the question of utility as if it could be completely abstracted from that of truth: on the contrary, it is, above all, because their doctrine is the "truth," that the knowledge or the belief of it is held to be so indispensable. There can be no fair discussion of the question of usefulness, when an argument so vital may be employed on one side, but not on the other. And in point of fact, when law or public feeling do not permit the truth of an opinion to be disputed, they are just as little tolerant of a denial of its usefulness. The utmost they allow is an extenuation of its absolute necessity, or of the positive guilt of rejecting it.

In order more fully to illustrate the mischief of denying a hearing to opinions because we, in our own judgment, have condemned them, it will be desirable to fix down the discussion to a concrete case; and I choose, by preference, the cases which are least favourable to me—in which the argument against freedom of opinion, both on the score of truth and on that of utility, is considered the strongest. Let the opinions impugned be the belief in God and in a future state, or any of the commonly received doctrines of morality. To fight the battle on such ground, gives a great advantage to an unfair antagonist; since he will be sure to say (and many who have no desire to be unfair will say it internally), Are these the doctrines which you do not deem sufficiently certain to be taken under the protection of law? Is the belief in a God one of the opinions, to feel sure of which, you hold to be assuming infallibility? But I must be permitted to observe, that it is not the feeling sure of a doctrine (be it what it may) which I call an assumption of infallibility. It is the undertaking to decide that question *for others*, without allowing them to hear what can be said on the contrary side. And I denounce and reprobate this pretension not the less, if put forth on the side of my most solemn convictions. However positive any one's persuasion may be, not only of the falsity but of the pernicious consequences—not only of the pernicious consequences, but (to adopt expressions which I altogether condemn) the immorality and impiety of an opinion; yet if, in pursuance of that private judgment, though backed by the public judgment of his country or his cotemporaries, he prevents the opinion from being heard in its defence, he assumes infallibility. And so far from the assumption being less objectionable or less dangerous because the opinion is called immoral or impious, this is the case of all others in which it is most fatal. These are exactly the occasions on which the men of one generation commit those dreadful mistakes, which excite the astonishment and horror of posterity. It is among such that we find the instances memorable in history, when the arm of the law has been employed to root out the best men and the noblest doctrines; with deplorable success as to the men, though some of the doctrines have survived to be (as if in mockery) invoked, in defence of similar conduct towards those who dissent from *them*, or from their received interpretation.

Mankind can hardly be too often reminded, that there was once a man named Socrates, between whom and the legal authorities and public opinion of his time, there took place a memorable collision. Born in an age and country abounding in individual greatness, this man has been handed down to us by those who best knew both him and the age, as the most virtuous man in it; while we know him as the head and prototype of all subsequent teachers of virtue, the source equally of the lofty inspiration of Plato and the judicious utilitarianism of Aristotle, "*i maestri di color che sanno*,"[3] the two headsprings of ethical as of all other philosophy. This acknowledged master of all the eminent thinkers who have since lived—whose fame, still growing after more than two thousand years, all but outweighs the whole remainder of the names which make his native city illustrious—was put to death by his countrymen, after a judicial conviction, for impiety and immorality. Impiety, in denying the gods recognised by the State; indeed his accuser asserted (see the *Apologia*) that he believed in no gods at all. Immorality, in being, by his doctrines and instructions, a "corrupter of youth."[4] Of these charges the tribunal, there is every ground for believing, honestly found him guilty, and condemned the man who probably of all then born had deserved best of mankind, to be put to death as a criminal.

To pass from this to the only other instance of judicial iniquity, the mention of which, after the condemnation of Socrates, would not be an

---

[3] [*i maestri di color che sanno*] "the masters of those who know." (Adapted from Dante's *Inferno*, Canto IV, 131, where the line, in the singular, refers to Aristotle.)

[4] See Plato's *Apology*. Socrates' accuser was Meletus.

anti-climax: the event which took place on Calvary rather more than eighteen hundred years ago. The man who left on the memory of those who witnessed his life and conversation, such an impression of his moral grandeur, that eighteen subsequent centuries have done homage to him as the Almighty in person, was ignominiously put to death, as what? As a blasphemer. Men did not merely mistake their benefactor; they mistook him for the exact contrary of what he was, and treated him as that prodigy of impiety, which they themselves are now held to be, for their treatment of him.[5] The feelings with which mankind now regard these lamentable transactions, especially the later of the two, render them extremely unjust in their judgment of the unhappy actors. These were, to all appearance, not bad men—not worse than men commonly are, but rather the contrary; men who possessed in a full, or somewhat more than a full measure, the religious, moral, and patriotic feelings of their time and people: the very kind of men who, in all times, our own included, have every chance of passing through life blameless and respected. The high-priest who rent his garments when the words were pronounced[6] which, according to all the ideas of his country, constituted the blackest guilt, was in all probability quite as sincere in his horror and indignation, as the generality of respectable and pious men now are in the religious and moral sentiments they profess; and most of those who now shudder at his conduct, if they had lived in his time, and been born Jews, would have acted precisely as he did. Orthodox Christians who are tempted to think that those who stoned to death the first martyrs must have been worse men than they themselves are, ought to remember that one of those persecutors was Saint Paul.[7]

Let us add one more example, the most striking of all, if the impressiveness of an error is measured by the wisdom and virtue of him who falls into it. If ever any one, possessed of power, had grounds for

[5] Mill's shadowy language suggests that he subscribed to the (long exploded) notion that it was the Jews, rather than the Romans, who were responsible for the sentencing and execution of Jesus.

[6] Caiaphas; see Matthew, 26:65.

[7] See Acts, 7:58–8:4.

thinking himself the best and most enlightened among his cotemporaries, it was the Emperor Marcus Aurelius. Absolute monarch of the whole civilized world, he preserved through life not only the most unblemished justice, but what was less to be expected from his Stoical breeding, the tenderest heart. The few failings which are attributed to him, were all on the side of indulgence: while his writings, the highest ethical product of the ancient mind, differ scarcely perceptibly, if they differ at all, from the most characteristic teachings of Christ. This man, a better Christian in all but the dogmatic sense of the word than almost any of the ostensibly Christian sovereigns who have since reigned, persecuted Christianity. Placed at the summit of all the previous attainments of humanity, with an open, unfettered intellect, and a character which led him of himself to embody in his moral writings the Christian ideal, he yet failed to see that Christianity was to be a good and not an evil to the world, with his duties to which he was so deeply penetrated. Existing society he knew to be in a deplorable state. But such as it was, he saw, or thought he saw, that it was held together, and prevented from being worse, by belief and reverence of the received divinities. As a ruler of mankind, he deemed it his duty not to suffer society to fall in pieces; and saw not how, if its existing ties were removed, any others could be formed which could again knit it together. The new religion openly aimed at dissolving these ties: unless, therefore, it was his duty to adopt that religion, it seemed to be his duty to put it down. Inasmuch then as the theology of Christianity did not appear to him true or of divine origin; inasmuch as this strange history of a crucified God was not credible to him, and a system which purported to rest entirely upon a foundation to him so wholly unbelievable, could not be foreseen by him to be that renovating agency which, after all abatements, it has in fact proved to be; the gentlest and most amiable of philosophers and rulers, under a solemn sense of duty, authorized the persecution of Christianity. To my mind this is one of the most tragical facts in all history. It is a bitter thought, how different a thing the Christianity of the world might have been, if the Christian faith had been adopted as the religion of the empire under the auspices of Marcus Aurelius instead of those of Constantine.[8] But it would be equally unjust to him and false to truth, to deny, that no one plea which can be urged for punishing anti-Christian teaching, was wanting to Marcus Aurelius for punishing, as he did, the propagation of Christianity. No Christian more firmly believes that Atheism is false, and tends to the dissolution of society, than Marcus Aurelius believed the same things of Christianity; he who, of all men then living, might have been thought the most capable of appreciating it. Unless any one who approves of punishment for the promulgation of opinions, flatters himself that he is a wiser and better man than Marcus Aurelius—more deeply versed in the wisdom of his time, more elevated in his intellect above it—more earnest in his search for truth, or more single-minded in his devotion to it when found;—let him abstain from that assumption of the joint infallibility of himself and the multitude, which the great Antoninus made with so unfortunate a result.

Aware of the impossibility of defending the use of punishment for restraining irreligious opinions, by any argument which will not justify Marcus Antoninus, the enemies of religious freedom, when hard pressed, occasionally accept this consequence, and say, with Dr. Johnson, that the persecutors of Christianity were in the right[9]; that persecution is an ordeal through which truth ought to pass, and always passes successfully, legal penalties being, in the end, powerless against truth, though sometimes beneficially effective against mischievous errors. This is a form of the argument for religious intolerance, sufficiently remarkable not to be passed without notice.

A theory which maintains that truth may justifiably be persecuted because persecution cannot possibly do it any harm, cannot be charged with being intentionally hostile to the reception of new truths; but we cannot commend the generosity of its dealing with the persons to whom mankind are indebted for them. To discover to the world something which deeply concerns it, and of which it was previously ignorant; to prove to it

[8] Constantine was the Roman Emperor (from 306–337) who adopted Christianity.

[9] See James Boswell, *Life of Johnson* (1791), vol. II. (Entry for 7 May 1773.)

that it had been mistaken on some vital point of temporal or spiritual interest, is as important a service as a human being can render to his fellow-creatures, and in certain cases, as in those of the early Christians and of the Reformers, those who think with Dr. Johnson believe it to have been the most precious gift which could be bestowed on mankind. That the authors of such splendid benefits should be requited by martyrdom; that their reward should be to be dealt with as the vilest of criminals, is not, upon this theory, a deplorable error and misfortune, for which humanity should mourn in sackcloth and ashes, but the normal and justifiable state of things. The propounder of a truth, according to this doctrine, should stand, as stood, in the legislation of the Locrians, the proposer of a new law, with a halter round his neck, to be instantly tightened if the public assembly did not, on hearing his reasons, then and there adopt his proposition.[10]

People who defend this mode of treating benefactors, cannot be supposed to set much value on the benefit; and I believe this view of the subject is mostly confined to the sort of persons who think that new truths may have been desirable once, but that we have had enough of them now.

But, indeed, the dictum that truth always triumphs over persecution, is one of those pleasant falsehoods which men repeat after one another till they pass into commonplaces, but which all experience refutes. History teems with instances of truth put down by persecution. If not suppressed for ever, it may be thrown back for centuries. To speak only of religious opinions: the Reformation broke out at least twenty times before Luther, and was put down. Arnold of Brescia was put down. Fra Dolcino was put down. Savonarola was put down. The Albigeois were put down. The Vaudois were put down. The Lollards were put down. The Hussites were put down.[11] Even after the era of Luther, wherever persecution was persisted in, it was successful. In Spain, Italy, Flanders, the Austrian empire, Protestantism was rooted out; and, most likely, would have been so in England, had Queen Mary lived, or Queen Elizabeth died. Persecution

---

[10] See Demosthenes, "Against Timocrates." Locris was a minor state in ancient Greece.

has always succeeded, save where the heretics were too strong a party to be effectually persecuted. No reasonable person can doubt that Christianity might have been extirpated in the Roman Empire. It spread, and became predominant, because the persecutions were only occasional, lasting but a short time, and separated by long intervals of almost undisturbed propagandism. It is a piece of idle sentimentality that truth, merely as truth, has any inherent power denied to error, of prevailing against the dungeon and the stake. Men are not more zealous for truth than they often are for error, and a sufficient application of legal or even of social penalties will generally succeed in stopping the propagation of either. The real advantage which truth has, consists in this, that when an opinion is true, it may be extinguished once, twice, or many times, but in the course of ages there will generally be found persons to rediscover it, until some one of its reappearances falls on a time when from favourable circumstances it escapes persecution until it has made such head as to withstand all subsequent attempts to suppress it.

It will be said, that we do not now put to death the introducers of new opinions: we are not like our fathers who slew the prophets, we even build sepulchres to them. It is true we no longer put heretics to death; and the amount of penal infliction which modern feeling would probably tolerate, even against the most obnoxious opinions, is not sufficient to extirpate them. But let us not flatter ourselves that we are yet free from the stain even of legal persecution. Penalties for opinion, or at least for its expression, still exist by law; and their enforcement is not, even in these times, so unexampled as to make it at all incredible that they may some day be

[11] The Italian religious reformers Arnold of Brescia, Fra Dolcino, and Girolamo Savonarola were put to death as heretics in the twelfth, fourteenth, and fifteenth centuries, respectively. The Albigeois, or Albigenses, were a religious sect that flourished in southern France in the twelfth and thirteen centuries, only to be murdered by the Inquisition under Pope Innocent III. The Vaudois, or Waldenses, were a Christian sect in southern France in the late twelfth century. The Lollards were a sect of English religious reformers in the fourteenth and fifteenth centuries, followers of John Wycliffe. Hussites followed the religious theories of John Huss, a Bohemian religious reformer burned at the stake.

revived in full force. In the year 1857, at the summer assizes of the county of Cornwall, an unfortunate man,[12] said to be of unexceptionable conduct in all relations of life, was sentenced to twenty-one months' imprisonment, for uttering, and writing on a gate, some offensive words concerning Christianity. Within a month of the same time, at the Old Bailey, two persons, on two separate occasions,[13] were rejected as jurymen, and one of them grossly insulted by the judge and by one of the counsel, because they honestly declared that they had no theological belief; and a third, a foreigner,[14] for the same reason, was denied justice against a thief. This refusal of redress took place in virtue of the legal doctrine, that no person can be allowed to give evidence in a court of justice, who does not profess belief in a God (any god is sufficient) and in a future state; which is equivalent to declaring such persons to be outlaws, excluded from the protection of the tribunals; who may not only be robbed or assaulted with impunity, if no one but themselves, or persons of similar opinions, be present, but any one else may be robbed or assaulted with impunity, if the proof of the fact depends on their evidence. The assumption on which this is grounded, is that the oath is worthless, of a person who does not believe in a future state; a proposition which betokens much ignorance of history in those who assent to it (since it is historically true that a large proportion of infidels in all ages have been persons of distinguished integrity and honour); and would be maintained by no one who had the smallest conception how many of the persons in greatest repute with the world, both for virtues and for attainments, are well known, at least to their intimates, to be unbelievers. The rule, besides, is suicidal, and cuts away its own foundation. Under pretence that atheists must be liars, it admits the testimony of all atheists who are willing to lie, and rejects only those who brave the obloquy of publicly confessing a detested creed rather than affirm a falsehood. A rule thus self-convicted of absurdity so far as regards

---

[12] Thomas Pooley, Bodmin Assizes, July 31, 1857. In December following, he received a free pardon from the Crown. (Mill's note.)

[13] George Jacob Holyoake, 17 August, 1857; Edward Truelove, July, 1857.

[14] Baron de Gleichen, Marlborough-street Police Court, 4 August 1857.

its professed purpose, can be kept in force only as a badge of hatred, a relic of persecution; a persecution, too, having the peculiarity, that the qualification for undergoing it, is the being clearly proved not to deserve it. The rule, and the theory it implies, are hardly less insulting to believers than to infidels. For if he who does not believe in a future state, necessarily lies, it follows that they who do believe are only prevented from lying, if prevented they are, by the fear of hell. We will not do the authors and abettors of the rule the injury of supposing, that the conception which they have formed of Christian virtue is drawn from their own consciousness.

These, indeed, are but rags and remnants of persecution, and may be thought to be not so much an indication of the wish to persecute, as an example of that very frequent infirmity of English minds, which makes them take a preposterous pleasure in the assertion of a bad principle, when they are no longer bad enough to desire to carry it really into practice. But unhappily there is no security in the state of the public mind, that the suspension of worse forms of legal persecution, which has lasted for about the space of a generation, will continue. In this age the quiet surface of routine is as often ruffled by attempts to resuscitate past evils, as to introduce new benefits. What is boasted of at the present time as the revival of religion, is always, in narrow and uncultivated minds, at least as much the revival of bigotry; and where there is the strong permanent leaven of intolerance in the feelings of a people, which at all times abides in the middle classes of this country, it needs but little to provoke them into actively persecuting those whom they have never ceased to think proper objects of persecution.[15]

For it is this—it is the opinions men entertain, and the feelings they cherish, respecting those who disown the beliefs they deem important, which makes this country not a place of mental freedom. For a long time past, the chief mischief of the legal penalties is that they strengthen the social stigma. It is that stigma which is really effective, and so effective is it, that the profession of opinions which are under the ban of society is much less common in England, than is, in many other countries, the avowal of those which incur risk of judicial punishment. In respect to all persons but those whose pecuniary circumstances make them independent of the good will of other people, opinion, on this subject, is as efficacious as law; men might as well be imprisoned, as excluded from the means of earning their bread. Those whose bread is already secured, and who desire no favours from men in power, or from bodies of men, or from the public, have nothing to fear from the open avowal of any opinions, but to be ill-thought of and ill-spoken of, and this it ought not to require a very heroic mould to enable them to bear. There is no room for any appeal *ad misericordiam*[16] in behalf

---

[15] Ample warning may be drawn from the large infusion of the passions of a persecutor, which mingled with the general display of the worst parts of our national character on the occasion of the Sepoy insurrection. The ravings of fanatics or charlatans from the pulpit may be unworthy of notice; but the heads of the Evangelical party have announced as their principle for the government of Hindoos and Mahomedans, that no schools be supported by public money in which the Bible is not taught, and by necessary consequence that no public employment be given to any but real or pretended Christians. An Under-Secretary of State [William N. Massey], in a speech delivered to his constituents on the 12th of November, 1857, is reported to have said: "Toleration of their faith" (the faith of a hundred millions of British subjects), "the superstition which they called religion, by the British Government, had had the effect of retarding the ascendancy of the British name, and preventing the salutary growth of Christianity....Toleration was the great corner-stone of the religious liberties of this country; but do not let them abuse that precious word toleration. As he understood it, it meant the complete liberty to all, freedom of worship, *among Christians, who worshipped upon the same foundation.* It meant toleration of all sects and denominations *of Christians who believed in the one mediation.*" [See *The Times*, 14 Nov., 1857, p. 4.] I desire to call attention to the fact, that a man who has been deemed fit to fill a high office in the government of this country, under a liberal Ministry, maintains the doctrine that all who do not believe in the divinity of Christ are beyond the pale of toleration. Who, after this imbecile display, can indulge the illusion that religious persecution has passed away, never to return? (Mill's note.) The Sepoy insurrection, also called the Indian Mutiny, was the revolt early in 1857 of 70,000 native troops (sepoys) in the Bengal army of the East India Company who objected to the issue of cartridges greased with animal fat, an act they took as insulting to their belief in the sacredness of animals. The revolt was suppressed in the following year, when the government of India was transferred from the East India Company to the Crown.

of such persons. But though we do not now inflict so much evil on those who think differently from us, as it was formerly our custom to do, it may be that we do ourselves as much evil as ever by our treatment of them. Socrates was put to death, but the Socratic philosophy rose like the sun in heaven, and spread its illumination over the whole intellectual firmament. Christians were cast to the lions, but the Christian church grew up a stately and spreading tree, overtopping the older and less vigorous growths, and stifling them by its shade. Our merely social intolerance kills no one, roots out no opinions, but induces men to disguise them, or to abstain from any active effort for their diffusion. With us, heretical opinions do not perceptibly gain, or even lose, ground in each decade or generation; they never blaze out far and wide, but continue to smoulder in the narrow circles of thinking and studious persons among whom they originate, without ever lighting up the general affairs of mankind with either a true or a deceptive light. And thus is kept up a state of things very satisfactory to some minds, because, without the unpleasant process of fining or imprisoning anybody, it maintains all prevailing opinions outwardly undisturbed, while it does not absolutely interdict the exercise of reason by dissentients afflicted with the malady of thought. A convenient plan for having peace in the intellectual world, and keeping all things going on therein very much as they do already. But the price paid for this sort of intellectual pacification, is the sacrifice of the entire moral courage of the human mind. A state of things in which a large portion of the most active and inquiring intellects find it advisable to keep the genuine principles and grounds of their convictions within their own breasts, and attempt, in what they address to the public, to fit as much as they can of their own conclusions to premises which they have internally renounced, cannot send forth the open, fearless characters, and logical, consistent intellects who once adorned the thinking world. The sort of men who can be looked for under it, are either mere conformers to commonplace, or time-servers for truth, whose arguments on all great subjects are meant for their hearers,

[16] [*ad misericordiam*] to pity. Said of an argument or appeal.

and are not those which have convinced themselves. Those who avoid this alternative, do so by narrowing their thoughts and interest to things which can be spoken of without venturing within the region of principles, that is, to small practical matters, which would come right of themselves, if but the minds of mankind were strengthened and enlarged, and which will never be made effectually right until then: while that which would strengthen and enlarge men's minds, free and daring speculation on the highest subjects, is abandoned.

Those in whose eyes this reticence on the part of heretics is no evil, should consider in the first place, that in consequence of it there is never any fair and thorough discussion of heretical opinions; and that such of them as could not stand such a discussion, though they may be prevented from spreading, do not disappear. But it is not the minds of heretics that are deteriorated most, by the ban placed on all inquiry which does not end in the orthodox conclusions. The greatest harm done is to those who are not heretics, and whose whole mental development is cramped, and their reason cowed, by the fear of heresy. Who can compute what the world loses in the multitude of promising intellects combined with timid characters, who dare not follow out any bold, vigorous, independent train of thought, lest it should land them in something which would admit of being considered irreligious or immoral? Among them we may occasionally see some man of deep conscientiousness, and subtle and refined understanding, who spends a life in sophisticating with an intellect which he cannot silence, and exhausts the resources of ingenuity in attempting to reconcile the promptings of his conscience and reason with orthodoxy, which yet he does not, perhaps, to the end succeed in doing. No one can be a great thinker who does not recognise, that as a thinker it is his first duty to follow his intellect to whatever conclusions it may lead. Truth gains more even by the errors of one who, with due study and preparation, thinks for himself, than by the true opinions of those who only hold them because they do not suffer themselves to think. Not that it is solely, or chiefly, to form great thinkers, that freedom of thinking is required. On the contrary, it is as much and even more indispensable, to enable average human beings to attain the mental stature which they are capable of. There have been, and may again be, great individual thinkers, in a general atmosphere of mental slavery. But there never has been, nor ever will be, in that atmosphere, an intellectually active people. When any people has made a temporary approach to such a character, it has been because the dread of heterodox speculation was for a time suspended. Where there is a tacit convention that principles are not to be disputed; where the discussion of the greatest questions which can occupy humanity is considered to be closed, we cannot hope to find that generally high scale of mental activity which has made some periods of history so remarkable. Never when controversy avoided the subjects which are large and important enough to kindle enthusiasm, was the mind of a people stirred up from its foundations, and the impulse given which raised even persons of the most ordinary intellect to something of the dignity of thinking beings. Of such we have had an example in the condition of Europe during the times immediately following the Reformation; another, though limited to the Continent and to a more cultivated class, in the speculative movement of the latter half of the eighteenth century;[17] and a third, of still briefer duration, in the intellectual fermentation of Germany during the Goethian and Fichtean period.[18] These periods differed widely in the particular opinions which they developed; but were alike in this, that during all three the yoke of authority was broken. In each, an old mental despotism had been thrown off, and no new one had yet taken its place. The impulse given at these three periods has made Europe what it now is. Every single improvement which has taken place either in the human mind or in institutions, may be traced distinctly to one or other of them. Appearances have for some time indicated that all three impulses are well nigh spent; and we can expect no fresh start, until we again assert our mental freedom.

[17] The Enlightenment.
[18] Johann Wolfgang von Goethe (1749–1832); Johann Gottlieb Fichte (1762–1814).

Let us now pass to the second division of the argument, and dismissing the supposition that any of the received opinions may be false, let us assume them to be true, and examine into the worth of the manner in which they are likely to be held, when their truth is not freely and openly canvassed. However unwillingly a person who has a strong opinion may admit the possibility that his opinion may be false, he ought to be moved by the consideration that however true it may be, if it is not fully, frequently, and fearlessly discussed, it will be held as a dead dogma, not a living truth.

There is a class of persons (happily not quite so numerous as formerly) who think it enough if a person assents undoubtingly to what they think true, though he has no knowledge whatever of the grounds of the opinion, and could not make a tenable defence of it against the most superficial objections. Such persons, if they can once get their creed taught from authority, naturally think that no good, and some harm, comes of its being allowed to be questioned. Where their influence prevails, they make it nearly impossible for the received opinion to be rejected wisely and considerately, though it may still be rejected rashly and ignorantly; for to shut out discussion entirely is seldom possible, and when it once gets in, beliefs not grounded on conviction are apt to give way before the slightest semblance of an argument. Waiving, however, this possibility—assuming that the true opinion abides in the mind, but abides as a prejudice, a belief independent of, and proof against, argument—this is not the way in which truth ought to be held by a rational being. This is not knowing the truth. Truth, thus held, is but one superstition the more, accidentally clinging to the words which enunciate a truth.

If the intellect and judgment of mankind ought to be cultivated, a thing which Protestants at least do not deny, on what can these faculties be more appropriately exercised by any one, than on the things which concern him so much that it is considered necessary for him to hold opinions on them? If the cultivation of the understanding consists in one thing more than in another, it is surely in learning the grounds of one's own opinions. Whatever people believe, on subjects on which it is of the first importance to believe rightly, they ought to be able to defend against at least the common objections. But, some one may say, "Let them be *taught* the grounds of their opinions. It does not follow that opinions must be merely parroted because they are never heard controverted. Persons who learn geometry do not simply commit the theorems to memory, but understand and learn likewise the demonstrations; and it would be absurd to say that they remain ignorant of the grounds of geometrical truths, because they never hear any one deny, and attempt to disprove them." Undoubtedly: and such teaching suffices on a subject like mathematics, where there is nothing at all to be said on the wrong side of the question. The peculiarity of the evidence of mathematical truths is, that all the argument is on one side. There are no objections, and no answers to objections. But on every subject on which difference of opinion is possible, the truth depends on a balance to be struck between two sets of conflicting reasons. Even in natural philosophy, there is always some other explanation possible of the same facts; some geocentric theory instead of heliocentric, some phlogiston instead of oxygen; and it has to be shown why that other theory cannot be the true one: and until this is shown, and until we know how it is shown, we do not understand the grounds of our opinion. But when we turn to subjects infinitely more complicated, to morals, religion, politics, social relations, and the business of life, three-fourths of the arguments for every disputed opinion consist in dispelling the appearances which favour some opinion different from it. The greatest orator, save one, of antiquity,[19] has left it on record that he always studied his adversary's case with as great, if not with still greater, intensity than even his own. What Cicero practiced as the means of forensic success, requires to be imitated by all who study any subject in order to arrive at the truth. He who knows only his own side of the case, knows little of that. His reasons may be good, and no one may have been able to refute them. But if he is equally unable to refute the reasons on the opposite side; if he does not so much as know what they are, he has no ground for preferring either opinion. The rational position for him would be suspension of judgment, and unless

---

[19] Cicero, e.g., in *De Oratore* II, xxiv. The one greater orator of antiquity was Demosthenes.

he contents himself with that, he is either led by authority, or adopts, like the generality of the world, the side to which he feels most inclination. Nor is it enough that he should hear the arguments of adversaries from his own teachers, presented as they state them, and accompanied by what they offer as refutations. That is not the way to do justice to the arguments, or bring them into real contact with his own mind. He must be able to hear them from persons who actually believe them; who defend them in earnest, and do their very utmost for them. He must know them in their most plausible and persuasive form; he must feel the whole force of the difficulty which the true view of the subject has to encounter and dispose of; else he will never really possess himself of the portion of truth which meets and removes that difficulty. Ninety-nine in a hundred of what are called educated men are in this condition; even of those who can argue fluently for their opinions. Their conclusion may be true, but it might be false for anything they know: they have never thrown themselves into the mental position of those who think differently from them, and considered what such persons may have to say; and consequently they do not, in any proper sense of the word, know the doctrine which they themselves profess. They do not know those parts of it which explain and justify the remainder; the considerations which show that a fact which seemingly conflicts with another is reconcilable with it, or that, of two apparently strong reasons, one and not the other ought to be preferred. All that part of the truth which turns the scale, and decides the judgment of a completely informed mind, they are strangers to; nor is it ever really known, but to those who have attended equally and impartially to both sides, and endeavoured to see the reasons of both in the strongest light. So essential is this discipline to a real understanding of moral and human subjects, that if opponents of all important truths do not exist, it is indispensable to imagine them, and supply them with the strongest arguments which the most skilful devil's advocate can conjure up.

To abate the force of these considerations, an enemy of free discussion may be supposed to say, that there is no necessity for mankind in general to know and understand all that can be said against or for their opinions by philosophers and theologians. That it is not needful for common men to be able to expose all the misstatements or fallacies of an ingenious opponent. That it is enough if there is always somebody capable of answering them, so that nothing likely to mislead uninstructed persons remains unrefuted. That simple minds, having been taught the obvious grounds of the truths inculcated on them, may trust to authority for the rest, and being aware that they have neither knowledge nor talent to resolve every difficulty which can be raised, may repose in the assurance that all those which have been raised have been or can be answered, by those who are specially trained to the task.

Conceding to this view of the subject the utmost that can be claimed for it by those most easily satisfied with the amount of understanding of truth which ought to accompany the belief of it; even so, the argument for free discussion is no way weakened. For even this doctrine acknowledges that mankind ought to have a rational assurance that all objections have been satisfactorily answered; and how are they to be answered if that which requires to be answered is not spoken? or how can the answer be known to be satisfactory, if the objectors have no opportunity of showing that it is unsatisfactory? If not the public, at least the philosophers and theologians who are to resolve the difficulties, must make themselves familiar with those difficulties in their most puzzling form; and this cannot be accomplished unless they are freely stated, and placed in the most advantageous light which they admit of. The Catholic Church has its own way of dealing with this embarrassing problem. It makes a broad separation between those who can be permitted to receive its doctrines on conviction, and those who must accept them on trust. Neither, indeed, are allowed any choice as to what they will accept; but the clergy, such at least as can be fully confided in, may admissibly and meritoriously make themselves acquainted with the arguments of opponents, in order to answer them, and may, therefore, read heretical books; the laity, not unless by special permission, hard to be obtained. This discipline recognises a knowledge of the enemy's case as beneficial to the teachers, but finds means, consistent with this, of denying it to the rest of the world: thus giving to the *elite* more mental culture, though not more mental freedom, than it allows to the mass. By this device it succeeds in obtaining the kind of mental superiority which its purposes require; for though culture without freedom never made a large and liberal mind, it can make a clever *nisi prius*[20] advocate of a cause. But in countries professing Protestantism, this resource is denied; since Protestants hold, at least in theory, that the responsibility for the choice of a religion must be borne by each for himself, and cannot be thrown off upon teachers. Besides, in the present state of the world, it is practically impossible that writings which are read by the instructed can be kept from the uninstructed. If the teachers of mankind are to be cognisant of all that they ought to know, everything must be free to be written and published without restraint.

If, however, the mischievous operation of the absence of free discussion, when the received opinions are true, were confined to leaving men ignorant of the grounds of those opinions, it might be thought that this, if an intellectual, is no moral evil, and does not affect the worth of the opinions, regarded in their influence on the character. The fact, however, is, that not only the grounds of the opinion are forgotten in the absence of discussion, but too often the meaning of the opinion itself. The words which convey it, cease to suggest ideas, or suggest only a small portion of those they were originally employed to communicate. Instead of a vivid conception and a living belief there remain only a few phrases retained by rote; or, if any part, the shell and husk only of the meaning is retained, the finer essence being lost. The great chapter in human history which this fact occupies and fills, cannot be too earnestly studied and meditated on.

It is illustrated in the experience of almost all ethical doctrines and religious creeds. They are all full of meaning and vitality to those who originate them, and to the direct disciples of the originators. Their meaning continues to be felt in undiminished strength, and is perhaps brought out into even fuller consciousness, so long as the struggle lasts to give the

[20] [*Nisi prius*] unless previously—a legal expression having several special uses. Mill probably means either a clever lawyer in a *nisi prius* court, or one who argues a cause on the grounds that it is valid unless shown to be invalid.

doctrine or creed an ascendancy over other creeds. At last it either prevails, and becomes the general opinion, or its progress stops; it keeps possession of the ground it has gained, but ceases to spread further. When either of these results has become apparent, controversy on the subject flags, and gradually dies away. The doctrine has taken its place, if not as a received opinion, as one of the admitted sects or divisions of opinion: those who hold it have generally inherited, not adopted it; and conversion from one of these doctrines to another, being now an exceptional fact, occupies little place in the thoughts of their professors. Instead of being, as at first, constantly on the alert either to defend themselves against the world, or to bring the world over to them, they have subsided into acquiescence, and neither listen, when they can help it, to arguments against their creed, nor trouble dissentients (if there be such) with arguments in its favour. From this time may usually be dated the decline in the living power of the doctrine. We often hear the teachers of all creeds lamenting the difficulty of keeping up in the minds of believers a lively apprehension of the truth which they nominally recognise, so that it may penetrate the feelings, and acquire a real mastery over the conduct. No such difficulty is complained of while the creed is still fighting for its existence: even the weaker combatants then know and feel what they are fighting for, and the difference between it and other doctrines; and in that period of every creed's existence, not a few persons may be found, who have realized its fundamental principles in all the forms of thought, have weighed and considered them in all their important bearings, and have experienced the full effect on the character, which belief in that creed ought produce in a mind thoroughly imbued with it. But when it has come to be an hereditary creed, and to be received passively, not actively—when the mind is no longer compelled, in the same degree as at first, to exercise its vital powers on the questions which its belief presents to it, there is a progressive tendency to forget all of the belief except the formularies, or to give it a dull and torpid assent, as if accepting it on trust dispensed with the necessity of realizing it in consciousness, or testing it by personal experience; until it almost ceases to connect itself at all with the inner life of the human being. Then are seen the cases, so frequent in this age of the world as almost to form the majority, in which the creed remains as it were outside the mind, incrusting and petrifying it against all other influences addressed to the higher parts of our nature; manifesting its power by not suffering any fresh and living conviction to get in, but itself doing nothing for the mind or heart, except standing sentinel over them to keep them vacant.

To what an extent doctrines intrinsically fitted to make the deepest impression upon the mind may remain in it as dead beliefs, without being ever realized in the imagination, the feelings, or the understanding, is exemplified by the manner in which the majority of believers hold the doctrines of Christianity. By Christianity I here mean what is accounted such by all churches and sects—the maxims and precepts contained in the New Testament. These are considered sacred, and accepted as laws, by all professing Christians. Yet it is scarcely too much to say that not one Christian in a thousand guides or tests his individual conduct by reference to those laws. The standard to which he does refer it, is the custom of his nation, his class, or his religious profession. He has thus, on the one hand, a collection of ethical maxims, which he believes to have been vouchsafed to him by infallible wisdom as rules for his government; and on the other, a set of every-day judgments and practices, which go a certain length with some of those maxims, not so great a length with others, stand in direct opposition to some, and are, on the whole, a compromise between the Christian creed and the interests and suggestions of worldly life. To the first of these standards he gives his homage; to the other his real allegiance. All Christians believe that the blessed are the poor and humble, and those who are ill-used by the world; that it is easier for a camel to pass through the eye of a needle than for a rich man to enter the kingdom of heaven; that they should judge not, lest they be judged; that they should swear not at all; that they should love their neighbour as themselves; that if one take their cloak, they should give him their coat also; that they should take no thought for the morrow; that if they would be perfect, they should sell all that they have and give it to the poor.[21] They are not insincere when they say that they believe these things. They do believe them, as people believe what they have always heard lauded and never discussed. But in the sense of that living belief which regulates conduct, they believe these doctrines just up to the point to which it is usual to act upon them. The doctrines in their integrity are serviceable to pelt adversaries with; and it is understood that they are to be put forward (when possible) as the reasons for whatever people do that they think laudable. But any one who reminded them that the maxims require an infinity of things which they never even think of doing, would gain nothing but to be classed among those very unpopular characters who affect to be better than other people. The doctrines have no hold on ordinary believers—are not a power in their minds. They have an habitual respect for the sound of them, but no feeling which spreads from the words to the things signified, and forces the mind to take *them* in, and make them conform to the formula. Whenever conduct is concerned, they look round for Mr. A and B to direct them how far to go in obeying Christ.

Now we may be well assured that the case was not thus, but far otherwise, with the early Christians. Had it been thus, Christianity never would have expanded from an obscure sect of the despised Hebrews into the religion of the Roman empire. When their enemies said, "See how these Christians love one another"[22] (a remark not likely to be made by anybody now), they assuredly had a much livelier feeling of the meaning of their creed than they have ever had since. And to this cause, probably, it is chiefly owing that Christianity now makes so little progress in extending its domain, and after eighteen centuries, is still nearly confined to Europeans and the descendants of Europeans. Even with the strictly religious, who are much in earnest about their doctrines, and attach a greater amount of meaning to many of them than people in general, it commonly happens that the part which is thus comparatively active in their minds is that which was made by Calvin, or Knox,[23] or some such person much nearer in character to themselves. The sayings of Christ coexist passively in their

[21] See, respectively, Luke, 6:20–3 and Matthew, 19:24, 7:1, 5:34, 19:19, 5:40, 6:34, 19:21.

[22] Tertullian, *Apologeticus* XXXIX, 7.

minds, producing hardly any effect beyond what is caused by mere listening to words so amiable and bland. There are many reasons, doubtless, why doctrines which are the badge of a sect retain more of their vitality than those common to all recognised sects, and why more pains are taken by teachers to keep their meaning alive; but one reason certainly is, that the peculiar doctrines are more questioned, and have to be oftener defended against open gainsayers.

Both teachers and learners go to sleep at their post, as soon as there is no enemy in the field.

The same thing holds true, generally speaking, of all traditional doctrines—those of prudence and knowledge of life, as well as of morals or religion. All languages and literatures are full of general observations on life, both as to what it is, and how to conduct oneself in it; observations which everybody knows, which everybody repeats, or hears with acquiescence, which are received as truisms, yet of which most people first truly learn the meaning, when experience, generally of a painful kind, has made it a reality to them. How often, when smarting under some unforeseen misfortune or disappointment, does a person call to mind some proverb or common saying, familiar to him all his life, the meaning of which, if he had ever before felt it as he does now, would have saved him from the calamity. There are indeed reasons for this, other than the absence of discussion: there are many truths of which the full meaning *cannot* be realized, until personal experience has brought it home. But much more of the meaning even of these would have been understood, and what was understood would have been far more deeply impressed on the mind, if the man had been accustomed to hear it argued *pro* and *con* by people who did understand it. The fatal tendency of mankind to leave off thinking about a thing when it is no longer doubtful, is the cause of half their errors. A cotemporary author has well spoken of "the deep slumber of a decided opinion."[24]

[23] John Calvin (1509–64), French theologian and religious reformer; John Knox (1505–72), Scottish Protestant reformer.
[24] Sir Arthur Helps, *Thoughts in the Cloister and the Crowd* (1835).

But what! (it may be asked) Is the absence of unanimity an indispensable condition of true knowledge? Is it necessary that some part of mankind should persist in error, to enable any to realize the truth? Does a belief cease to be real and vital as soon as it is generally received—and is a proposition never thoroughly understood and felt unless some doubt of it remains? As soon as mankind have unanimously accepted a truth, does the truth perish within them? The highest aim and best result of improved intelligence, it has hitherto been thought, is to unite mankind more and more in the acknowledgment of all important truths: and does the intelligence only last as long as it has not achieved its object? Do the fruits of conquest perish by the very completeness of the victory?

I affirm no such thing. As mankind improve, the number of doctrines which are no longer disputed or doubted will be constantly on the increase: and the well-being of mankind may almost be measured by the number and gravity of the truths which have reached the point of being uncontested. The cessation, on one question after another, of serious controversy, is one of the necessary incidents of the consolidation of opinion; a consolidation as salutary in the case of true opinions, as it is dangerous and noxious when the opinions are erroneous. But though this gradual narrowing of the bounds of diversity of opinion is necessary in both senses of the term, being at once inevitable and indispensable, we are not therefore obliged to conclude that all its consequences must be beneficial. The loss of so important an aid to the intelligent and living apprehension of a truth, as is afforded by the necessity of explaining it to, or defending it against, opponents, though not sufficient to outweigh, is no trifling drawback from, the benefit of its universal recognition. Where this advantage can no longer be had, I confess I should like to see the teachers of mankind endeavouring to provide a substitute for it; some contrivance for making the difficulties of the question as present to the learner's consciousness, as if they were pressed upon him by a dissentient champion, eager for his conversion.

But instead of seeking contrivances for this purpose, they have lost those they formerly had. The Socratic dialectics, so magnificently exemplified in the dialogues of Plato, were a contrivance of this description.

They were essentially a negative discussion of the great questions of philosophy and life, directed with consummate skill to the purpose of convincing any one who had merely adopted the commonplaces of received opinion, that he did not understand the subject—that he as yet attached no definite meaning to the doctrines he professed; in order that, becoming aware of his ignorance, he might be put in the way to attain a stable belief, resting on a clear apprehension both of the meaning of doctrines and of their evidence. The school disputations of the middle ages had a somewhat similar object. They were intended to make sure that the pupil understood his own opinion, and (by necessary correlation) the opinion opposed to it, and could enforce the grounds of the one and confute those of the other. These last-mentioned contests had indeed the incurable defect, that the premises appealed to were taken from authority, not from reason; and, as a discipline to the mind, they were in every respect inferior to the powerful dialectics which formed the intellects of the "Socratici viri":[25] but the modern mind owes far more to both than it is generally willing to admit, and the present modes of education contain nothing which in the smallest degree supplies the place either of the one or of the other. A person who derives all his instruction from teachers or books, even if he escape the besetting temptation of contenting himself with cram, is under no compulsion to hear both sides; accordingly it is far from a frequent accomplishment, even among thinkers, to know both sides; and the weakest part of what everybody says in defence of his opinion, is what he intends as a reply to antagonists. It is the fashion of the present time to disparage negative logic—that which points out weaknesses in theory or errors in practice, without establishing positive truths. Such negative criticism would indeed be poor enough as an ultimate result; but as a means to attaining any positive knowledge or conviction worthy the name, it cannot be valued too highly; and until people are again systematically trained to it, there will be few great thinkers, and a low general average of intellect, in any but the mathematical and physical departments of speculation. On any

[25] [*Socratici viri*] disciples of Socrates.

other subject no one's opinions deserve the name of knowledge, except so far as he has either had forced upon him by others, or gone through of himself, the same mental process which would have been required of him in carrying on an active controversy with opponents. That, therefore, which when absent, it is so indispensable, but so difficult, to create, how worse than absurd it is to forego, when spontaneously offering itself! If there are any persons who contest a received opinion, or who will do so if law or opinion will let them, let us thank them for it, open our minds to listen to them, and rejoice that there is some one to do for us what we otherwise ought, if we have any regard for either the certainty or the vitality of our convictions, to do with much greater labour for ourselves.

It still remains to speak of one of the principal causes which make diversity of opinion advantageous, and will continue to do so until mankind shall have entered a stage of intellectual advancement which at present seems at an incalculable distance. We have hitherto considered only two possibilities: that the received opinion may be false, and some other opinion, consequently, true; or that, the received opinion being true, a conflict with the opposite error is essential to a clear apprehension and deep feeling of its truth. But there is a commoner case than either of these; when the conflicting doctrines, instead of being one true and the other false, share the truth between them; and the nonconforming opinion is needed to supply the remainder of the truth, of which the received doctrine embodies only a part. Popular opinions, on subjects not palpable to sense, are often true, but seldom or never the whole truth. They are a part of the truth; sometimes a greater, sometimes a smaller part, but exaggerated, distorted, and disjoined from the truths by which they ought to be accompanied and limited. Heretical opinions, on the other hand, are generally some of these suppressed and neglected truths, bursting the bonds which kept them down, and either seeking reconciliation with the truth contained in the common opinion, or fronting it as enemies, and setting themselves up, with similar exclusiveness, as the whole truth. The latter case is hitherto the most frequent, as, in the human mind, one-sidedness has always been the rule, and many-sidedness the exception. Hence, even in revolutions of opinion, one part of the truth usually sets while another rises. Even progress, which ought to superadd, for the most part only substitutes, one partial and incomplete truth for another; improvement consisting chiefly in this, that the new fragment of truth is more wanted, more adapted to the needs of the time, than that which it displaces. Such being the partial character of prevailing opinions, even when resting on a true foundation, every opinion which embodies somewhat of the portion of truth which the common opinion omits, ought to be considered precious, with whatever amount of error and confusion that truth may be blended. No sober judge of human affairs will feel bound to be indignant because those who force on our notice truths which we should otherwise have overlooked, overlook some of those which we see. Rather, he will think that so long as popular truth is one-sided, it is more desirable than otherwise that unpopular truth should have one-sided asserters too; such being usually the most energetic, and the most likely to compel reluctant attention to the fragment of wisdom which they proclaim as if it were the whole.

Thus, in the eighteenth century, when nearly all the instructed, and all those of the uninstructed who were led by them, were lost in admiration of what is called civilization, and of the marvels of modern science, literature, and philosophy, and while greatly overrating the amount of unlikeness between the men of modern and those of ancient times, indulged the belief that the whole of the difference was in their own favour; with what a salutary shock did the paradoxes of Rousseau explode like bombshells in the midst, dislocating the compact mass of one-sided opinion, and forcing its elements to recombine in a better form and with additional ingredients. Not that the current opinions were on the whole farther from the truth than Rousseau's were; on the contrary, they were nearer to it; they contained more of positive truth, and very much less of error. Nevertheless there lay in Rousseau's doctrine, and has floated down the stream of opinion along with it, a considerable amount of exactly those truths which the popular opinion wanted; and these are the deposit which was left behind when the flood subsided. The superior worth of simplicity of life, the enervating and demoralizing effect of the trammels and hypocrisies of artificial society, are ideas which have never been entirely absent from cultivated minds since Rousseau wrote; and they will in time produce their due effect, though at present needing to be asserted as much as ever, and to be asserted by deeds, for words, on this subject, have nearly exhausted their power.

In politics, again, it is almost a commonplace, that a party of order or stability, and a party of progress or reform, are both necessary elements of a healthy state of political life; until the one or the other shall have so enlarged its mental grasp as to be a party equally of order and of progress, knowing and distinguishing what is fit to be preserved from what ought to be swept away. Each of these modes of thinking derives its utility from the deficiencies of the other; but it is in a great measure the opposition of the other that keeps each within the limits of reason and sanity. Unless opinions favourable to democracy and to aristocracy, to property and to equality, to co-operation and to competition, to luxury and to abstinence, to sociality and individuality, to liberty and discipline, and all the other standing antagonisms of practical life, are expressed with equal freedom, and enforced and defended with equal talent and energy, there is no chance of both elements obtaining their due; one scale is sure to go up, and the other down. Truth, in the great practical concerns of life, is so much a question of the reconciling and combining of opposites, that very few have minds sufficiently capacious and impartial to make the adjustment with an approach to correctness, and it has to be made by the rough process of a struggle between combatants fighting under hostile banners. On any of the great open questions just enumerated, if either of the two opinions has a better claim than the other, not merely to be tolerated, but to be encouraged and countenanced, it is the one which happens at the particular time and place to be in a minority. That is the opinion which, for the time being, represents the neglected interests, the side of human well-being which is in danger of obtaining less than its share. I am aware that there is not, in this country, any intolerance of differences of opinion on most of these topics. They are adduced to show, by admitted and multiplied examples, the universality of the fact, that only through diversity of opinion is there, in the existing state of human intellect, a chance of fair play to all sides of the truth. When there are persons to be found, who form an exception to the apparent unanimity of the world on any subject, even if the world is in the right, it is always probable that dissentients have something worth hearing to say for themselves, and that truth would lose something by their silence.

It may be objected, "But *some* received principles, especially on the highest and most vital subjects, are more than half-truths. The Christian morality, for instance, is the whole truth on that subject, and if any one teaches a morality which varies from it, he is wholly in error." As this is of all cases the most important in practice, none can be fitter to test the general maxim. But before pronouncing what Christian morality is or is not, it would be desirable to decide what is meant by Christian morality. If it means the morality of the New Testament, I wonder that any one who derives his knowledge of this from the book itself, can suppose that it was announced, or intended, as a complete doctrine of morals. The Gospel always refers to a pre-existing morality, and confines its precepts to the particulars in which that morality was to be corrected, or superseded by a wider and higher; expressing itself, moreover, in terms most general, often impossible to be interpreted literally, and possessing rather the impressiveness of poetry or eloquence than the precision of legislation. To extract from it a body of ethical doctrine, has never been possible without eking it out from the Old Testament, that is, from a system elaborate indeed, but in many respects barbarous, and intended only for a barbarous people. St. Paul, a declared enemy to this Judaical mode of interpreting the doctrine and filling up the scheme of his Master, equally assumes a pre-existing morality, namely that of the Greeks and Romans; and his advice to Christians is in a great measure a system of accommodation to that; even to the extent of giving an apparent sanction to slavery.[26] What is called

---

[26] See, for example, Colossians, 3:22 – 4:1. Mill, one of the prominent feminists of his age, delicately refrains from mentioning that St. Paul also says, in the same paragraph (Colossians,3:18): "Wives, be subject to your husbands, as is fitting in the Lord."

Christian, but should rather be termed theological, morality, was not the work of Christ or the Apostles, but is of much later origin, having been gradually built up by the Catholic church of the first five centuries, and though not implicitly adopted by moderns and Protestants, has been much less modified by them than might have been expected. For the most part, indeed, they have contented themselves with cutting off the additions which had been made to it in the middle ages, each sect supplying the place by fresh additions, adapted to its own character and tendencies. That mankind owe a great debt to this morality, and to its early teachers, I should be the last person to deny; but I do not scruple to say of it, that it is, in many important points, incomplete and one-sided, and that unless ideas and feelings, not sanctioned by it, had contributed to the formation of European life and character, human affairs would have been in a worse condition than they now are. Christian morality (so called) has all the characters of a reaction; it is, in great part, a protest against Paganism. Its ideal is negative rather than positive; passive rather than active; Innocence rather than Nobleness; Abstinence from Evil, rather than energetic Pursuit of Good: in its precepts (as has been well said) "thou shalt not" predominates unduly over "thou shalt." In its horror of sensuality, it made an idol of asceticism, which has been gradually compromised away into one of legality. It holds out the hope of heaven and the threat of hell, as the appointed and appropriate motives to a virtuous life: in this falling far below the best of the ancients, and doing what lies in it to give to human morality an essentially selfish character, by disconnecting each man's feelings of duty from the interests of his fellow-creatures, except so far as a self-interested inducement is offered to him for consulting them. It is essentially a doctrine of passive obedience; it inculcates submission to all authorities found established; who indeed are not to be actively obeyed when they command what religion forbids, but who are not to be resisted, far less rebelled against, for any amount of wrong to ourselves. And while, in the morality of the best Pagan nations, duty to the State holds even a disproportionate place, infringing on the just liberty of the individual; in purely Christian ethics, that grand department of duty is scarcely noticed or acknowledged. It is in the Koran, not the New Testament, that we read the maxim—"A ruler who appoints any man to an office, when there is in his dominions another man better qualified for it, sins against God and against the State."[27] What little recognition the idea of obligation to the public obtains in modern morality, is derived from Greek and Roman sources, not from Christian; as, even in the morality of private life, whatever exists of magnanimity, highmindedness, personal dignity, even the sense of honour, is derived from the purely human, not the religious part of our education, and never could have grown out of a standard of ethics in which the only worth, professedly recognised, is that of obedience.

I am as far as any one from pretending that these defects are necessarily inherent in the Christian ethics, in every manner in which it can be conceived, or that the many requisites of a complete moral doctrine which it does not contain, do not admit of being reconciled with it. Far less would I insinuate this of the doctrines and precepts of Christ himself. I believe that the sayings of Christ are all, that I can see any evidence of their having been intended to be; that they are irreconcilable with nothing which a comprehensive morality requires; that everything which is excellent in ethics may be brought within them, with no greater violence to their language than has been done to it by all who have attempted to deduce from them any practical system of conduct whatever. But it is quite consistent with this, to believe that they contain, and were meant to contain, only a part of the truth; that many essential elements of the highest morality are among the things which are not provided for, nor intended to be provided for, in the recorded deliverances of the Founder of Christianity, and which have been entirely thrown aside in the system of ethics erected on the basis of those deliverances by the Christian Church. And this being so, I think it a great error to persist in attempting to find in the Christian doctrine that complete rule for our guidance, which its author intended it to sanction and force, but only partially to provide. I believe, too, that this narrow theory is becoming a grave practical evil, detracting greatly from

[27] Mill errs; the passage is not in the Koran.

the value of the moral training and instruction, which so many well-meaning persons are now at length exerting themselves to promote. I much fear that by attempting to form the mind and feelings on an exclusively religious type, and discarding those secular standards (as for want of a better name they may be called) which heretofore co-existed with and supplemented the Christian ethics, receiving some of its spirit, and infusing into it some of theirs, there will result, and is even now resulting, a low, abject, servile type of character, which, submit itself as it may to what it deems the Supreme Will, is incapable of rising to or sympathizing in the conception of Supreme Goodness. I believe that other ethics than any which can be evolved from exclusively Christian sources, must exist side by side with Christian ethics to produce the moral regeneration of mankind; and that the Christian system is no exception to the rule, that in an imperfect state of the human mind, the interests of truth require a diversity of opinions. It is not necessary that in ceasing to ignore the moral truths not contained in Christianity, men should ignore any of those which it does contain. Such prejudice, or oversight, when it occurs, is altogether an evil; but it is one from which we cannot hope to be always exempt, and must be regarded as the price paid for an inestimable good. The exclusive pretension made by a part of the truth to be the whole, must and ought to be protested against; and if a reactionary impulse should make the protectors unjust in their turn, this one-sidedness, like the other, may be lamented, but must be tolerated. If Christians would teach infidels to be just to Christianity, they should themselves be just to infidelity. It can do truth no service to blink the fact, known to all who have the most ordinary acquaintance with literary history, that a large portion of the noblest and most valuable moral teaching has been the work, not only of men who did not know, but of men who knew and rejected, the Christian faith.

I do not pretend that the most unlimited use of the freedom of enunciating all possible opinions would put an end to the evils of religious or philosophical sectarianism. Every truth which men of narrow capacity are in earnest about, is sure to be asserted, inculcated, and in many ways even acted on, as if no other truth existed in the world, or at all events none that could limit or qualify the first. I acknowledge that the tendency of all opinions to become sectarian is not cured by the freest discussion, but is often heightened and exacerbated thereby; the truth which ought to have been, but was not, seen, being rejected all the more violently because proclaimed by persons regarded as opponents. But it is not on the impassioned partisan, it is on the calmer and more disinterested bystander, that this collision of opinions works its salutary effect. Not the violent conflict between parts of the truth, but the quiet suppression of half of it, is the formidable evil; there is always hope when people are forced to listen to both sides; it is when they attend only to one that errors harden into prejudices, and truth itself ceases to have the effect of truth, by being exaggerated into falsehood. And since there are few mental attributes more rare than that judicial faculty which can sit in intelligent judgment between two sides of a question, of which only one is represented by an advocate before it, truth has no chance but in proportion as every side of it, every opinion which embodies any fraction of the truth, not only finds advocates, but is so advocated as to be listened to.

We have now recognised the necessity to the mental well-being of mankind (on which all their other well-being depends) of freedom of opinion, and freedom of the expression of opinion, on four distinct grounds; which we will now briefly recapitulate.

First, if any opinion is compelled to silence, that opinion may, for aught we can certainly know, be true. To deny this is to assume our own infallibility.

Secondly, though the silenced opinion be an error, it may, and very commonly does, contain a portion of truth; and since the general or prevailing opinion on any subject is rarely or never the whole truth, it is only by the collision of adverse opinions that the remainder of the truth has any chance of being supplied.

Thirdly, even if the received opinion be not only true, but the whole truth; unless it is suffered to be, and actually is, vigorously and earnestly contested, it will, by most of those who receive it, be held in the manner of a prejudice, with little comprehension or feeling of its rational grounds.

And not only this, but, fourthly, the meaning of the doctrine itself will be in danger of being lost, or enfeebled, and deprived of its vital effect on the character and conduct: the dogma becoming a mere formal profession, inefficacious for good, but cumbering the ground, and preventing the growth of any real and heartfelt conviction, from reason or personal experience.

Before quitting the subject of freedom of opinion, it is fit to take some notice of those who say, that the free expression of all opinions should be permitted, on condition that the manner be temperate, and do not pass the bounds of fair discussion. Much might be said on the impossibility of fixing where these supposed bounds are to be placed; for if the test be offence to those whose opinion is attacked, I think experience testifies that this offence is given whenever the attack is telling and powerful, and that every opponent who pushes them hard, and whom they find it difficult to answer, appears to them, if he shows any strong feeling on the subject, an intemperate opponent. But this, though an important consideration in a practical point of view, merges in a more fundamental objection. Undoubtedly the manner of asserting an opinion, even though it be a true one, may be very objectionable, and may justly incur severe censure. But the principal offences of the kind are such as it is mostly impossible, unless by accidental self-betrayal, to bring home to conviction. The gravest of them is, to argue sophistically, to suppress facts or arguments, to misstate the elements of the case, or misrepresent the opposite opinion. But all this, even to the most aggravated degree, is so continually done in perfect good faith, by persons who are not considered, and in many other respects may not deserve to be considered, ignorant or incompetent, that it is rarely possible on adequate grounds conscientiously to stamp the misrepresentation as morally culpable; and still less could law presume to interfere with this kind of controversial misconduct. With regard to what is commonly meant by intemperate discussion, namely invective, sarcasm, personality, and the like, the denunciation of these weapons would deserve more sympathy if it were ever proposed to interdict them equally to both sides; but it is only desired to restrain the employment of them against the prevailing opinion: against the unprevailing they may not only be used without general disapproval, but will be likely to obtain for him who uses them the praise of honest zeal and righteous indignation. Yet whatever mischief arises from their use, is greatest when they are employed against the comparatively defenceless; and whatever unfair advantage can be derived by any opinion from this mode of asserting it, accrues almost exclusively to received opinions. The worst offence of this kind which can be committed by a polemic, is to stigmatize those who hold the contrary opinion as bad and immoral men. To calumny of this sort, those who hold any unpopular opinion are peculiarly exposed, because they are in general few and uninfluential, and nobody but themselves feels much interested in seeing justice done them; but this weapon is, from the nature of the case, denied to those who attack a prevailing opinion: they can neither use it with safety to themselves, nor, if they could, would it do anything but recoil on their own cause. In general, opinions contrary to those commonly received can only obtain a hearing by studied moderation of language, and the most cautious avoidance of unnecessary offence, from which they hardly ever deviate even in a slight degree without losing ground: while unmeasured vituperation employed on the side of the prevailing opinion, really does deter people from professing contrary opinions, and from listening to those who profess them. For the interest, therefore, of truth and justice, it is far more important to restrain this employment of vituperative language than the other; and, for example, if it were necessary to choose, there would be much more need to discourage offensive attacks on infidelity, than on religion. It is, however, obvious that law and authority have no business with restraining either, while opinion ought, in every instance, to determine its verdict by the circumstances of the individual case; condemning every one, on whichever side of the argument he places himself, in whose mode of advocacy either want of candour, or malignity, bigotry, or intolerance of feeling manifest themselves; but not inferring these vices from the side which a person takes, though it be the contrary side of the question to our own: and giving merited honour to every one, whatever opinion he may hold, who has calmness to see and honesty to state what his opponents and their opinions really are, exaggerating nothing to their discredit, keeping nothing back which tells, or can be supposed to tell, in their favour. This is the real morality of public discussion and if often violated, I am happy to think that there are many controversialists who to a great extent observe it, and a still greater number who conscientiously strive towards it.

Chapter III:
Of Individuality, as One of the
Elements of Well-Being

SUCH being the reasons which make it imperative that human beings should be free to form opinions, and to express their opinions without reserve; and such the baneful consequences to the intellectual, and through that to the moral nature of man, unless this liberty is either conceded, or asserted in spite of prohibition; let us next examine whether the same reasons do not require that men should be free to act upon their opinions—to carry these out in their lives, without hindrance, either physical or moral, from their fellow-men, so long as it is at their own risk and peril. This last proviso is of course indispensable. No one pretends that actions should be as free as opinions. On the contrary, even opinions lose their immunity, when the circumstances in which they are expressed are such as to constitute their expression a positive instigation to some mischievous act. An opinion that corn-dealers are starvers of the poor, or that private property is robbery, ought to be unmolested when simply circulated through the press, but may justly incur punishment when delivered orally to an excited mob assembled before the house of a corn-dealer, or when handed about among the same mob in the form of a placard. Acts, of whatever kind, which, without justifiable cause, do harm to others, may be, and in the more important cases absolutely require to be, controlled by the unfavourable sentiments, and, when needful, by the active interference of mankind. The liberty of the individual must be thus far limited; he must not make himself a nuisance to other people. But if he refrains from molesting others in what concerns them, and merely acts according to his own inclination and judgment in things which concern himself, the same reasons which show that opinion should be free, prove also that he should be allowed, without molestation, to carry his opinions into practice at his own cost. That mankind are not infallible; that their truths, for the most part, are only half-truths; that unity of opinion, unless resulting from the fullest and freest comparison of opposite opinions, is not desirable, and diversity not an evil, but a good, until mankind are much more capable than at present of recognising all sides of the truth, are principles applicable to men's modes of action, not less than to their opinions. As it is useful that while mankind are imperfect there should be different opinions, so is it that there should be different experiments of living; that free scope should be given to varieties of character, short of injury to others; and that the worth of different modes of life should be proved practically, when any one thinks fit to try them. It is desirable, in short, that in things which do not primarily concern others, individuality should assert itself. Where, not the person's own character, but the traditions or customs of other people are the rule of conduct, there is wanting one of the principal ingredients of human happiness, and quite the chief ingredient of individual and social progress.

In maintaining this principle, the greatest difficulty to be encountered does not lie in the appreciation of means towards an acknowledged end, but in the indifference of persons in general to the end itself. If it were felt that the free development of individuality is one of the leading essentials of well-being; that it is not only a co-ordinate element with all that is designated by the terms civilization, instruction, education, culture, but is itself a necessary part and condition of all those things; there would be no danger that liberty should be undervalued, and the adjustment of the boundaries between it and social control would present no extraordinary difficulty. But the evil is, that individual spontaneity is hardly recognised by the common modes of thinking, as having any intrinsic worth, or deserving any regard on its own account. The majority, being satisfied with the ways of mankind as they now are (for it is they who make them what they are), cannot comprehend why those ways should not be good enough for everybody; and what is more, spontaneity forms no part of the ideal of the majority of moral and social reformers, but is rather looked on with jealousy, as a troublesome and perhaps rebellious obstruction to the general acceptance of what these reformers, in their own judgment, think would be best for mankind. Few persons, out of Germany, even comprehend the meaning of the doctrine which Wilhelm Von Humboldt, so eminent both as a savant and as a politician, made the text of a treatise—that "the end of man, or that which is prescribed by the eternal or immutable dictates of reason, and not suggested by vague and transient desires, is the highest and most harmonious development of his powers to a complete and consistent whole;" that, therefore, the object "towards which every human being must ceaselessly direct his efforts, and on which especially those who design to influence their fellow-men must ever keep their eyes, is the individuality of power and development;" that for this there are two requisites, "freedom, and a variety of situations;" and that from the union of these arise "individual vigour and manifold diversity," which combine themselves in "originality."[1]

Little, however, as people are accustomed to a doctrine like that of Von Humboldt, and surprising as it may be to them to find so high a value attached to individuality, the question, one must nevertheless think, can only be one of degree. No one's idea of excellence in conduct is that people should do absolutely nothing but copy one another. No one would assert that people ought not to put into their mode of life, and into the conduct of their concerns, any impress whatever of their own judgment, or of their own individual character. On the other hand, it would be absurd to pretend that people ought to live as if nothing whatever had been known in the world before they came into it; as if experience had as yet done nothing towards showing that one mode of existence, or of conduct, is preferable to another. Nobody denies that people should be so taught and trained in youth, as to know and benefit by the ascertained results of human experience. But it is the privilege and proper condition of a human being,

[1] *The Sphere and Duties of Government*, from the German of Baron Wilhelm von Humboldt, pp. 11, 13. (Mill's note.) Humboldt (1767–1835) was a German statesman, philologist, and educational reformer.

arrived at the maturity of his faculties, to use and interpret experience in his own way. It is for him to find out what part of recorded experience is properly applicable to his own circumstances and character. The traditions and customs of other people are, to a certain extent, evidence of what their experience has taught *them*; presumptive evidence, and as such, have a claim to his deference: but, in the first place, their experience may be too narrow; or they may not have interpreted it rightly. Secondly, their interpretation of experience may be correct, but unsuitable to him. Customs are made for customary circumstances, and customary characters; and his circumstances or his character may be uncustomary. Thirdly, though the customs be both good as customs, and suitable to him, yet to conform to custom, merely as custom, does not educate or develope in him any of the qualities which are the distinctive endowment of a human being. The human faculties of perception, judgment, discriminative feeling, mental activity, and even moral preference, are exercised only in making a choice. He who does anything because it is the custom, makes no choice. He gains no practice either in discerning or in desiring what is best. The mental and moral, like the muscular powers, are improved only by being used. The faculties are called into no exercise by doing a thing merely because others do it, no more than by believing a thing only because others believe it. If the grounds of an opinion are not conclusive to the person's own reason, his reason cannot be strengthened, but is likely to be weakened, by his adopting it: and if the inducements to an act are not such as are consentaneous to his own feelings and character (where affection, or the rights of others, are not concerned) it is so much done towards rendering his feelings and character inert and torpid, instead of active and energetic.

He who lets the world, or his own portion of it, choose his plan of life for him, has no need of any other faculty than the ape-like one of imitation. He who chooses his plan for himself, employs all his faculties. He must use observation to see, reasoning and judgment to foresee, activity to gather materials for decision, discrimination to decide, and when he has decided, firmness and self-control to hold to his deliberate decision. And these qualities he requires and exercises exactly in proportion as the part of his conduct which he determines according to his own judgment and feelings is a large one. It is possible that he might be guided in some good path, and kept out of harm's way, without any of these things. But what will be his comparative worth as a human being? It really is of importance, not only what men do, but also what manner of men they are that do it. Among the works of man, which human life is rightly employed in perfecting and beautifying, the first in importance surely is man himself. Supposing it were possible to get houses built, corn grown, battles fought, causes tried, and even churches erected and prayers said, by machinery—by automatons in human form—it would be a considerable loss to exchange for these automatons even the men and women who at present inhabit the more civilized parts of the world, and who assuredly are but starved specimens of what nature can and will produce. Human nature is not a machine to be built after a model, and set to do exactly the work prescribed for it, but a tree, which requires to grow and develope itself on all sides, according to the tendency of the inward forces which make it a living thing.

It will probably be conceded that it is desirable people should exercise their understandings, and that an intelligent following of custom, or even occasionally an intelligent deviation from custom, is better than a blind and simply mechanical adhesion to it. To a certain extent it is admitted, that our understanding should be our own: but there is not the same willingness to admit that our desires and impulses should be our own likewise; or that to possess impulses of our own, and of any strength, is anything but a peril and a snare. Yet desires and impulses are as much a part of a perfect human being, as beliefs and restraints: and strong impulses are only perilous when not properly balanced; when one set of aims and inclinations is developed into strength, while others, which ought to co-exist with them, remain weak and inactive. It is not because men's desires are strong that they act ill; it is because their consciences are weak. There is no natural connexion between strong impulses and a weak conscience. The natural connexion is the other way. To say that one person's desires and feelings are stronger and more various than those of another, is merely to say that he has more of the raw material of human nature, and is therefore capable, perhaps of more evil, but certainly of more good. Strong impulses are but another name for energy. Energy may be turned to bad uses; but more good may always be made of an energetic nature, than of an indolent and impassive one. Those who have most natural feeling, are always those whose cultivated feelings may be made the strongest. The same strong susceptibilities which make the personal impulses vivid and powerful, are also the source from whence are generated the most passionate love of virtue, and the sternest self-control. It is through the cultivation of these, that society both does its duty and protects its interests: not by rejecting the stuff of which heroes are made, because it knows not how to make them. A person whose desires and impulses are his own—are the expression of his own nature, as it has been developed and modified by his own culture—is said to have a character. One whose desires and impulses are not his own, has no character, no more than a steam-engine has a character. If, in addition to being his own, his impulses are strong, and are under the government of a strong will, he has an energetic character. Whoever thinks that individuality of desires and impulses should not be encouraged to unfold itself must maintain that society has no need of strong natures—is not the better for containing many persons who have much character— and that a high general average of energy is not desirable.

In some early states of society, these forces might be, and were too much ahead of the power which society then possessed of disciplining and controlling them. There has been a time when the element of spontaneity and individuality was in excess, and the social principle had a hard struggle with it. The difficulty then was, to induce men of strong bodies or minds to pay obedience to any rules which required them to control their impulses. To overcome this difficulty, law and discipline, like the Popes struggling against the Emperors, asserted a power over the whole man claiming to control all his life in order to control his character—which society had not found any other sufficient means of binding. But society has now fairly got the better of individuality; and the danger which threatens human nature is not the excess, but the deficiency, of personal impulses and preferences. Things are vastly changed, since the passions of those who were strong by station or by personal endowment were in a state of habitual rebellion against laws and ordinances, and required to be rigorously chained up to enable the persons within their reach to enjoy any particle of security. In our times, from the highest class of society down to the lowest, every one lives as under the eye of a hostile and dreaded censorship. Not only in what concerns others, but in what concerns only themselves, the individual or the family do not ask themselves—what do I prefer? or, what would suit my character and disposition? or, what would allow the best and highest in me to have fair play, and enable it to grow and thrive? They ask themselves, what is suitable to my position? what is usually done by persons of my station and pecuniary circumstances? or (worse still) what is usually done by persons of a station and circumstances superior to mine? I do not mean that they choose what is customary, in preference to what suits their own inclination. It does not occur to them to have any inclination, except for what is customary. Thus the mind itself is bowed to the yoke: even in what people do for pleasure, conformity is the first thing thought of; they like in crowds; they exercise choice only among things commonly done: peculiarity of taste, eccentricity of conduct, are shunned equally with crimes: until by dint of not following their own nature, they have no nature to follow: their human capacities are withered and starved: they become incapable of any strong wishes or native pleasures, and are generally without either opinions or feelings of home growth, or properly their own. Now is this, or is it not, the desirable condition of human nature?

It is so, on the Calvinistic theory. According to that, the one great offence of man is self-will. All the good of which humanity is capable, is comprised in obedience. You have no choice; thus you must do, and no otherwise: "whatever is not a duty, is a sin." Human nature being radically corrupt, there is no redemption for any one until human nature is killed within him. To one holding this theory of life, crushing out any of the human faculties, capacities, and susceptibilities, is no evil: man needs no capacity, but that of surrendering himself to the will of God: and if he uses any of his faculties for any other purpose but to do that supposed will more effectually, he is better without them. This is the theory of Calvinism;

and it is held, in a mitigated form, by many who do not consider themselves Calvinists; the mitigation consisting in giving a less ascetic interpretation to the alleged will of God; asserting it to be his will that mankind should gratify some of their inclinations; of course not in the manner they themselves prefer, but in the way of obedience, that is, in a way prescribed to them by authority; and, therefore, by the necessary conditions of the case, the same for all.

In some such insidious form there is at present a strong tendency to this narrow theory of life, and to the pinched and hidebound type of human character which it patronizes. Many persons, no doubt, sincerely think that human beings thus cramped and dwarfed, are as their Maker designed them to be; just as many have thought that trees are a much finer thing when clipped into pollards, or cut out into figures of animals, than as nature made them. But if it be any part of religion to believe that man was made by a good Being, it is more consistent with that faith to believe, that this Being gave all human faculties that they might be cultivated and unfolded, not rooted out and consumed, and that he takes delight in every nearer approach made by his creatures to the ideal conception embodied in them, every increase in any of their capabilities of comprehension, of action, or of enjoyment. There is a different type of human excellence from the Calvinistic; a conception of humanity as having its nature bestowed on it for other purposes than merely to be abnegated. "Pagan self-assertion" is one of the elements of human worth, as well as "Christian self-denial."[2] There is a Greek ideal of self-development, which the Platonic and Christian ideal of self-government blends with, but does not supersede. It may be better to be a John Knox than an Alcibiades,[3] but it is better to be a Pericles[4] than either; nor would a Pericles, if we had one in these days, be without anything good which belonged to John Knox.

---

[2] Sterling's *Essays*. (Mill's note.) He refers to John Sterling's *Essays and Tales*, ed., J.C. Hare (1848) I, 190.

[3] Alcibiades (450–404 BCE), Athenian general, protégé of Socrates; held by some to be responsible for the decline of Athens.

[4] Pericles (495?–429 BCE), Athenian statesman, orator, and general.

It is not by wearing down into uniformity all that is individual in themselves, but by cultivating it and calling it forth, within the limits imposed by the rights and interests of others, that human beings become a noble and beautiful object of contemplation; and as the works partake the character of those who do them, by the same process human life also becomes rich, diversified, and animating, furnishing more abundant aliment to high thoughts and elevating feelings, and strengthening the tie which binds every individual to the race, by making the race infinitely better worth belonging to. In proportion to the development of his individuality, each person becomes more valuable to himself, and is therefore capable of being more valuable to others. There is a greater fulness of life about his own existence, and when there is more life in the units there is more in the mass which is composed of them. As much compression as is necessary to prevent the stronger specimens of human nature from encroaching on the rights of others, cannot be dispensed with; but for this there is ample compensation even in the point of view of human development. The means of development which the individual loses by being prevented from gratifying his inclinations to the injury of others, are chiefly obtained at the expense of the development of other people. And even to himself there is a full equivalent in the better development of the social part of his nature, rendered possible by the strains put upon the selfish part. To be held to rigid rules of justice for the sake of others, developes the feelings and capacities which have the good of others for their object. But to be restrained in things not affecting their good, by their mere displeasure, developes nothing valuable, except such force of character as may unfold itself in resisting the restraint. If acquiesced in, it dulls and blunts the whole nature. To give any fair play to the nature of each, it is essential that different persons should be allowed to lead different lives. In proportion as this latitude has been exercised in any age, has that age been noteworthy to posterity. Even despotism does not produce its worst effects, so long as individuality exists under it; and whatever crushes individuality is despotism, by whatever name it may be called, and whether it professes to be enforcing the will of God or the injunctions of men.

Having said that individuality is the same thing with development, and that it is only the cultivation of individuality which produces, or can produce, well-developed human beings, I might here close the argument: for what more or better can be said of any condition of human affairs, than that it brings human beings themselves nearer to the best thing they can be? or what worse can be said of any obstruction to good, than that it prevents this? Doubtless, however, these considerations will not suffice to convince those who most need convincing; and it is necessary further to show, that these developed human beings are of some use to the undeveloped—to point out to those who do not desire liberty, and would not avail themselves of it, that they may be in some intelligible manner rewarded for allowing other people to make use of it without hindrance.

In the first place, then, I would suggest that they might possibly learn something from them. It will not be denied by anybody, that originality is a valuable element in human affairs. There is always need of persons not only to discover new truths, and point out when what were once truths are true no longer, but also to commence new practices, and set the example of more enlightened conduct, and better taste and sense in human life. This cannot well be gainsaid by anybody who does not believe that the world has already attained perfection in all its ways and practices. It is true that this benefit is not capable of being rendered by everybody alike: there are but few persons, in comparison with the whole of mankind, whose experiments, if adopted by others, would be likely to be any improvement on established practice. But these few are the salt of the earth; without them, human life would become a stagnant pool. Not only is it they who introduce good things which did not before exist; it is they who keep the life in those which already existed. If there were nothing new to be done, would human intellect cease to be necessary? Would it be a reason why those who do the old things should forget why they are done, and do them like cattle, not like human beings? There is only too great a tendency in the best beliefs and practices to degenerate into the mechanical; and unless there were a succession of persons whose ever-recurring originality prevents the grounds of those beliefs and practices from becoming merely traditional, such dead matter would not resist the smallest shock from anything really alive, and there would be no reason why civilization should not die out, as in the Byzantine Empire. Persons of genius, it is true, are, and are always likely to be, a small minority, but in order to have them, it is necessary to preserve the soil in which they grow. Genius can only breathe freely in an *atmosphere* of freedom. Persons of genius are, *ex vi termini,*[5] more individual than any other people—less capable, consequently, of fitting themselves, without hurtful compression, into any of the small number of moulds which society provides in order to save its members the trouble of forming their own character. If from timidity they consent to be forced into one of these moulds, and to let all that part of themselves which cannot expand under the pressure remain unexpanded, society will be little the better for their genius. If they are of a strong character, and break their fetters, they become a mark for the society which has not succeeded in reducing them to commonplace, to point at with solemn warning as "wild," "erratic," and the like; much as if one should complain of the Niagara river for not flowing smoothly between its banks like a Dutch canal.

I insist thus emphatically on the importance of genius, and the necessity of allowing it to unfold itself freely both in thought and in practice, being well aware that no one will deny the position in theory, but knowing also that almost every one, in reality, is totally indifferent to it. People think genius a fine thing if it enables a man to write an exciting poem, or paint a picture. But in its true sense, that of originality in thought and action, though no one says that it is not a thing to be admired, nearly all, at heart, think that they can do very well without it. Unhappily this is too natural to be wondered at. Originality is the one thing which unoriginal minds cannot feel the use of. They cannot see what it is to do for them: how should they? If they could see what it would do for them, it would not be originality. The first service which originality has to render them, is that of opening their eyes: which being once fully done, they would have a chance of being themselves original. Meanwhile, recollecting that nothing

[5] [*ex vi termini*] by definition.

was ever yet done which some one was not the first to do, and that all good things which exist are the fruits of originality, let them be modest enough to believe that there is something still left for it to accomplish, and assure themselves that they are more in need of originality, the less they are conscious of the want.

In sober truth, whatever homage may be professed, or even paid, to real or supposed mental superiority, the general tendency of things throughout the world is to render mediocrity the ascendant power among mankind. In ancient history, in the middle ages, and in a diminishing degree through the long transition from feudality to the present time, the individual was a power in himself; and if he had either great talents or a high social position he was a considerable power. At present individuals are lost in the crowd. In politics it is almost a triviality to say that public opinion now rules the world. The only power deserving the name is that of masses, and of governments while they make themselves the organ of the tendencies and instincts of masses. This is as true in the moral and social relations of private life as in public transactions. Those whose opinions go by the name of public opinion, are not always the same sort of public: in America they are the whole white population; in England, chiefly the middle class. But they are always a mass, that is to say, collective mediocrity. And what is a still greater novelty, the mass do not now take their opinions from dignitaries in Church or State, from ostensible leaders, or from books. Their thinking is done for them by men much like themselves, addressing them or speaking in their name, on the spur of the moment, through the newspapers. I am not complaining of all this. I do not assert that anything better is compatible, as a general rule, with the present low state of the human mind. But that does not hinder the government of mediocrity from being mediocre government. No government by a democracy or a numerous aristocracy, either in its political acts or in the opinions, qualities, and tone of mind which it fosters, ever did or could rise above mediocrity, except in so far as the sovereign Many have let themselves be guided (which in their best times they always have done) by the counsels and influence of a more highly gifted and instructed

One or Few. The initiation of all wise or noble things, comes and must come from individuals; generally at first from some one individual. The honour and glory of the average man is that he is capable of following that initiative, that he can respond internally to wise and noble things, and be led to them with his eyes open. I am not countenancing the sort of "hero-worship" which applauds the strong man of genius for forcibly seizing on the government of the world and making it do his bidding in spite of itself.[6] All he can claim is, freedom to point out the way. The power of compelling others into it, is not only inconsistent with the freedom and development of all the rest, but corrupting to the strong man himself. It does seem, however, that when the opinions of masses of merely average men are everywhere become or becoming the dominant power, the counterpoise and corrective to that tendency would be, the more and more pronounced individuality of those who stand on the higher eminences of thought. It is in these circumstances most especially, that exceptional individuals, instead of being deterred, should be encouraged in acting differently from the mass. In other times there was no advantage in their doing so, unless they acted not only differently, but better. In this age, the mere example of nonconformity, the mere refusal to bend the knee to custom, is itself a service. Precisely because the tyranny of opinion is such as to make eccentricity a reproach, it is desirable, in order to break through that tyranny, that people should be eccentric. Eccentricity has always abounded when and where strength of character has abounded; and the amount of eccentricity in a society has generally been proportional to the amount of genius, mental vigour, and moral courage which it contained. That so few now dare to be eccentric, marks the chief danger of the time.

I have said that it is important to give the freest scope possible to uncustomary things, in order that it may in time appear which of these are fit to be converted into customs. But independence of action, and disregard of custom, are not solely deserving of encouragement for the chance they

[6] Very likely a reference to Carlyle, especially *On Heroes, Hero-Worship, and the Heroic in History* (1841).

afford that better modes of action, and customs more worthy of general adoption, may be struck out; nor is it only persons of decided mental superiority who have a just claim to carry on their lives in their own way. There is no reason that all human existence should be constructed on some one or some small number of patterns. If a person possesses any tolerable amount of common sense and experience, his own mode of laying out his existence is the best, not because it is the best in itself, but because it is his own mode. Human beings are not like sheep; and even sheep are not undistinguishably alike. A man cannot get a coat or a pair of boots to fit him, unless they are either made to his measure, or he has a whole warehouseful to choose from: and is it easier to fit him with a life than with a coat, or are human beings more like one another in their whole physical and spiritual conformation than in the shape of their feet? If it were only that people have diversities of taste, that is reason enough for not attempting to shape them all after one model. But different persons also require different conditions for their spiritual development; and can no more exist healthily in the same moral, than all the variety of plants can in the same physical, atmosphere and climate. The same things which are helps to one person towards the cultivation of his higher nature, are hindrances to another. The same mode of life is a healthy excitement to one, keeping all his faculties of action and enjoyment in their best order, while to another it is a distracting burthen, which suspends or crushes all internal life. Such are the differences among human beings in their sources of pleasure, their susceptibilities of pain, and the operation on them of different physical and moral agencies, that unless there is a corresponding diversity in their modes of life, they neither obtain their fair share of happiness, nor grow up to the mental, moral, and aesthetic stature of which their nature is capable. Why then should tolerance, as far as the public sentiment is concerned, extend only to tastes and modes of life which extort acquiescence by the multitude of their adherents? Nowhere (except in some monastic institutions) is diversity of taste entirely unrecognised; a person may, without blame, either like or dislike rowing, or smoking, or music, or athletic exercises, or chess, or cards, or study, because both those who like each of these things, and those who dislike them, are too numerous to be put down. But the man, and still more the woman, who can be accused either of doing "what nobody does," or of not doing "what everybody does," is the subject of as much depreciatory remark as if he or she had committed some grave moral delinquency. Persons require to possess a title, or some other badge of rank, or of the consideration of people of rank, to be able to indulge somewhat in the luxury of doing as they like without detriment to their estimation. To indulge somewhat, I repeat: for whoever allow themselves much of that indulgence, incur the risk of something worse than disparaging speeches—they are in peril of a commission *de lunatico*,[7] and of having their property taken from them and given to their relations.[8] There is one characteristic of the present

---

[7] [*de lunatico*] A "commission *de lunatico*" is a court authorization to inquire into the sanity of an individual.

[8] There is something both contemptible and frightful in the sort of evidence on which, of late years, any person can be judicially declared unfit for the management of his affairs; and after his death, his disposal of his property can be set aside, if there is enough of it to pay the expenses of litigation—which are charged on the property itself. All the minute details of his daily life are pried into, and whatever is found which, seen through the medium of the perceiving and describing faculties of the lowest of the low, bears an appearance unlike absolute commonplace, is laid before the jury as evidence of insanity, and often with success; the jurors being little, if at all, less vulgar and ignorant than the witnesses; while the judges, with that extraordinary want of knowledge of human nature and life which continually astonishes us in English lawyers, often help to mislead them. These trials speak volumes as to the state of feeling and opinion among the vulgar with regard to human liberty. So far from setting any value on individuality—so far from respecting the right of each individual to act, in things indifferent, as seems good to his own judgment and inclinations, judges and juries cannot even conceive that a person in a state of sanity can desire such freedom. In former days, when it was proposed to burn atheists, charitable people used to suggest putting them in a mad-house instead: it would be nothing surprising now-a-days were we to see this done, and the doers applauding themselves, because, instead of persecuting for religion, they had adopted so humane and Christian a mode of treating these unfortunates, not without a silent satisfaction at their having thereby obtained their deserts. (Mill's note.)

direction of public opinion, peculiarly calculated to make it intolerant of any marked demonstration of individuality. The general average of mankind are not only moderate in intellect, but also moderate in inclinations: they have no tastes or wishes strong enough to incline them to do anything unusual, and they consequently do not understand those who have, and class all such with the wild and intemperate whom they are accustomed to look down upon. Now, in addition to this fact which is general, we have only to suppose that a strong movement has set in towards the improvement of morals, and it is evident what we have to expect. In these days such a movement has set in; much has actually been effected in the way of increased regularity of conduct, and discouragement of excesses; and there is a philanthropic spirit abroad, for the exercise of which there is no more inviting field than the moral and prudential improvement of our fellow–creatures. These tendencies of the times cause the public to be more disposed than at most former periods to prescribe general rules of conduct, and endeavour to make every one conform to the approved standard. And that standard, express or tacit, is to desire nothing strongly. Its ideal of character is to be without any marked character; to maim by compression, like a Chinese lady's foot, every part of human nature which stands out prominently, and tends to make the person markedly dissimilar in outline to commonplace humanity.

As is usually the case with ideals which exclude one-half of what is desirable, the present standard of approbation produces only an inferior imitation of the other half. Instead of great energies guided by vigorous reason, and strong feelings strongly controlled by a conscientious will, its result is weak feelings and weak energies, which therefore can be kept in outward conformity to rule without any strength either of will or of reason. Already energetic characters on any large scale are becoming merely traditional. There is now scarcely any outlet for energy in this country except business. The energy expended in this may still be regarded as considerable. What little is left from that employment, is expended on some hobby; which may be a useful, even a philanthropic hobby, but is always some one thing, and generally a thing of small dimensions. The greatness of England is now all collective: individually small, we only appear capable of anything great by our habit of combining; and with this our moral and religious philanthropists are perfectly contented. But it was men of another stamp than this that made England what it has been; and men of another stamp will be needed to prevent its decline.

The despotism of custom is everywhere the standing hindrance to human advancement, being in unceasing antagonism to that disposition to aim at something better than customary, which is called, according to circumstances, the spirit of liberty, or that of progress or improvement. The spirit of improvement is not always a spirit of liberty, for it may aim at forcing improvements on an unwilling people; and the spirit of liberty, in so far as it resists such attempts, may ally itself locally and temporarily with the opponents of improvement; but the only unfailing and permanent source of improvement is liberty, since by it there are as many possible independent centres of improvement as there are individuals. The progressive principle, however, in either shape, whether as the love of liberty or of improvement, is antagonistic to the sway of Custom, involving at least emancipation from that yoke; and the contest between the two constitutes the chief interest of the history of mankind. The greater part of the world has, properly speaking, no history, because the despotism of Custom is complete. This is the case over the whole East. Custom is there, in all things, the final appeal; justice and right mean conformity to custom; the argument of custom no one, unless some tyrant intoxicated with power, thinks of resisting. And we see the result. Those nations must once have had originality; they did not start out of the ground populous, lettered, and versed in many of the arts of life; they made themselves all this, and were then the greatest and most powerful nations of the world. What are they now? The subjects or dependents of tribes whose forefathers wandered in the forests when theirs had magnificent palaces and gorgeous temples, but over whom custom exercised only a divided rule with liberty and progress. A people, it appears, may be progressive for a certain length of time, and then stop: when does it stop? When it ceases to possess individuality. If a similar change should befall the nations of Europe, it will not be in exactly the same shape: the despotism of custom with which these nations are threatened is not precisely stationariness. It proscribes singularity, but it does not preclude change, provided all change together. We have discarded the fixed costumes of our forefathers; every one must still dress like other people, but the fashion may change once or twice a year. We thus take care that when there is change it shall be for change's sake, and not from any idea of beauty or convenience; for the same idea of beauty or convenience would not strike all the world at the same moment, and be simultaneously thrown aside by all at another moment. But we are progressive as well as changeable: we continually make new inventions in mechanical things, and keep them until they are again superseded by better; we are eager for improvement in politics, in education, even in morals, though in this last our idea of improvement chiefly consists in persuading or forcing other people to be as good as ourselves. It is not progress that we object to; on the contrary, we flatter ourselves that we are the most progressive people who ever lived. It is individuality that we war against: we should think we had done wonders if we had made ourselves all alike; forgetting that the unlikeness of one person to another is generally the first thing which draws the attention of either to the imperfection of his own type, and the superiority of another, or the possibility, by combining the advantages of both, of producing something better than either. We have a warning example in China—a nation of much talent, and, in some respects, even wisdom, owing to the rare good fortune of having been provided at an early period with a particularly good set of customs, the work, in some measure, of men to whom even the most enlightened European must accord, under certain limitations, the title of sages and philosophers. They are remarkable, too, in the excellence of their apparatus for impressing, as far as possible, the best wisdom they possess upon every mind in the community, and securing that those who have appropriated most of it shall occupy the posts of honour and power. Surely the people who did this have discovered the secret of human progressiveness, and must have kept themselves steadily at the head of the movement of the world. On the contrary, they have become stationary—have remained so for thousands of years; and if they are ever to be farther improved, it must be by foreigners. They have succeeded beyond all hope in what English philanthropists are so industriously working at—in making a people all alike, all governing their thoughts and conduct by the same maxims and rules; and these are the fruits. The modern *regime* of public opinion is, in an unorganized form, what the Chinese educational and political systems are in an organized; and unless individuality shall be able successfully to assert itself against this yoke, Europe, notwithstanding its noble antecedents and its professed Christianity, will tend to become another China.

What is it that has hitherto preserved Europe from this lot? What has made the European family of nations an improving, instead of a stationary portion of mankind? Not any superior excellence in them, which, when it exists, exists as the effect, not as the cause; but their remarkable diversity of character and culture. Individuals, classes, nations, have been extremely unlike one another: they have struck out a great variety of paths, each leading to something valuable; and although at every period those who travelled in different paths have been intolerant of one another, and each would have thought it an excellent thing if all the rest could have been compelled to travel his road, their attempts to thwart each other's development have rarely had any permanent success, and each has in time endured to receive the good which the others have offered. Europe is, in my judgment, wholly indebted to this plurality of paths for its progressive and many-sided development. But it already begins to possess this benefit in a considerably less degree. It is decidedly advancing towards the Chinese ideal of making all people alike. M. de Tocqueville, in his last important work, remarks how much more the Frenchmen of the present day resemble one another, than did those even of the last generation.[9] The same remark might be made of Englishmen in a far greater degree. In a passage already quoted from Wilhelm von Humboldt, he points out two things as necessary conditions of human development, because necessary to render people

[9] See Alexis de Tocqueville, *L'Ancien régime et la révolution* (1856), chap. viii.

unlike one another; namely, freedom, and variety of situations. The second of these two conditions is in this country every day diminishing. The circumstances which surround different classes and individuals, and shape their characters, are daily becoming more assimilated. Formerly, different ranks, different neighbourhoods, different trades and professions, lived in what might be called different worlds; at present, to a great degree in the same. Comparatively speaking, they now read the same things, listen to the same things, see the same things, go to the same places, have their hopes and fears directed to the same objects, have the same rights and liberties, and the same means of asserting them. Great as are the differences of position which remain, they are nothing to those which have ceased. And the assimilation is still proceeding. All the political changes of the age promote it, since they all tend to raise the low and to lower the high. Every extension of education promotes it, because education brings people under common influences, and gives them access to the general stock of facts and sentiments. Improvements in the means of communication promote it, by bringing the inhabitants of distant places into personal contact, and keeping up a rapid flow of changes of residence between one place and another. The increase of commerce and manufactures promotes it, by diffusing more widely the advantages of easy circumstances, and opening all objects of ambition, even the highest, to general competition, whereby the desire of rising becomes no longer the character of a particular class, but of all classes. A more powerful agency than even all these, in bringing about a general similarity among mankind, is the complete establishment, in this and other free countries, of the ascendancy of public opinion in the State. As the various social eminences which enabled persons entrenched on them to disregard the opinion of the multitude, gradually become levelled; as the very idea of resisting the will of the public, when it is positively known that they have a will, disappears more and more from the minds of practical politicians; there ceases to be any social support for nonconformity—any substantive power in society, which, itself opposed to the ascendancy of numbers, is interested in taking under its protection opinions and tendencies at variance with those of the public.

The combination of all these causes forms so great a mass of influences hostile to Individuality, that it is not easy to see how it can stand its ground. It will do so with increasing difficulty, unless the intelligent part of the public can be made to feel its value—to see that it is good there should be differences, even though not for the better, even though, as it may appear to them, some should be for the worse. If the claims of Individuality are ever to be asserted, the time is now, while much is still wanting to complete the enforced assimilation. It is only in the earlier stages that any stand can be successfully made against the encroachment. The demand that all other people shall resemble ourselves, grows by what it feeds on. If resistance waits till life is reduced *nearly* to one uniform type, all deviations from that type will come to be considered impious, immoral, even monstrous and contrary to nature. Mankind speedily become unable to conceive diversity, when they have been for some time unaccustomed to see it.

Chapter IV:
Of the Limits to the Authority
of Society over the Individual

WHAT, then, is the rightful limit to the sovereignty of the individual over himself? Where does the authority of society begin? How much of human life should be assigned to individuality, and how much to society?

Each will receive its proper share, if each has that which more particularly concerns it. To individuality should belong the part of life in which it is chiefly the individual that is interested; to society, the part which chiefly interests society.

Though society is not founded on a contract, and though no good purpose is answered by inventing a contract in order to deduce social obligations from it, every one who receives the protection of society owes a return for the benefit, and the fact of living in society renders it indispensable that each should be bound to observe a certain line of conduct towards the rest. This conduct consists first, in not injuring the interests of one another; or rather certain interests, which, either by express legal provision or by tacit understanding, ought to be considered as rights; and secondly, in each person's bearing his share (to be fixed on some equitable principle) of the labours and sacrifices incurred for defending the society or its members from injury and molestation. These conditions society is justified in enforcing at all costs to those who endeavour to withhold fulfilment. Nor is this all that society may do. The acts of an individual may be hurtful to others, or wanting in due consideration for their welfare, without going the length of violating any of their constituted rights. The offender may then be justly punished by opinion, though not by law. As soon as any part of a person's conduct affects prejudicially the interests of others, society has jurisdiction over it, and the question whether the general welfare will or will not be promoted by interfering with it, becomes open to discussion. But there is no room for entertaining any such question when a person's conduct affects the interests of no persons besides himself, or needs not affect them unless they like (all the persons concerned being of full age, and the ordinary amount of understanding). In all such cases there should be perfect freedom, legal and social, to do the action and stand the consequences.

It would be a great misunderstanding of this doctrine to suppose that it is one of selfish indifference, which pretends that human beings have no business with each other's conduct in life, and that they should not concern themselves about the well-doing or well-being of one another, unless their own interest is involved. Instead of any diminution, there is need of a great increase of disinterested exertion to promote the good of others. But disinterested benevolence can find other instruments to persuade people to their good, than whips and scourges, either of the literal or the metaphorical sort. I am the last person to undervalue the self-regarding virtues; they are only second in importance, if even second, to the social. It is equally the business of education to cultivate both. But even education works by conviction and persuasion as well as by compulsion, and it is by the former only that, when the period of education is past, the self-regarding virtues should be inculcated. Human beings owe to each other help to distinguish the better from the worse, and encouragement to choose the former and avoid the latter. They should be for ever stimulating each other to increased exercise of their higher faculties, and increased direction of their feelings and aims towards wise instead of foolish, elevating instead of degrading, objects and contemplations. But neither one person, nor any number of persons, is warranted in saying to another human creature of ripe years, that he shall not do with his life for his own benefit what he chooses to do with it. He is the person most interested in his own well-being: the interest which any other person, except in cases of strong personal attachment, can have in it, is trifling, compared with that which he himself has; the interest which society has in him individually (except as to his conduct to others) is fractional, and altogether indirect: while, with respect to his own feelings and circumstances, the most ordinary man or woman has means of knowledge immeasurably surpassing those that can be possessed by any one else. The interference of society to overrule his judgment and purposes in what only regards himself, must be grounded on general presumptions; which may be altogether wrong, and even if right, are as likely as not to be misapplied to individual cases, by persons no better acquainted with the circumstances of such cases than those are who look at them merely from without. In this department, therefore, of human affairs, Individuality has its proper field of action. In the conduct of human beings towards one another, it is necessary that general rules should for the most part be observed, in order that people may know what they have to expect; but in each person's own concerns, his individual spontaneity is entitled to free exercise. Considerations to aid his judgment, exhortations to strengthen his will, may be offered to him, even obtruded on him, by others; but he himself is the final judge. All errors which he is likely to commit against advice and warning, are far outweighed by the evil of allowing others to constrain him to what they deem his good.

I do not mean that the feelings with which a person is regarded by others, ought not to be in any way affected by his self-regarding qualities or deficiencies. This is neither possible nor desirable. If he is eminent in any of the qualities which conduce to his own good, he is, so far, a proper object of admiration. He is so much the nearer to the ideal perfection of human nature. If he is grossly deficient in those qualities, a sentiment the opposite of admiration will follow. There is a degree of folly, and a degree of what may be called (though the phrase is not unobjectionable) lowness or depravation of taste, which, though it cannot justify doing harm to the person who manifests it, renders him necessarily and properly a subject of distaste, or, in extreme cases, even of contempt: a person could not have the opposite qualities in due strength without entertaining these feelings. Though doing no wrong to any one, a person may so act as to compel us to judge him, and feel to him, as a fool, or as a being of an inferior order:

and since this judgment and feeling are a fact which he would prefer to avoid, it is doing him a service to warn him of it beforehand, as of any other disagreeable consequence to which he exposes himself. It would be well, indeed, if this good office were much more freely rendered than the common notions of politeness at present permit, and if one person could honestly point out to another that he thinks him in fault, without being considered unmannerly or presuming. We have a right, also, in various ways, to act upon our unfavourable opinion of any one, not to the oppression of his individuality, but in the exercise of ours. We are not bound, for example, to seek his society; we have a right to avoid it (though not to parade the avoidance), for we have a right to choose the society most acceptable to us. We have a right, and it may be our duty, to caution others against him, if we think his example or conversation likely to have a pernicious effect on those with whom he associates. We may give others a preference over him in optional good offices, except those which tend to his improvement. In these various modes a person may suffer very severe penalties at the hands of others, for faults which directly concern only himself; but he suffers these penalties only in so far as they are the natural, and, as it were, the spontaneous consequences of the faults themselves, not because they are purposely inflicted on him for the sake of punishment. A person who shows rashness, obstinacy, self-conceit—who cannot live within moderate means—who cannot restrain himself from hurtful indulgences—who pursues animal pleasures at the expense of those of feeling and intellect—must expect to be lowered in the opinion of others, and to have a less share of their favourable sentiments; but of this he has no right to complain, unless he has merited their favour by special excellence in his social relations, and has thus established a title to their good offices, which is not affected by his demerits towards himself.

What I contend for is, that the inconveniences which are strictly inseparable from the unfavourable judgment of others, are the only ones to which a person should ever be subjected for that portion of his conduct and character which concerns his own good, but which does not affect the interests of others in their relations with him. Acts injurious to others require a totally different treatment. Encroachment on their rights; infliction on them of any loss or damage not justified by his own rights; falsehood or duplicity in dealing with them; unfair or ungenerous use of advantages over them; even selfish abstinence from defending them against injury—these are fit objects of moral reprobation, and, in grave cases, of moral retribution and punishment. And not only these acts, but the dispositions which lead to them, are properly immoral, and fit subjects of disapprobation which may rise to abhorrence. Cruelty of disposition; malice and ill-nature; that most anti-social and odious of all passions, envy; dissimulation and insincerity; irascibility on insufficient cause, and resentment disproportioned to the provocation; the love of domineering over others; the desire to engross more than one's share of advantages (the πλεονεξία[1] of the Greeks); the pride which derives gratification from the abasement of others; the egotism which thinks self and its concerns more important than everything else, and decides all doubtful questions in its own favour;—these are moral vices, and constitute a bad and odious moral character: unlike the self-regarding faults previously mentioned, which are not properly immoralities, and to whatever pitch they may be carried, do not constitute wickedness. They may be proofs of any amount of folly, or want of personal dignity and self-respect; but they are only a subject of moral reprobation when they involve a breach of duty to others, for whose sake the individual is bound to have care for himself. What are called duties to ourselves are not socially obligatory, unless circumstances render them at the same time duties to others. The term duty to oneself, when it means anything more than prudence, means self-respect or self-development; and for none of these is any one accountable to his fellow creatures, because for none of them is it for the good of mankind that he be held accountable to them.

The distinction between the loss of consideration which a person may rightly incur by defect of prudence or of personal dignity, and the reprobation which is due to him for an offence against the rights of others,

---

[1] [πλεονεξία] greediness.

is not a merely nominal distinction. It makes a vast difference both in our feelings and in our conduct towards him, whether he displeases us in things in which we think we have a right to control him, or in things in which we know that we have not. If he displeases us, we may express our distaste, and we may stand aloof from a person as well as from a thing that displeases us; but we shall not therefore feel called on to make his life uncomfortable. We shall reflect that he already bears, or will bear, the whole penalty of his error; if he spoils his life by mismanagement, we shall not, for that reason, desire to spoil it still further: instead of wishing to punish him, we shall rather endeavour to alleviate his punishment, by showing him how he may avoid or cure the evils his conduct tends to bring upon him. He may be to us an object of pity, perhaps of dislike, but not of anger or resentment; we shall not treat him like an enemy of society: the worst we shall think ourselves justified in doing is leaving him to himself, if we do not interfere benevolently by showing interest or concern for him. It is far otherwise if he has infringed the rules necessary for the protection of his fellow-creatures, individually or collectively. The evil consequences of his acts do not then fall on himself, but on others; and society, as the protector of all its members, must retaliate on him; must inflict pain on him for the express purpose of punishment, and must take care that it be sufficiently severe. In the one case, he is an offender at our bar, and we are called on not only to sit in judgment on him, but, in one shape or another, to execute our own sentence: in the other case, it is not our part to inflict any suffering on him, except what may incidentally follow from our using the same liberty in the regulation of our own affairs, which we allow to him in his.

The distinction here pointed out between the part of a person's life which concerns only himself, and that which concerns others, many persons will refuse to admit. How (it may be asked) can any part of the conduct of a member of society be a matter of indifference to the other members? No person is an entirely isolated being; it is impossible for a person to do anything seriously or permanently hurtful to himself, without mischief reaching at least to his near connexions, and often far beyond them. If he injures his property, he does harm to those who directly or indirectly derived support from it, and usually diminishes, by a greater or less amount, the general resources of the community. If he deteriorates his bodily or mental faculties, he not only brings evil upon all who depended on him for any portion of their happiness, but disqualifies himself for rendering the services which he owes to his fellow-creatures generally; perhaps becomes a burthen on their affection or benevolence; and if such conduct were very frequent, hardly any offence that is committed would detract more from the general sum of good. Finally, if by his vices or follies a person does no direct harm to others, he is nevertheless (it may be said) injurious by his example; and ought to be compelled to control himself, for the sake of those whom the sight or knowledge of his conduct might corrupt or mislead.

And even (it will be added) if the consequences of misconduct could be confined to the vicious or thoughtless individual, ought society to abandon to their own guidance those who are manifestly unfit for it? If protection against themselves is confessedly due to children and persons under age, is not society equally bound to afford it to persons of mature years who are equally incapable of self-government? If gambling, or drunkenness, or incontinence, or idleness, or uncleanliness, are as injurious to happiness, and as great a hindrance to improvement, as many or most of the acts prohibited by law, why (it may be asked) should not law, so far as is consistent with practicability and social convenience, endeavour to repress these also? And as a supplement to the unavoidable imperfections of law, ought not opinion at least to organize a powerful police against these vices, and visit rigidly with social penalties those who are known to practise them? There is no question here (it may be said) about restricting individuality, or impeding the trial of new and original experiments in living. The only things it is sought to prevent are things which have been tried and condemned from the beginning of the world until now; things which experience has shown not to be useful or suitable to any person's individuality. There must be some length of time and amount of experience, after which a moral or prudential truth may be regarded as established: and it is merely desired to prevent generation after generation from falling over the same precipice which has been fatal to their predecessors.

I fully admit that the mischief which a person does to himself may seriously affect, both through their sympathies and their interests, those nearly connected with him, and in a minor degree, society at large. When, by conduct of this sort, a person is led to violate a distinct and assignable obligation to any other person or persons, the case is taken out of the self-regarding class, and becomes amenable to moral disapprobation in the proper sense of the term. If, for example, a man, through intemperance or extravagance, becomes unable to pay his debts, or, having undertaken the moral responsibility of a family, becomes from the same cause incapable of supporting or educating them, he is deservedly reprobated, and might be justly punished; but it is for the breach of duty to his family or creditors, not for the extravagance. If the resources which ought to have been devoted to them, had been diverted from them for the most prudent investment, the moral culpability would have been the same. George Barnwell murdered his uncle to get money for his mistress, but if he had done it to set himself up in business, he would equally have been hanged.[2] Again, in the frequent case of a man who causes grief to his family by addiction to bad habits, he deserves reproach for his unkindness or ingratitude; but so he may for cultivating habits not in themselves vicious, if they are painful to those with whom he passes his life, or who from personal ties are dependent on him for their comfort. Whoever fails in the consideration generally due to the interests and feelings of others, not being compelled by some more imperative duty, or justified by allowable self-preference, is a subject of moral disapprobation for that failure, but not for the cause of it, nor for the errors, merely personal to himself, which may have remotely led to it. In like manner, when a person disables himself, by conduct purely self-regarding, from the performance of some definite duty incumbent on him to the public, he is guilty of a social offence. No person ought to be punished simply for being drunk; but a soldier or a policeman should be punished for being drunk on duty. Whenever, in short, there is a definite damage,

[2] George Barnwell was the apprentice in the ballad "George Barnwell" and George Lillo's play *The London Merchant; or, the History of George Barnwell* (1731).

or a definite risk of damage, either to an individual or to the public, the case is taken out of the province of liberty, and placed in that of morality or law.

But with regard to the merely contingent, or, as it may be called, constructive injury which a person causes to society, by conduct which neither violates any specific duty to the public, nor occasions perceptible hurt to any assignable individual except himself; the inconvenience is one which society can afford to bear, for the sake of the greater good of human freedom. If grown persons are to be punished for not taking proper care of themselves, I would rather it were for their own sake, than under pretence of preventing them from impairing their capacity of rendering to society benefits which society does not pretend it has a right to exact. But I cannot consent to argue the point as if society had no means of bringing its weaker members up to its ordinary standard of rational conduct, except waiting till they do something irrational, and then punishing them, legally or morally, for it. Society has had absolute power over them during all the early portion of their existence: it has had the whole period of childhood and nonage in which to try whether it could make them capable of rational conduct in life. The existing generation is master both of the training and the entire circumstances of the generation to come; it cannot indeed make them perfectly wise and good, because it is itself so lamentably deficient in goodness and wisdom; and its best efforts are not always, in individual cases, its most successful ones; but it is perfectly well able to make the rising generation, as a whole, as good as, and a little better than, itself. If society lets any considerable number of its members grow up mere children, incapable of being acted on by rational consideration of distant motives, society has itself to blame for the consequences. Armed not only with all the powers of education, but with the ascendancy which the authority of a received opinion always exercises over the minds who are least fitted to judge for themselves; and aided by the *natural* penalties which cannot be prevented from falling on those who incur the distaste or the contempt of those who know them; let not society pretend that it needs, besides all this, the power to issue commands and enforce obedience in the personal concerns of individuals, in which, on all principles of justice and policy, the decision ought to rest with those who are to abide the consequences. Nor is there anything which tends more to discredit and frustrate the better means of influencing conduct, than a resort to the worse. If there be among those whom it is attempted to coerce into prudence or temperance, any of the material of which vigorous and independent character are made, they will infallibly rebel against the yoke. No such person will ever feel that others have a right to control him in his concerns, such as they have to prevent him from injuring them in theirs; and it easily comes to be considered a mark of spirit and courage to fly in the face of such usurped authority, and do with ostentation the exact opposite of what it enjoins; as in the fashion of grossness which succeeded, in the time of Charles II, to the fanatical moral intolerance of the Puritans. With respect to what is said of the necessity of protecting society from the bad example set to others by the vicious or self-indulgent; it is true that bad example may have a pernicious effect, especially the example of doing wrong to others with impunity to the wrong-doer. But we are now speaking of conduct which, while it does no wrong to others, is supposed to do great harm to the agent himself: and I do not see how those who believe this, can think otherwise than that the example, on the whole, must be more salutary than hurtful, since, if it displays the misconduct, it displays also the painful or degrading consequences which, if the conduct is justly censured, must be supposed to be in all or most cases attendant on it.

But the strongest of all the arguments against the interference of the public with purely personal conduct, is that when it does interfere, the odds are that it interferes wrongly, and in the wrong place. On questions of social morality, of duty to others, the opinion of the public, that is, of an overruling majority, though often wrong, is likely to be still oftener right; because on such questions they are only required to judge of their own interests; of the manner in which some mode of conduct, if allowed to be practised, would affect themselves. But the opinion of a similar majority, imposed as a law on the minority, on questions of self-regarding conduct, is quite as likely to be wrong as right; for in these cases public opinion means, at the best, some people's opinion of what is good or bad for other people; while very often it does not even mean that; the public, with the most perfect indifference, passing over the pleasure or convenience of those whose conduct they censure, and considering only their own preference. There are many who consider as an injury to themselves any conduct which they have a distaste for, and resent it as an outrage to their feelings; as a religious bigot, when charged with disregarding the religious feelings of others, has been known to retort that they disregard his feelings, by persisting in their abominable worship or creed. But there is no parity between the feeling of a person for his own opinion, and the feeling of another who is offended at his holding it; no more than between the desire of a thief to take a purse, and the desire of the right owner to keep it. And a person's taste is as much his own peculiar concern as his opinion or his purse. It is easy for any one to imagine an ideal public, which leaves the freedom and choice of individuals in all uncertain matters undisturbed, and only requires them to abstain from modes of conduct which universal experience has condemned. But where has there been seen a public which set any such limit to its censorship? or when does the public trouble itself about universal experience? In its interferences with personal conduct it is seldom thinking of anything but the enormity of acting or feeling differently from itself; and this standard of judgment, thinly disguised, is held up to mankind as the dictate of religion and philosophy, by nine-tenths of all moralists and speculative writers. Those teach that things are right because they are right; because we feel them to be so. They tell us to search in our own minds and hearts for laws of conduct binding on ourselves and on all others. What can the poor public do but apply these instructions, and make their own personal feelings of good and evil, if they are tolerably unanimous in them, obligatory on all the world?

The evil here pointed out is not one which exists only in theory; and it may perhaps be expected that I should specify the instances in which the public of this age and country improperly invests its own preferences with the character of moral laws. That is too weighty a subject to be discussed parenthetically, and by way of illustration. Yet examples are necessary, to show that the principle I maintain is of serious and practical moment, and that I am not endeavouring to erect a barrier against imaginary evils. And it is not difficult to show, by abundant instances, that to extend the bounds of what may be called moral police, until it encroaches on the most unquestionably legitimate liberty of the individual, is one of the most universal of all human propensities.

As a first instance, consider the antipathies which men cherish on no better grounds than that persons whose religious opinions are different from theirs, do not practise their religious observances, especially their religious abstinences. To cite a rather trivial example, nothing in the creed or practice of Christians does more to envenom the hatred of Mahomedans against them, than the fact of their eating pork. There are few acts which Christians and Europeans regard with more unaffected disgust, than Mussulmans regard this particular mode of satisfying hunger. It is, in the first place, an offence against their religion; but this circumstance by no means explains either the degree or the kind of their repugnance; for wine also is forbidden by their religion, and to partake of it is by all Mussulmans accounted wrong, but not disgusting. Their aversion to the flesh of the "unclean beast" is, on the contrary, of that peculiar character, resembling an instinctive antipathy, which the idea of uncleanness, when once it thoroughly sinks into the feelings, seems always to excite even in those whose personal habits are anything but scrupulously cleanly, and of which the sentiment of religious impurity, so intense in the Hindoos, is a remarkable example. Suppose now that in a people, of whom the majority were Mussulmans, that majority should insist upon not permitting pork to be eaten within the limits of the country. This would be nothing new in Mahomedan countries.[3] Would it be a legitimate exercise of the moral authority of public opinion? and if not, why not? The practice is really revolting to such a public. They also sincerely think that it is forbidden and abhorred by the Deity. Neither could the prohibition be censured as religious persecution. It might be religious in its origin, but it would not be persecution for religion, since nobody's religion makes it a duty to eat pork. The only tenable ground of condemnation would be, that with the personal tastes and self-regarding concerns of individuals the public has no business to interfere.

To come somewhat nearer home; the majority of Spaniards consider it a gross impiety, offensive in the highest degree to the Supreme Being, to worship him in any other manner than the Roman Catholic; and no other public worship is lawful on Spanish soil. The people of all Southern Europe look upon a married clergy as not only irreligious, but unchaste, indecent, gross, disgusting. What do Protestants think of these perfectly sincere feelings, and of the attempt to enforce them against non-Catholics? Yet, if mankind are justified in interfering with each other's liberty in things which do not concern the interests of others, on what principle is it possible consistently to exclude these cases? or who can blame people for desiring to suppress what they regard as a scandal in the sight of God and man? No stronger case can be shown for prohibiting anything which is regarded as a personal immorality, than is made out for suppressing these practices in the eyes of those who regard them as impieties; and unless we are willing to adopt the logic of persecutors, and to say that we may persecute others because we are right, and that they must not persecute us because they are wrong, we must beware of admitting a principle of which we should resent as a gross injustice the application to ourselves.

The preceding instances may be objected to, although unreasonably, as drawn from contingencies impossible among us: opinion, in this country, not being likely to enforce abstinence from meats, or to interfere with

[3] The case of the Bombay Parsees is a curious instance in point. When this industrious and enterprising tribe, the descendants of the Persian fire-worshippers, flying from their native country before the Caliphs, arrived in Western India, they were admitted to toleration by the Hindoo sovereigns, on condition of not eating beef. When those regions afterwards fell under the dominion of Mahomedan conquerors, the Parsees obtained from them a continuance of indulgence, on condition of refraining from pork. What was at first obedience became a second nature, and the Parsees to this day abstain both from beef and pork. Though not required by their religion, the double abstinence has had time to grow into a custom of their tribe; and custom, in the East, is a religion. (Mill's note.)

people for worshipping, and for either marrying or not marrying, according to their creed or inclination. The next example, however, shall be taken from an interference with liberty which we have by no means passed all danger of. Wherever the Puritans have been sufficiently powerful, as in New England, and in Great Britain at the time of the Commonwealth, they have endeavoured, with considerable success, to put down all public, and nearly all private, amusements: especially music, dancing, public games, or other assemblages for purposes of diversion, and the theatre. There are still in this country large bodies of persons by whose notions of morality and religion these recreations are condemned; and those persons belonging chiefly to the middle class, who are the ascendant power in the present social and political condition of the kingdom, it is by no means impossible that persons of these sentiments may at some time or other command a majority in Parliament. How will the remaining portion of the community like to have the amusements that shall be permitted to them regulated by the religious and moral sentiments of the stricter Calvinists and Methodists? Would they not, with considerable peremptoriness, desire these intrusively pious members of society to mind their own business? This is precisely what should be said to every government and every public, who have the pretension that no person shall enjoy any pleasure which they think wrong. But if the principle of the pretension be admitted, no one can reasonably object to its being acted on in the sense of the majority, or other preponderating power in the country; and all persons must be ready to conform to the idea of a Christian commonwealth, as understood by the early settlers in New England, if a religious profession similar to theirs should ever succeed in regaining its lost ground, as religions supposed to be declining have so often been known to do.

To imagine another contingency more likely to be realized than the one last mentioned. There is confessedly a strong tendency in the modern world towards a democratic constitution of society, accompanied or not by popular political institutions. It is affirmed that in the country where this tendency is most completely realized—where both society and the government are most democratic—the United States—the feeling of the majority, to whom any appearance of a more showy or costly style of living than they can hope to rival is disagreeable, operates as a tolerably effectual sumptuary law, and that in many parts of the Union it is really difficult for a person possessing a very large income, to find any mode of spending it, which will not incur popular disapprobation. Though such statements as these are doubtless much exaggerated as a representation of existing facts, the state of things they describe is not only a conceivable and possible, but a probable result of democratic feeling, combined with the notion that the public has a right to a veto on the manner in which individuals shall spend their incomes. We have only further to suppose a considerable diffusion of Socialist opinions, and it may become infamous in the eyes of the majority to possess more property than some very small amount, or any income not earned by manual labour. Opinions similar in principle to these, already prevail widely among the artizan class, and weigh oppressively on those who are amenable to the opinion chiefly of that class, namely, its own members. It is known that the bad workmen who form the majority of the operatives in many branches of industry, are decidedly of opinion that bad workmen ought to receive the same wages as good, and that no one ought to be allowed, through piecework or otherwise, to earn by superior skill or industry more than others can without it. And they employ a moral police, which occasionally becomes a physical one, to deter skilful workmen from receiving, and employers from giving, a larger remuneration for a more useful service. If the public have any jurisdiction over private concerns, I cannot see that these people are in fault, or that any individual's particular public can be blamed for asserting the same authority over his individual conduct, which the general public asserts over people in general.

But, without dwelling upon supposititious cases, there are, in our own day, gross usurpations upon the liberty of private life actually practised, and still greater ones threatened with some expectation of success, and opinions propounded which assert an unlimited right in the public not only to prohibit by law everything which it thinks wrong, but in order to get at what it thinks wrong, to prohibit any number of things which it admits to be innocent.

Under the name of preventing intemperance, the people of one English colony, and of nearly half the United States, have been interdicted by law from making any use whatever of fermented drinks, except for medical purposes: for prohibition of their sale is in fact, as it is intended to be, prohibition of their use. And though the impracticability of executing the law has caused its repeal in several of the States which had adopted it, including the one from which it derives its name,[4] an attempt has notwithstanding been commenced, and is prosecuted with considerable zeal by many of the professed philanthropists, to agitate for a similar law in this country. The association, or "Alliance" as it terms itself, which has been formed for this purpose, has acquired some notoriety through the publicity given to a correspondence between its Secretary and one of the very few English public men who hold that a politician's opinions ought to be founded on principles.[5] Lord Stanley's share in this correspondence is calculated to strengthen the hopes already built on him, by those who know how rare such qualities as are manifested in some of his public appearances, unhappily are among those who figure in political life. The organ of the Alliance, who would "deeply deplore the recognition of any principle which could be wrested to justify bigotry and persecution," undertakes to point out the "broad and impassable barrier" which divides such principles from those of the association. "All matters relating to thought, opinion, conscience, appear to me," he says, "to be without the sphere of legislation; all pertaining to social act, habit, relation, subject only to a discretionary power vested in the State itself, and not in the individual, to be within it." No mention is made of a third class, different from either of these, viz. acts and habits which are not social, but individual; although it is to this class, surely, that the act of drinking fermented liquors

---

[4] That is, Maine. New Brunswick and thirteen of the states had prohibition laws in the 1850s. Because Maine was the first state to adopt it, "Maine Law" became the general term for prohibition.

[5] Edward John Stanley, second Baron Stanley of Alderley, a Whig politician, was at this time president of the Board of Trade. The United Kingdom Alliance for the Legislative Suppression of the Sale of Intoxicating Liquors was founded in 1853.

belongs. Selling fermented liquors, however, is trading, and trading is a social act. But the infringement complained of is not on the liberty of the seller, but on that of the buyer and consumer; since the State might just as well forbid him to drink wine, as purposely make it impossible for him to obtain it. The Secretary, however, says, "I claim, as a citizen, a right to legislate whenever my social rights are invaded by the social act of another." And now for the definition of these "social rights." "If anything invades my social rights, certainly the traffic in strong drink does. It destroys my primary right of security, by constantly creating and stimulating social disorder. It invades my right of equality, by deriving a profit from the creation of a misery I am taxed to support. It impedes my right to free moral and intellectual development, by surrounding my path with dangers, and by weakening and demoralizing society, from which I have a right to claim mutual aid and intercourse." A theory of "social rights," the like of which probably never before found its way into distinct language: being nothing short of this—that it is the absolute social right of every individual, that every other individual shall act in every respect exactly as he ought; that whosoever fails thereof in the smallest particular, violates my social right, and entitles me to demand from the legislature the removal of the grievance. So monstrous a principle is far more dangerous than any single interference with liberty; there is no violation of liberty which it would not justify; it acknowledges no right to any freedom whatever, except perhaps to that of holding opinions in secret, without ever disclosing them: for, the moment an opinion which I consider noxious passes any one's lips, it invades all the "social rights" attributed to me by the Alliance. The doctrine ascribes to all mankind a vested interest in each other's moral, intellectual, and even physical perfection, to be defined by each claimant according to his own standard.

Another important example of illegitimate interference with the rightful liberty of the individual, not simply threatened, but long since carried into triumphant effect, is Sabbatarian legislation. Without doubt, abstinence on one day in the week, so far as the exigencies of life permit, from the usual daily occupation, though in no respect religiously binding on any except Jews,[6] is a highly beneficial custom. And inasmuch as this custom cannot be observed without a general consent to that effect among the industrious classes, therefore, in so far as some persons by working may impose the same necessity on others, it may be allowable and right that the law should guarantee to each the observance by others of the custom, by suspending the greater operations of industry on a particular day. But this justification, grounded on the direct interest which others have in each individual's observance of the practice, does not apply to the self-chosen occupations in which a person may think fit to employ his leisure; nor does it hold good, in the smallest degree, for legal restrictions on amusements. It is true that the amusement of some is the day's work of others; but the pleasure, not to say the useful recreation, of many, is worth the labour of a few, provided the occupation is freely chosen, and can be freely resigned. The operatives are perfectly right in thinking that if all worked on Sunday, seven days' work would have to be given for six days' wages: but so long as the great mass of employments are suspended, the small number who for the enjoyment of others must still work, obtain a proportional increase of earnings; and they are not obliged to follow those occupations, if they prefer leisure to emolument. If a further remedy is sought, it might be found in the establishment by custom of a holiday on some other day of the week for those particular classes of persons. The only ground, therefore, on which restrictions on Sunday amusements can be defended, must be that they are religiously wrong; a motive of legislation which never can be too earnestly protested against. "Deorum injuriae Diis curae."[7] It remains to be proved that society or any of its officers holds a commission from on high to avenge any supposed offence to Omnipotence, which is not also a wrong to our fellow creatures. The notion that it is one man's duty that another should be religious, was the foundation of all the religious persecutions ever perpetrated, and if admitted, would fully justify

[6] For Jews, the Sabbath (sundown Friday to sundown Saturday) is a day of rest and prayer; work and travel are prohibited.

[7] [*Deorum injuriae Diis curae*] "The gods can avenge their own wrongs" (Tacitus, Annals, I, lxxiii).

them. Though the feeling which breaks out in the repeated attempts to stop railway travelling on Sunday, in the resistance to the opening of Museums, and the like, has not the cruelty of the old persecutors, the state of mind indicated by it is fundamentally the same. It is a determination not to tolerate others in doing what is permitted by their religion, because it is not permitted by the persecutor's religion. It is a belief that God not only abominates the act of the misbeliever, but will not hold us guiltless if we leave him unmolested.

I cannot refrain from adding to these examples of the little account commonly made of human liberty, the language of downright persecution which breaks out from the press of this country, whenever it feels called on to notice the remarkable phenomenon of Mormonism.[8] Much might be said on the unexpected and instructive fact, that an alleged new revelation, and a religion founded on it, the product of palpable imposture, not even supported by the *prestige* of extraordinary qualities in its founder, is believed by hundreds of thousands, and has been made the foundation of a society, in the age of newspapers, railways, and the electric telegraph. What here concerns us is, that this religion, like other and better religions, has its martyrs; that its prophet and founder was, for his teaching, put to death by a mob; that others of its adherents lost their lives by the same lawless violence; that they were forcibly expelled, in a body, from the country in which they first grew up; while, now that they have been chased into a solitary recess in the midst of a desert, many in this country openly declare that it would be right (only that it is not convenient) to send an expedition against them, and compel them by force to conform to the opinions of other people. The article of the Mormonite doctrine which is the chief provocative to the antipathy which thus breaks through the ordinary restraints of religious tolerance, is its sanction of polygamy; which, though permitted to Mahomedans, and Hindoos, and Chinese, seems to

---

[8] The Mormon religion (Church of Jesus Christ of Latter-Day Saints) was founded by Joseph Smith (1805–44) in Manchester, New York, in 1830, based on the *Book of Mormon*, which he claimed to have found in 1827 following an angelic visitation.

excite unquenchable animosity when practised by persons who speak English, and profess to be a kind of Christians. No one has a deeper disapprobation than I have of this Mormon institution; both for other reasons, and because, far from being in any way countenanced by the principle of liberty, it is a direct infraction of that principle, being a mere rivetting of the chains of one-half of the community, and an emancipation of the other from reciprocity of obligation towards them. Still, it must be remembered that this relation is as much voluntary on the part of the women concerned in it, and who may be deemed the sufferers by it, as is the case with any other form of the marriage institution; and however surprising this fact may appear, it has its explanation in the common ideas and customs of the world, which teaching women to think marriage the one thing needful, make it intelligible that many a woman should prefer being one of several wives, to not being a wife at all. Other countries are not asked to recognise such unions, or release any portion of their inhabitants from their own laws on the score of Mormonite opinions. But when the dissentients have conceded to the hostile sentiments of others, far more than could justly be demanded; when they have left the countries to which their doctrines were unacceptable, and established themselves in a remote corner of the earth, which they have been the first to render habitable to human beings; it is difficult to see on what principles but those of tyranny they can be prevented from living there under what laws they please, provided they commit no aggression on other nations, and allow perfect freedom of departure to those who are dissatisfied with their ways. A recent writer, in some respects of considerable merit, proposes (to use his own words) not a crusade, but a *civilizade*, against this polygamous community, to put an end to what seems to him a retrograde step in civilization. It also appears so to me, but I am not aware that any community has a right to force another to be civilized. So long as the sufferers by the bad law do not invoke assistance from other communities, I cannot admit that persons entirely unconnected with them ought to step in and require that a condition of things with which all who are directly interested appear to be satisfied, should be put an end to because it is a scandal to persons some thousands of miles distant, who have no part or concern in it. Let them send missionaries, if they please, to preach against it; and let them, by any fair means (of which silencing the teachers is not one,) oppose the progress of similar doctrines among their own people. If civilization has got the better of barbarism when barbarism had the world to itself, it is too much to profess to be afraid lest barbarism, after having been fairly got under, should revive and conquer civilization. A civilization that can thus succumb to its vanquished enemy, must first have become so degenerate, that neither its appointed priests and teachers, nor anybody else, has the capacity, or will take the trouble, to stand up for it. If this be so, the sooner such a civilization receives notice to quit, the better. It can only go on from bad to worse, until destroyed and regenerated (like the Western Empire[9]) by energetic barbarians.

---

[9] The Western portion of the Roman Empire, after the division into East and West in 364, which fell before the barbarian invasions of the fifth century.

Chapter V:
Applications

Thin principles asserted in these pages must be more generally admitted as the basis for discussion of details, before a consistent application of them to all the various departments of government and morals can be attempted with any prospect of advantage. The few observations I propose to make on questions of detail, are designed to illustrate the principles, rather than to follow them out to their consequences. I offer, not so much applications, as specimens of application; which may serve to bring into greater clearness the meaning and limits of the two maxims which together form the entire doctrine of this Essay, and to assist the judgment in holding the balance between them, in the cases where it appears doubtful which of them is applicable to the case.

The maxims are, first, that the individual is not accountable to society for his actions, in so far as these concern the interests of no person but himself. Advice, instruction, persuasion, and avoidance by other people if thought necessary by them for their own good, are the only measures by which society can justifiably express its dislike or disapprobation of his conduct. Secondly, that for such actions as are prejudicial to the interests of others, the individual is accountable, and may be subjected either to social or to legal punishment, if society is of opinion that the one or the other is requisite for its protection.

In the first place, it must by no means be supposed, because damage, or probability of damage, to the interests of others, can alone justify the interference of society, that therefore it always does justify such interference. In many cases, an individual, in pursuing a legitimate object, necessarily and therefore legitimately causes pain or loss to others, or intercepts a good which they had a reasonable hope of obtaining. Such oppositions of interest between individuals often arise from bad social institutions, but are unavoidable while those institutions last; and some would be unavoidable under any institutions. Whoever succeeds in an overcrowded profession, or in a competitive examination; whoever is preferred to another in any contest for an object which both desire, reaps benefit from the loss of others, from their wasted exertion and their disappointment. But it is, by common admission, better for the general interest of mankind, that persons should pursue their objects undeterred by this sort of consequences. In other words, society admits no right, either legal or moral, in the disappointed competitors, to immunity from this kind of suffering; and feels called on to interfere, only when means of success have been employed which it is contrary to the general interest to permit—namely, fraud or treachery, and force.

Again, trade is a social act. Whoever undertakes to sell any description of goods to the public, does what affects the interest of other persons, and of society in general; and thus his conduct, in principle, comes within the jurisdiction of society: accordingly, it was once held to be the duty of governments, in all cases which were considered of importance, to fix prices, and regulate the processes of manufacture. But it is now recognised, though not till after a long struggle, that both the cheapness and the good quality of commodities are most effectually provided for by leaving the producers and sellers perfectly free, under the sole check of equal freedom to the buyers for supplying themselves elsewhere. This is the so-called doctrine of Free Trade,[1] which rests on grounds different from, though equally solid with, the principle of individual liberty asserted in this Essay. Restrictions on trade, or on production for purposes of trade, are indeed restraints; and all restraint, *quâ* restraint, is an evil: but the restraints in question affect only that part of conduct which society is competent to restrain, and are wrong solely because they do not really produce the results which it is desired to produce by them. As the principle of individual liberty is

---

[1] The doctrine that there should be no duties or restrictions on international trade.

not involved in the doctrine of Free Trade, so neither is it in most of the questions which arise respecting the limits of that doctrine; as for example, what amount of public control is admissible for the prevention of fraud by adulteration; how far sanitary precautions, or arrangements to protect workpeople employed in dangerous occupations, should be enforced on employers. Such questions involve considerations of liberty, only in so far as leaving people to themselves is always better, *caeteris paribus*,[2] than controlling them: but that they may be legitimately controlled for these ends, is in principle undeniable. On the other hand, there are questions relating to interference with trade, which are essentially questions of liberty; such as the Maine Law, already touched upon; the prohibition of the importation of opium into China; the restriction of the sale of poisons; all cases, in short, where the object of the interference is to make it impossible or difficult to obtain a particular commodity. These interferences are objectionable, not as infringements on the liberty of the producer or seller, but on that of the buyer.

One of these examples, that of the sale of poisons, opens a new question; the proper limits of what may be called the functions of police; how far liberty may legitimately be invaded for the prevention of crime, or of accident. It is one of the undisputed functions of government to take precautions against crime before it has been committed, as well as to detect and punish it afterwards. The preventive function of government, however, is far more liable to be abused, to the prejudice of liberty, than the punitory function; for there is hardly any part of the legitimate freedom of action of a human being which would not admit of being represented, and fairly too, as increasing the facilities for some form or other of delinquency. Nevertheless, if a public authority, or even a private person, sees any one evidently preparing to commit a crime, they are not bound to look on inactive until the crime is committed, but may interfere to prevent it. If poisons were never bought or used for any purpose except the commission of murder, it would be right to prohibit their manufacture and sale. They

[2] [*caeteris paribus*] other things being equal.

may, however, be wanted not only for innocent but for useful purposes, and restrictions cannot be imposed in the one case without operating in the other. Again, it is a proper office of public authority to guard against accidents. If either a public officer or any one else saw a person attempting to cross a bridge which had been ascertained to be unsafe, and there were no time to warn him of his danger, they might seize him and turn him back, without any real infringement of his liberty; for liberty consists in doing what one desires, and he does not desire to fall into the river. Nevertheless, when there is not a certainty, but only a danger of mischief, no one but the person himself can judge of the sufficiency of the motive which may prompt him to incur the risk: in this case, therefore, (unless he is a child, or delirious, or in some state of excitement or absorption incompatible with the full use of the reflecting faculty) he ought, I conceive, to be only warned of the danger; not forcibly prevented from exposing himself to it. Similar considerations, applied to such a question as the sale of poisons, may enable us to decide which among the possible modes of regulation are or are not contrary to principle. Such a precaution, for example, as that of labelling the drug with some word expressive of its dangerous character, may be enforced without violation of liberty: the buyer cannot wish not to know that the thing he possesses has poisonous qualities. But to require in all cases the certificate of a medical practitioner, would make it sometimes impossible, always expensive, to obtain the article for legitimate uses. The only mode apparent to me, in which difficulties may be thrown in the way of crime committed through this means, without any infringement, worth taking into account, upon the liberty of those who desire the poisonous substance for other purposes, consists in providing what, in the apt language of Bentham, is called "preappointed evidence." This provision is familiar to every one in the case of contracts. It is usual and right that the law, when a contract is entered into, should require as the condition of its enforcing performance, that certain formalities should be observed, such as signatures, attestation of witnesses, and the like, in order that in case of subsequent dispute, there may be evidence to prove that the contract was really entered into, and that there was nothing in the circumstances to render it legally invalid; the effect being, to throw great obstacles in the way of fictitious contracts made in circumstances which, if known, would destroy their validity. Precautions of a similar nature might be enforced in the sale of articles adapted to be instruments of crime. The seller, for example, might be required to enter in a register the exact time of the transaction, the name and address of the buyer, the precise quality and quantity sold; to ask the purpose for which it was wanted, and record the answer he received. When there was no medical prescription, the presence of some third person might be required, to bring home the fact to the purchaser, in case there should afterwards be reason to believe that the article had been applied to criminal purposes. Such regulations would in general be no material impediment to obtaining the article, but a very considerable one to making an improper use of it without detection.

The right inherent in society, to ward off crimes against itself by antecedent precautions, suggests the obvious limitations to the maxim, that purely self-regarding misconduct cannot properly be meddled with in the way of prevention or punishment. Drunkenness, for example, in ordinary cases, is not a fit subject for legislative interference; but I should deem it perfectly legitimate that a person, who had once been convicted of violence to others under the influence of drink, should be placed under a special legal restriction, personal to himself; that if he were afterwards found drunk, he should be liable to a penalty, and that if when in that state he committed another offence, the punishment to which he would be liable for that other offence should be increased in severity. The making himself drunk, in a person whom drunkenness excites to do harm to others, is a crime against others. So, again, idleness, except in a person receiving support from the public, or except when it constitutes a breach of contract, cannot without tyranny be made a subject of legal punishment; but if, either from idleness or from any other avoidable cause, a man fails to support his children, it is not tyranny to force him to fulfil that obligation, by compulsory labour, if no other means are available.

Again, there are many acts which, being directly injurious only to the agents themselves, ought not to be legally interdicted, but which, if done publicly, are a violation of good manners, and coming thus within the category of offences against others, may rightfully be prohibited. Of this kind are offences against decency; on which it is unnecessary to dwell, the rather as they are only connected indirectly with our subject, the objection to publicity being equally strong in the case of many actions not in themselves condemnable, nor supposed to be so.

There is another question to which an answer must be found, consistent with the principles which have been laid down. In cases of personal conduct supposed to be blameable, but which respect for liberty precludes society from preventing or punishing, because the evil directly resulting falls wholly on the agent; what the agent is free to do, ought other persons to be equally free to counsel or instigate? This question is not free from difficulty. The case of a person who solicits another to do an act, is not strictly a case of self-regarding conduct. To give advice or offer inducements to any one, is a social act, and may, therefore, like actions in general which affect others, be supposed amenable to social control. But a little reflection corrects the first impression, by showing that if the case is not strictly within the definition of individual liberty, yet the reasons on which the principle of individual liberty is grounded, are applicable to it. If people must be allowed, in whatever concerns only themselves, to act as seems best to themselves at their own peril, they must equally be free to consult with one another about what is fit to be so done; to exchange opinions, and give and receive suggestions. Whatever it is permitted to do, it must be permitted to advise to do. The question is doubtful, only when the instigator derives a personal benefit from his advice; when he makes it his occupation, for subsistence or pecuniary gain, to promote what society and the State consider to be an evil. Then, indeed, a new element of complication is introduced; namely, the existence of classes of persons with an interest opposed to what is considered as the public weal, and whose mode of living is grounded on the counteraction of it. Ought this to be interfered with, or not? Fornication, for example, must be tolerated, and so must gambling; but should a person be free to be a pimp, or to keep a gambling-house? The case is one of those which lie on the exact boundary line between two principles, and it is not at once apparent to which of the two it properly belongs. There are arguments on both sides. On the side of toleration it may be said, that the fact of following anything as an occupation, and living or profiting by the practice of it, cannot make that criminal which would otherwise be admissible; that the act should either be consistently permitted or consistently prohibited; that if the principles which we have hitherto defended are true, society has no business, as society, to decide anything to be wrong which concerns only the individual; that it cannot go beyond dissuasion, and that one person should be as free to persuade, as another to dissuade. In opposition to this it may be contended, that although the public, or the State, are not warranted in authoritatively deciding, for purposes of repression or punishment, that such or such conduct affecting only the interests of the individual is good or bad, they are fully justified in assuming, if they regard it as bad, that its being so or not is at least a disputable question: That, this being supposed, they cannot be acting wrongly in endeavouring to exclude the influence of solicitations which are not disinterested, of instigators who cannot possibly be impartial—who have a direct personal interest on one side, and that side the one which the State believes to be wrong, and who confessedly promote it for personal objects only. There can surely, it may be urged, be nothing lost, no sacrifice of good, by so ordering matters that persons shall make their election, either wisely or foolishly, on their own prompting, as free as possible from the arts of persons who stimulate their inclinations for interested purposes of their own. Thus (it may be said) though the statutes respecting unlawful games are utterly indefensible—though all persons should be free to gamble in their own or each other's houses, or in any place of meeting established by their own subscriptions, and open only to the members and their visitors—yet public gambling-houses should not be permitted. It is true that the prohibition is never effectual, and that, whatever amount of tyrannical power may be given to the police, gambling-houses can always be maintained under other pretences; but they may be compelled to conduct their operations with a certain degree of secrecy and mystery, so that nobody knows anything about them but those who seek them; and more than this, society ought not to aim at. There is considerable force in these arguments. I will not venture to decide whether they are sufficient to justify the moral anomaly of punishing the accessary, when the principal is (and must be) allowed to go free; of fining or imprisoning the procurer, but not the fornicator, the gambling-house keeper, but not the gambler. Still less ought the common operations of buying and selling to be interfered with on analogous grounds. Almost every article which is bought and sold may be used in excess, and the sellers have a pecuniary interest in encouraging that excess; but no argument can be founded on this, in favour, for instance, of the Maine Law; because the class of dealers in strong drinks, though interested in their abuse, are indispensably required for the sake of their legitimate use. The interest, however, of these dealers in promoting intemperance is a real evil, and justifies the State in imposing restrictions and requiring guarantees which, but for that justification, would be infringements of legitimate liberty.

A further question is, whether the State, while it permits, should nevertheless indirectly discourage conduct which it deems contrary to the best interests of the agent; whether, for example, it should take measures to render the means of drunkenness more costly, or add to the difficulty of procuring them by limiting the number of the places of sale. On this as on most other practical questions, many distinctions require to be made. To tax stimulants for the sole purpose of making them more difficult to be obtained, is a measure differing only in degree from their entire prohibition; and would be justifiable only if that were justifiable. Every increase of cost is a prohibition, to those whose means do not come up to the augmented price; and to those who do, it is a penalty laid on them for gratifying a particular taste. Their choice of pleasures, and their mode of expending their income, after satisfying their legal and moral obligations to the State and to individuals, are their own concern, and must rest with their own judgement. These considerations may seem at first sight to condemn the selection of stimulants as special subjects of taxation for purposes of revenue. But it must be remembered that taxation for fiscal purposes is absolutely inevitable; that in most countries it is necessary that a considerable part of that taxation should be indirect; that the State, therefore, cannot help imposing penalties, which to some persons may be prohibitory, on the use of some articles of consumption. It is hence the duty of the State to consider, in the imposition of taxes, what commodities the consumers can best spare; and *à fortiori*[3], to select in preference those of which it deems the use, beyond a very moderate quantity, to be positively injurious. Taxation, therefore, of stimulants, up to the point which produces the largest amount of revenue (supposing that the State needs all the revenue which it yields) is not only admissible, but to be approved of.

The question of making the sale of these commodities a more or less exclusive privilege, must be answered differently, according to the purposes to which the restriction is intended to be subservient. All places of public resort require the restraint of a police, and places of this kind peculiarly, because offences against society are especially apt to originate there. It is, therefore, fit to confine the power of selling these commodities (at least for consumption on the spot) to persons, of known or vouched-for respectability of conduct; to make such regulations respecting hours of opening and closing as may be requisite for public surveillance, and to withdraw the licence if breaches of the peace repeatedly take place through the connivance or incapacity of the keeper of the house, or if it becomes a rendez-vous for concocting and preparing offences against the law. Any further restriction I do not conceive to be, in principle, justifiable. The limitation in number, for instance, of beer and spirit houses, for the express purpose of rendering them more difficult of access, and diminishing the occasions of temptation, not only exposes all to an inconvenience because there are some by whom the facility would be abused, but is suited only to a state of society in which the labouring classes are avowedly treated as children or savages, and placed under an education of restraint, to fit them for future admission to the privileges of freedom. This is not the principle on which the labouring classes are professedly governed in any free country; and no person who sets due value on freedom will give his adhesion to

---

[3] [*à fortiori*] with stronger reason, i.e., more justifiably.

their being so governed, unless after all efforts have been exhausted to educate them for freedom and govern them as freemen, and it has been definitively proved that they can only be governed as children. The bare statement of the alternative shows the absurdity of supposing that such efforts have been made in any case which needs be considered here. It is only because the institutions of this country are a mass of inconsistencies, that things find admittance into our practice which belong to the system of despotic, or what is called paternal, government, while the general freedom of our institutions precludes the exercise of the amount of control necessary to render the restraint of any real efficacy as a moral education.

It was pointed out in an early part of this Essay, that the liberty of the individual, in things wherein the individual is alone concerned, implies a corresponding liberty in any number of individuals to regulate by mutual agreement such things as regard them jointly, and regard no persons but themselves. This question presents no difficulty, so long as the will of all the persons implicated remains unaltered; but since that will may change, it is often necessary, even in things in which they alone are concerned, that they should enter into engagements with one another; and when they do, it is fit, as a general rule, that those engagements should be kept. Yet, in the laws, probably, of every country, this general rule has some exceptions. Not only persons are not held to engagements which violate the rights of third parties, but it is sometimes considered a sufficient reason for releasing them from an engagement, that it is injurious to themselves. In this and most other civilized countries, for example, an engagement by which a person should sell himself, or allow himself to be sold, as a slave, would be null and void; neither enforced by law nor by opinion. The ground for thus limiting his power of voluntarily disposing of his own lot in life, is apparent, and is very clearly seen in this extreme case. The reason for not interfering, unless for the sake of others, with a person's voluntary acts, is consideration for his liberty. His voluntary choice is evidence that what he so chooses is desirable, or at the least endurable, to him, and his good is on the whole best provided for by allowing him to take his own means of pursuing it. But by selling himself for a slave, he abdicates his liberty; he foregoes any future use of it beyond that single act. He therefore defeats, in his own case, the very purpose which is the justification of allowing him to dispose of himself. He is no longer free; but is thenceforth in a position which has no longer the presumption in its favour, that would be afforded by his voluntarily remaining in it. The principle of freedom cannot require that he should be free not to be free. It is not freedom, to be allowed to alienate his freedom. These reasons, the force of which is so conspicuous in this peculiar case, are evidently of far wider application; yet a limit is everywhere set to them by the necessities of life, which continually require, not indeed that we should resign our freedom, but that we should consent to this and the other limitation of it. The principle, however, which demands uncontrolled freedom of action in all that concerns only the agents themselves, requires that those who have become bound to one another, in things which concern no third party, should be able to release one another from the engagement: and even without such voluntary release, there are perhaps no contracts or engagements, except those that relate to money or money's worth, of which one can venture to say that there ought to be no liberty whatever of retractation. Baron Wilhelm von Humboldt, in the excellent essay from which I have already quoted, states it as his conviction, that engagements which involve personal relations or services, should never be legally binding beyond a limited duration of time; and that the most important of these engagements, marriage, having the peculiarity that its objects are frustrated unless the feelings of both the parties are in harmony with it, should require nothing more than the declared will of either party to dissolve it. This subject is too important, and too complicated, to be discussed in a parenthesis, and I touch on it only so far as is necessary for purposes of illustration. If the conciseness and generality of Baron Humboldt's dissertation had not obliged him in this instance to content himself with enunciating his conclusion without discussing the premises, he would doubtless have recognised that the question cannot be decided on grounds so simple as those to which he confines himself. When a person, either by express promise or by conduct, has encouraged another to rely upon his continuing to act in a certain way—to build expectations and calculations, and stake any part of his plan of life upon that supposition—a new series of moral obligations arises on his part towards that person, which may possibly be overruled, but cannot be ignored. And again, if the relation between two contracting parties has been followed by consequences to others; if it has placed third parties in any peculiar position, or, as in the case of marriage, has even called third parties into existence, obligations arise on the part of both the contracting parties towards those third persons, the fulfilment of which, or at all events the mode of fulfilment, must be greatly affected by the continuance or disruption of the relation between the original parties to the contract. It does not follow, nor can I admit, that these obligations extend to requiring the fulfilment of the contract at all costs to the happiness of the reluctant party; but they are a necessary element in the question; and even if, as Von Humboldt maintains, they ought to make no difference in the *legal* freedom of the parties to release themselves from the engagement (and I also hold that they ought not to make *much* difference), they necessarily make a great difference in the *moral* freedom. A person is bound to take all these circumstances into account, before resolving on a step which may affect such important interests of others; and if he does not allow proper weight to those interests, he is morally responsible for the wrong. I have made these obvious remarks for the better illustration of the general principle of liberty, and not because they are at all needed on the particular question, which, on the contrary, is usually discussed as if the interest of children was everything, and that of grown persons nothing.

I have already observed that, owing to the absence of any recognised general principles, liberty is often granted where it should be withheld, as well as withheld where it should be granted; and one of the cases in which, in the modern European world, the sentiment of liberty is the strongest, is a case where, in my view, it is altogether misplaced. A person should be free to do as he likes in his own concerns; but he ought not to be free to do as he likes in acting for another, under the pretext that the affairs of the other are his own affairs. The State, while it respects the liberty of each in what specially regards himself, is bound to maintain a vigilant control over his exercise of any power which it allows him to possess over others. This obligation is almost entirely disregarded in the case of the family relations, a case, in its direct influence on human happiness, more important than all others taken together. The almost despotic power of husbands over wives needs not be enlarged upon here, because nothing more is needed for the complete removal of the evil, than that wives should have the same rights, and should receive the protection of law in the same manner, as all other persons; and because, on this subject, the defenders of established injustice do not avail themselves of the plea of liberty, but stand forth openly as the champions of power. It is in the case of children, that misapplied notions of liberty are a real obstacle to the fulfilment by the State of its duties. One would almost think that a man's children were supposed to be literally, and not metaphorically, a part of himself, so jealous is opinion of the smallest interference of law with his absolute and exclusive control over them; more jealous than of almost any interference with his own freedom of action: so much less do the generality of mankind value liberty than power. Consider, for example, the case of education. Is it not almost a self-evident axiom, that the State should require and compel the education, up to a certain standard, of every human being who is born its citizen? Yet who is there that is not afraid to recognise and assert this truth? Hardly any one indeed will deny that it is one of the most sacred duties of the parents (or, as law and usage now stand, the father), after summoning a human being into the world, to give to that being an education fitting him to perform his part well in life towards others and towards himself. But while this is unanimously declared to be the father's duty, scarcely anybody, in this country, will bear to hear of obliging him to perform it. Instead of his being required to make any exertion or sacrifice for securing education to the child, it is left to his choice to accept it or not when it is provided gratis! It still remains unrecognised, that to bring a child into existence without a fair prospect of being able, not only to provide food for its body, but instruction and training for its mind, is a moral crime, both against the unfortunate offspring and against society; and that if the parent does not fulfil this obligation, the State ought to see it fulfilled, at the charge, as far as possible, of the parent.

Were the duty of enforcing universal education once admitted, there would be an end to the difficulties about what the State should teach, and how it should teach, which now convert the subject into a mere battle-field for sects and parties, causing the time and labour which should have been spent in educating, to be wasted in quarrelling about education. If the government would make up its mind to *require* for every child a good education, it might save itself the trouble of *providing* one. It might leave to parents to obtain the education where and how they pleased, and content itself with helping to pay the school fees of the poorer classes of children, and defraying the entire school expenses of those who have no one else to pay for them. The objections which are urged with reason against State education, do not apply to the enforcement of education by the State, but to the State's taking upon itself to direct that education: which is a totally different thing. That the whole or any large part of the education of the people should be in State hands, I go as far as any one in deprecating. All that has been said of the importance of individuality of character, and diversity in opinions and modes of conduct, involves, as of the same unspeakable importance, diversity of education. A general State education is a mere contrivance for moulding people to be exactly like one another: and as the mould in which it casts them is that which pleases the predominant power in the government, whether this be a monarch, a priesthood, an aristocracy, or the majority of the existing generation, in proportion as it is efficient and successful, it establishes a despotism over the mind, leading by natural tendency to one over the body. An education established and controlled by the State should only exist, if it exist at all, as one among many competing experiments, carried on for the purpose of example and stimulus, to keep the others up to a certain standard of excellence. Unless, indeed, when society in general is in so backward a state that it could not or would not provide for itself any proper institutions of education, unless the government undertook the task: then, indeed, the government may, as the less of two great evils, take upon itself the business of schools and universities, as it may that of joint stock companies, when private enterprise, in a shape fitted for undertaking great works of industry, does not exist in the country. But in general, if the country contains a sufficient number of persons qualified to provide education under government auspices, the same persons would be able and willing to give an equally good education on the voluntary principle, under the assurance of remuneration afforded by a law rendering education compulsory, combined with State aid to those unable to defray the expense.

The instrument for enforcing the law could be no other than public examinations, extending to all children, and beginning at an early age. An age might be fixed at which every child must be examined, to ascertain if he (or she) is able to read. If a child proves unable, the father, unless he has some sufficient ground of excuse, might be subjected to a moderate fine, to be worked out, if necessary, by his labour, and the child might be put to school at his expense. Once in every year the examination should be renewed, with a gradually extending range of subjects, so as to make the universal acquisition, and what is more, retention, of a certain minimum of general knowledge, virtually compulsory. Beyond that minimum, there should be voluntary examinations on all subjects, at which all who come up to a certain standard of proficiency might claim a certificate. To prevent the State from exercising, through these arrangements, an improper influence over opinion, the knowledge required for passing an examination (beyond the merely instrumental parts of knowledge, such as languages and their use) should, even in the higher classes of examinations, be confined to facts and positive science exclusively. The examinations on religion, politics, or other disputed topics, should not turn on the truth or falsehood of opinions, but on the matter of fact that such and such an opinion is held, on such grounds, by such authors, or schools, or churches. Under this system, the rising generation would be no worse off in regard to all disputed truths, than they are at present; they would be brought up either churchmen or dissenters[4] as they now are, the State merely taking

[4] Members of the (Established) Church of England or Nonconformist dissenters from it, such as Methodists, Congregationalists, Presbyterians, etc.

care that they should be instructed churchmen, or instructed dissenters. There would be nothing to hinder them from being taught religion, if their parents chose, at the same schools where they were taught other things. All attempts by the State to bias the conclusions of its citizens on disputed subjects, are evil; but it may very properly offer to ascertain and certify that a person possesses the knowledge, requisite to make his conclusions, on any given subject, worth attending to. A student of philosophy would be the better for being able to stand an examination both in Locke and in Kant, whichever of the two he takes up with, or even if with neither: and there is no reasonable objection to examining an atheist in the evidences of Christianity, provided he is not required to profess a belief in them. The examinations, however, in the higher branches of knowledge should, I conceive, be entirely voluntary. It would be giving too dangerous a power to governments, were they allowed to exclude any one from professions, even from the profession of teacher, for alleged deficiency of qualifications: and I think, with Wilhelm von Humboldt, that degrees, or other public certificates of scientific or professional acquirements, should be given to all who present themselves for examination, and stand the test; but that such certificates should confer no advantage over competitors, other than the weight which may be attached to their testimony by public opinion.

It is not in the matter of education only, that misplaced notions of liberty prevent moral obligations on the part of parents from being recognised, and legal obligations from being imposed, where there are the strongest grounds for the former always, and in many cases for the latter also. The fact itself, of causing the existence of a human being, is one of the most responsible actions in the range of human life. To undertake this responsibility—to bestow a life which may be either a curse or a blessing—unless the being on whom it is to be bestowed will have at least the ordinary chances of a desirable existence, is a crime against that being. And in a country either overpeopled, or threatened with being so, to produce children, beyond a very small number, with the effect of reducing the reward of labour by their competition, is a serious offence against all who live by the remuneration of their labour. The laws which, in many countries on the Continent, forbid marriage unless the parties can show that they have the means of supporting a family, do not exceed the legitimate powers of the State: and whether such laws be expedient or not (a question mainly dependent on local circumstances and feelings), they are not objectionable as violations of liberty. Such laws are interferences of the State to prohibit a mischievous act—an act injurious to others, which ought to be a subject of reprobation, and social stigma, even when it is not deemed expedient to superadd legal punishment. Yet the current ideas of liberty, which bend so easily to real infringements of the freedom of the individual in things which concern only himself, would repel the attempt to put any restraint upon his inclinations when the consequence of their indulgence is a life or lives of wretchedness and depravity to the offspring, with manifold evils to those sufficiently within reach to be in any way affected by their actions. When we compare the strange respect of mankind for liberty, with their strange want of respect for it, we might imagine that a man had an indispensable right to do harm to others, and no right at all to please himself without giving pain to any one.

I have reserved for the last place a large class of questions respecting the limits of government interference, which, though closely connected with the subject of this Essay, do not, in strictness, belong to it. These are cases in which the reasons against interference do not turn upon the principle of liberty: the question is not about restraining the actions of individuals, but about helping them: it is asked whether the government should do, or cause to be done, something for their benefit, instead of leaving it to be done by themselves, individually, or in voluntary combination.

The objections to government interference, when it is not such as to involve infringement of liberty, may be of three kinds.

The first is, when the thing to be done is likely to be better done by individuals than by the government. Speaking generally, there is no one so fit to conduct any business, or to determine how or by whom it shall be conducted, as those who are personally interested in it. This principle condemns the interferences, once so common, of the legislature, or the officers of government, with the ordinary processes of industry. But this part of the subject has been sufficiently enlarged upon by political economists, and is not particularly related to the principles of this Essay.

The second objection is more nearly allied to our subject. In many cases, though individuals may not do the particular thing so well, on the average, as the officers of government, it is nevertheless desirable that it should be done by them, rather than by the government, as a means to their own mental education—a mode of strengthening their active faculties, exercising their judgment, and giving them a familiar knowledge of the subjects with which they are thus left to deal. This is a principal, though not the sole, recommendation of jury trial (in cases not political); of free and popular local and municipal institutions; of the conduct of industrial and philanthropic enterprises by voluntary associations. These are not questions of liberty, and are connected with that subject only by remote tendencies; but they are questions of development. It belongs to a different occasion from the present to dwell on these things as parts of national education; as being, in truth, the peculiar training of a citizen, the practical part of the political education of a free people, taking them out of the narrow circle of personal and family selfishness, and accustoming them to the comprehension of joint interests, the management of joint concerns— habituating them to act from public or semi-public motives, and guide their conduct by aims which unite instead of isolating them from one another. Without these habits and powers, a free constitution can neither be worked nor preserved; as is exemplified by the too-often transitory nature of political freedom in countries where it does not rest upon a sufficient basis of local liberties. The management of purely local business by the localities, and of the great enterprises of industry by the union of those who voluntarily supply the pecuniary means, is further recommended by all the advantages which have been set forth in this Essay as belonging to individuality of development, and diversity of modes of action. Government operations tend to be everywhere alike. With individuals and voluntary associations, on the contrary, there are varied experiments, and endless diversity of experience. What the State can usefully do, is to make itself a central depository, and active circulator and diffuser, of the experience resulting from many trials. Its business is to enable each experimentalist to benefit by the experiments of others; instead of tolerating no experiments but its own.

The third, and most cogent reason for restricting the interference of government, is the great evil of adding unnecessarily to its power. Every function superadded to those already exercised by the government, causes its influence over hopes and fears to be more widely diffused, and converts, more and more, the active and ambitious part of the public into hangers-on of the government, or of some party which aims at becoming the government. If the roads, the railways, the banks, the insurance offices, the great joint-stock companies, the universities, and the public charities, were all of them branches of the government; if, in addition, the municipal corporations and local boards, with all that now devolves on them, became departments of the central administration; if the employés of all these different enterprises were appointed and paid by the government, and looked to the government for every rise in life; not all the freedom of the press and popular constitution of the legislature would make this or any other country free otherwise than in name. And the evil would be greater, the more efficiently and scientifically the administrative machinery was constructed—the more skilful the arrangements for obtaining the best qualified hands and heads with which to work it. In England it has of late been proposed that all the members of the civil service of government should be selected by competitive examination, to obtain for those employments the most intelligent and instructed persons procurable; and much has been said and written for and against this proposal.[5] One of the arguments most insisted on by its opponents, is that the occupation of a permanent official servant of the State does not hold out sufficient prospects of emolument and importance to attract the highest talents, which will always be able to find a more inviting career in the professions, or in the service of companies and other public bodies. One would not have been

[5] See, for example, Mill's own essay, "Reform of the Civil Service."

surprised if this argument had been used by the friends of the proposition, as an answer to its principal difficulty. Coming from the opponents it is strange enough. What is urged as an objection is the safety-valve of the proposed system. If indeed all the high talent of the country *could* be drawn into the service of the government, a proposal tending to bring about that result might well inspire uneasiness. If every part of the business of society which required organized concert, or large and comprehensive views, were in the hands of the government, and if government offices were universally filled by the ablest men, all the enlarged culture and practised intelligence in the country, except the purely speculative, would be concentrated in a numerous bureaucracy, to whom alone the rest of the community would look for all things: the multitude for direction and dictation in all they had to do; the able and aspiring for personal advancement. To be admitted into the ranks of this bureaucracy, and when admitted, to rise therein, would be the sole objects of ambition. Under this regime, not only is the outside public ill-qualified, for want of practical experience, to criticize or check the mode of operation of the bureaucracy, but even if the accidents of despotic or the natural working of popular institutions occasionally raise to the summit a ruler or rulers of reforming inclinations, no reform can be effected which is contrary to the interest of the bureaucracy. Such is the melancholy condition of the Russian empire, as shown in the accounts of those who have had sufficient opportunity of observation. The Czar himself is powerless against the bureaucratic body; he can send any one of them to Siberia, but he cannot govern without them, or against their will. On every decree of his they have a tacit veto, by merely refraining from carrying it into effect. In countries of more advanced civilization and of a more insurrectionary spirit, the public, accustomed to expect everything to be done for them by the State, or at least to do nothing for themselves without asking from the State not only leave to do it, but even how it is to be done, naturally hold the State responsible for all evil which befals them, and when the evil exceeds their amount of patience, they rise against the government and make what is called a revolution; whereupon somebody else, with or without legitimate authority from the nation, vaults into the seat, issues his orders to the bureaucracy, and everything goes on much as it did before; the bureaucracy being unchanged, and nobody else being capable of taking their place.

A very different spectacle is exhibited among a people accustomed to transact their own business. In France, a large part of the people having been engaged in military service, many of whom have held at least the rank of non-commissioned officers, there are in every popular insurrection several persons competent to take the lead, and improvise some tolerable plan of action. What the French are in military affairs, the Americans are in every kind of civil business; let them be left without a government, every body of Americans is able to improvise one, and to carry on that or any other public business with a sufficient amount of intelligence, order, and decision. This is what every free people ought to be: and a people capable of this is certain to be free; it will never let itself be enslaved by any man or body of men because these are able to seize and pull the reins of the central administration. No bureaucracy can hope to make such a people as this do or undergo anything that they do not like. But where everything is done through the bureaucracy, nothing to which the bureaucracy is really adverse can be done at all. The constitution of such countries is an organization of the experience and practical ability of the nation, into a disciplined body for the purpose of governing the rest; and the more perfect that organization is in itself, the more successful in drawing to itself and educating for itself the persons of greatest capacity from all ranks of the community, the more complete is the bondage of all, the members of the bureaucracy included. For the governors are as much the slaves of their organization and discipline, as the governed are of the governors. A Chinese mandarin is as much the tool and creature of a despotism as the humblest cultivator. An individual Jesuit is to the utmost degree of abasement the slave of his order, though the order itself exists for the collective power and importance of its members.

It is not, also, to be forgotten, that the absorption of all the principal ability of the country into the governing body is fatal, sooner or later, to the mental activity and progressiveness of the body itself. Banded together as they are—working a system which, like all systems, necessarily proceeds in a great measure by fixed rules—the official body are under the constant temptation of sinking into indolent routine, or, if they now and then desert that millhorse round, of rushing into some half-examined crudity which has struck the fancy of some leading member of the corps: and the sole check to these closely allied, though seemingly opposite, tendencies, the only stimulus which can keep the ability of the body itself up to a high standard, is liability to the watchful criticism of equal ability outside the body. It is indispensable, therefore, that the means should exist, independently of the government, of forming such ability, and furnishing it with the opportunities and experience necessary for a correct judgment of great practical affairs. If we would possess permanently a skilful and efficient body of functionaries—above all, a body able to originate and willing to adopt improvements; if we would not have our bureaucracy degenerate into a pedantocracy, this body must not engross all the occupations which form and cultivate the faculties required for the government of mankind.

To determine the point at which evils, so formidable to human freedom and advancement, begin, or rather at which they begin to predominate over the benefits attending the collective application of the force of society, under its recognised chiefs, for the removal of the obstacles which stand in the way of its well-being; to secure as much of the advantages of centralized power and intelligence, as can be had without turning into governmental channels too great a proportion of the general activity—is one of the most difficult and complicated questions in the art of government. It is, in a great measure, a question of detail, in which many and various considerations must be kept in view, and no absolute rule can be laid down. But I believe that the practical principle in which safety resides, the ideal to be kept in view, the standard by which to test all arrangements intended for overcoming the difficulty, may be conveyed in these words: the greatest dissemination of power consistent with efficiency; but the greatest possible centralization of information, and diffusion of it from the centre. Thus, in municipal administration, there would be, as in the New England States, a very minute division among separate officers, chosen by the localities, of all business which is not better left to the persons directly interested; but besides this, there would be, in each department of local affairs, a central superintendence, forming a branch of the general government. The organ of this superintendence would concentrate, as in a focus, the variety of information and experience derived from the conduct of that branch of public business in all the localities, from everything analogous which is done in foreign countries, and from the general principles of political science. This central organ should have a right to know all that is done, and its special duty should be that of making the knowledge acquired in one place available for others. Emancipated from the petty prejudices and narrow views of a locality by its elevated position and comprehensive sphere of observation, its advice would naturally carry much authority; but its actual power, as a permanent institution, should, I conceive, be limited to compelling the local officers to obey the laws laid down for their guidance. In all things not provided for by general rules, those officers should be left to their own judgment, under responsibility to their constituents. For the violation of rules, they should be responsible to law, and the rules themselves should be laid down by the legislature; the central administrative authority only watching over their execution, and if they were not properly carried into effect, appealing, according to the nature of the case, to the tribunals to enforce the law, or to the constituencies to dismiss the functionaries who had not executed it according to its spirit. Such, in its general conception, is the central superintendence which the Poor Law Board is intended to exercise over the administrators of the Poor Rate throughout the country. Whatever powers the Board exercises beyond this limit, were right and necessary in that peculiar case, for the cure of rooted habits of maladministration in matters deeply affecting not the localities merely, but the whole community; since no locality has a moral right to make itself by mismanagement a nest of pauperism, necessarily overflowing into other localities, and impairing the moral and physical condition of the whole labouring community. The powers of administrative coercion and subordinate legislation possessed by the Poor Law Board (but which, owing to the state of opinion on the subject, are very scantily exercised by them), though perfectly justifiable in a case of first-rate national interest, would be wholly out of place in the superintendence of interests purely local. But a central organ of information and instruction for all the localities, would be equally valuable in all departments of administration. A government cannot have too much of the kind of activity which does not impede, but aids and stimulates, individual exertion and development. The mischief begins when, instead of calling forth the activity and powers of individuals and bodies, it substitutes its own activity for theirs; when, instead of informing, advising, and, upon occasion, denouncing, it makes them work in fetters, or bids them stand aside and does their work instead of them. The worth of a State, in the long run, is the worth of the individuals composing it; and a State which postpones the interests of *their* mental expansion and elevation, to a little more of administrative skill, or of that semblance of it which practice gives, in the details of business; a State which dwarfs its men, in order that they may be more docile instruments in its hands even for beneficial purposes—will find that with small men no great thing can really be accomplished; and that the perfection of machinery to which it has sacrificed everything, will in the end avail it nothing, for want of the vital power which, in order that the machine might work more smoothly, it has preferred to banish.

Appendix A:
Preludes to *On Liberty*

1. Alexis de Tocqueville,[1] "Unlimited Power of the Majority in the United States, and its Consequences." *Democracy in America*. Trans. Henry Reeve (1835), vol.I, chapter XV.

Tyranny of the Majority

I hold it to be an impious and detestable maxim that, politically speaking, the people have a right to do anything; and yet I have asserted that all authority originates in the will of the majority. Am I, then, in contradiction with myself?... When I refuse to obey an unjust law, I do not contest the right of the majority to command, but I simply appeal from the sovereignty of the people to the sovereignty of mankind. Some have not feared to assert that a people can never outstep the boundaries of justice and reason in those affairs which are peculiarly its own; and that consequently full power may be given to the majority by which it is represented. But this is the language of a slave.

A majority taken collectively is only an individual, whose opinions, and frequently whose interests, are opposed to those of another individual, who is styled a minority. If it be admitted that a man possessing absolute power may misuse that power by wronging his adversaries, why should not a majority be liable to the same reproach? Men do not change their characters by uniting with one another; nor does their patience in the presence of obstacles increase with their strength. For my own part, I cannot believe it; the power to do everything, which I should refuse to one of my equals, I will never grant to any number of them....I am...of the opinion that social power superior to all others must always be placed somewhere; but I think that liberty is endangered when this power finds no obstacle which can retard its course and give it time to moderate its own vehemence.

Unlimited power is in itself a bad and dangerous thing. Human beings are not competent to exercise it with discretion. God alone can be

---

[1] Alexis-Henri-Charles-Maurice Clerel, Comte de Tocqueville (1805–59), was sent in 1831 as an assistant magistrate by the French government on a mission to examine prisons in America. On his return he wrote his classic *Democracy in America* (1835–40), the first comprehensive study of the political and social institutions of the United States.

omnipotent, because his wisdom and his justice are always equal to his power. There is no power on earth so worthy of honor in itself or clothed with rights so sacred that I would admit its uncontrolled and all-predominant authority. When I see that the right and the means of absolute command are conferred on any power whatever, be it called a people or a king, an aristocracy or a democracy, a monarchy or a republic, I say there is the germ of tyranny, and I seek to live elsewhere, under other laws.

In my opinion, the main evil of the present democratic institutions of the United States does not arise, as is often asserted in Europe, from their weakness, but from their irresistible strength. I am not so much alarmed at the excessive liberty which reigns in that country as at the inadequate securities which one finds there against tyranny.

When an individual or a party is wronged in the United States, to whom can he apply for redress? If to public opinion, public opinion constitutes the majority; if to the legislature, it represents the majority and implicitly obeys it; if to the executive power, it is appointed by the majority and serves as a passive tool in its hands. The public force consists of the majority under arms; the jury is the majority invested with the right of hearing judicial cases; and in certain states even the judges are elected by the majority. However iniquitous or absurd the measure of which you complain, you must submit to it as well as you can.

If, on the other hand, a legislative power could be so constituted as to represent the majority without necessarily being the slave of its passions, an executive so as to retain a proper share of authority, and a judiciary so as to remain independent of the other two powers, a government would be formed which would still be democratic while incurring scarcely any risk of tyranny.

I do not say that there is a frequent use of tyranny in America at the present day; but I maintain that there is no sure barrier against it, and that the causes which mitigate the government there are to be found in the circumstances and the manners of the country more than in its laws....

Power Exercised By The Majority In America Upon Opinion. In America, when the majority has once irrevocably decided a question, all discussion ceases—Reason for this—Moral power exercised by the majority upon opinion—Democratic republics have applied despotism to the minds of men.

It is in the examination of the exercise of thought in the United States that we clearly perceive how far the power of the majority surpasses all the powers with which we are acquainted in Europe. Thought is an invisible and subtle power that mocks all the efforts of tyranny. At the present time the most absolute monarchs in Europe cannot prevent certain opinions hostile to their authority from circulating in secret through their dominions and even in their courts. It is not so in America; as long as the majority is still undecided, discussion is carried on; but as soon as its decision is irrevocably pronounced, everyone is silent, and the friends as well as the opponents of the measure unite in assenting to its propriety. The reason for this is perfectly clear: no monarch is so absolute as to combine all the powers of society in his own hands and to conquer all opposition, as a majority is able to do, which has the right both of making and of executing the laws.

The authority of a king is physical and controls the actions of men without subduing their will. But the majority possesses a power that is physical and moral at the same time, which acts upon the will as much as upon the actions and represses not only all contest, but all controversy.

I know of no country in which there is so little independence of mind and real freedom of discussion as in America....In America the majority raises formidable barriers around the liberty of opinion; within these barriers an author may write what he pleases, but woe to him if he goes beyond them. Not that he is in danger of an *auto-da-fe*,[2] but he is exposed to continued obloquy and persecution. His political career is closed forever, since he has offended the only authority that is able to open it. Every sort of compensation, even that of celebrity, is refused to him. Before making public his opinions he thought he had sympathizers; now it seems to him that he has none any more since he has revealed himself to everyone; then those who blame him criticize loudly and those who think as he does keep quiet and move away without courage. He yields at length, overcome by the daily effort which he has to make, and subsides into silence, as if he felt remorse for having spoken the truth.

Fetters and headsmen were the coarse instruments that tyranny formerly employed; but the civilization of our age has perfected despotism itself, though it seemed to have nothing to learn. Monarchs, had, so to speak, materialized oppression; the democratic republics of the present day have rendered it as entirely an affair of the mind as the will which it is intended to coerce. Under the absolute sway of one man the body was attacked in order to subdue the soul; but the soul escaped the blows which were directed against it and rose proudly superior. Such is not the course adopted by tyranny in democratic republics; there the body is left free, and the soul is enslaved. The master no longer says: "You shall think as I do or you shall die"; but he says: "You are free to think differently from me and to retain your life, your property, and all that you possess; but you are hence forth a stranger among

---

[2] [*auto-da-fe*] act of the faith: burning of heretics, tried and sentenced by the Inquisition, at the stake.

your people. You may retain your civil rights, but they will be useless to you, for you will never be chosen by your fellow citizens if you solicit their votes; and they will affect to scorn you if you ask for their esteem. You will remain among men, but you will be deprived of the rights of mankind. Your fellow creatures will shun you like an impure being; and even those who believe in your innocence will abandon you, lest they should be shunned in their turn. Go in peace! I have given you your life, but it is an existence worse than death.". . .

If America has not as yet had any great writers, the reason is given in these facts; there can be no literary genius without freedom of opinion, and freedom of opinion does not exist in America. The Inquisition has never been able to prevent a vast number of anti-religious books from circulating in Spain. The empire of the majority succeeds much better in the United States, since it actually removes any wish to publish them. Unbelievers are to be met with in America, but there is no public organ of infidelity. . . .

If ever the free institutions of America are destroyed, that event may be attributed to the omnipotence of the majority, which may at some future time urge the minorities to desperation and oblige them to have recourse to physical force. Anarchy will then be the result, but it will have been brought about by despotism.

2. Early Essays and Letters by Mill.

a. "On the Oxford Movement." Letter to *The Morning Chronicle,* 1 January 1842.

Sir,

I address you as one of, I believe, many who although most remote from any connection, either personal, or through their opinions, with Puseyism,[1] have seen with pleasure the letters of "PhiloPuseyite," in the first place, because we agree with that writer in a large portion of his sentiments, but also, and still more, because we approve of the tone of mind, which is less eager to hold up to obloquy the errors of an adversary, than conscientiously to examine what portion of truth exists in those errors, and gives them their plausibility. We not only esteem it a more healthful exercise of the mind to employ itself in learning from an enemy, than in inveighing against him; but, we believe, that the extirpation of what is erroneous in any system of belief is in no way so much promoted as by extricating from it, and

[1] One of several labels for the High Church or Oxford or Tractarian Movement, after one of its leading figures, the theologian Edward B. Pusey (1800–82).

incorporating into our own systems, whatever in it is true. If your correspondent, "Miso-Jesuit," had taken heed of these things, he would probably have spared you his ill-tempered and uncourteous second letter— a document which would prove, if such proof were required, that there is nothing which a zealot, Christian or infidel, dissenter or churchman, can so little pardon, or on which he is so incapable of putting a candid interpretation as the offence of not going with him to the full length of his narrow-minded antipathies.

It was scarcely needful for your correspondent to remind "Philo-Puseyite" that the Oxford theologians would not thank him for such advocacy as his, and that whoever stands up for toleration or charity in their behalf claims for the Puseyites what the Puseyites would not be willing to bestow. The leaders of this sect, for a sect it is, are, as it is evident that "Miso-Jesuit" himself is, conscientious bigots: like him, however, they are not bigots to error, but to one-half of the truth; and are, in the present writer's estimation, entitled to the approbation and goodwill which he cannot but feel towards all such persons, provided that the portion of truth they contend for is one which the age specially needs, and provided (he must add) they have not the power of burning him for heresy, a fate which, to say truth, if their doctrines ever obtained the ascendancy in this country, he does not well see how he could hope to escape. It is not, therefore, out of any special partiality to them that he undertakes their apology. But not to our friends alone is justice due from us and to the Puseyites; permit me to say, it is more particularly due from your paper, inasmuch as you have repeatedly in your leading articles done them cruel injustice, of the kind likely to be most severely felt by conscientious men, and most likely also to prejudice impartial bystanders against your good cause, by your perpetual denunciations of them as hypocrites and mammon-servers, because, holding doctrines which you (not they) deem inconsistent with the articles of the church, they yet do not secede from it.

Can you be serious, sir, in addressing this particular reproach to men of whom it is the distinctive feature, among all other religious parties, to maintain that no difference of opinion whatever is capable of justifying the sin of schism? That the first command of Christ is adherence to the standard which he has erected upon earth, and for the recognition of which he has appointed certain criteria, of which the profession of a particular set of theological tenets is *not* one; that even if the whole human race, one person excepted, should desert that standard and set up another, by proclaiming a church of man's ordinance, not God's, it is they who apostatize, and he, that one person, be his opinions what they may, is the Christian church upon earth; or if, instead of themselves seceding from the communion, they forcibly exclude him from it (as the Roman church did Luther), he refusing and protesting, they, by so doing, constitute their church a schismatic body, while he remains a member of the church as before! In common candour, sir, ask yourself whether persons of whose belief this is a correct expression, are sacrificing their principles to lucre because they do not take upon their consciences what they esteem a deadly sin.

And since we are on the subject of interested motives, give me leave to ask you, as a man acquainted with the world, and aware of the ordinary course of affairs in political life, whether you do or can think other of these men than that by professing their opinions they are abandoning all hope of further advancement in worldly advantages? If the extraordinary acquirements and powers, for example, of Mr. Newman[2] had been employed in any of the modes in which able men in the Church of England usually seek to distinguish themselves—in the paths, for instance, by which Dr. Blomfield or Dr. Philpotts[3] rose to eminence, is there any dignity in the Establishment to which he might not have aspired? And do you believe that either the present government, or any other ministry that could be formed, would dare to raise an avowed and active Puseyite to episcopal, or any other high ecclesiastical honors? Let me answer for you, sir. You know the contrary: you are not ignorant of the sort of feelings with which practical politicians of every class invariably regard the speculative men who formulize either into philosophic theories or religious dogmas the extreme doctrines of their own party. You know that those whose business is conciliation and compromise, the smoothing of difficulties and the allaying of apprehensions, do not hold their most determined adversaries in so much dread as they do those who display to public view all the vulnerable points in their system of opinions, in the manner most fertile of misgiving to friends, and irritation to opponents, and proclaim as sacred principles, to be acted upon, without qualification or reserve, all which *they* in their practice not only sedulously guard by countless modifications and restrictions, but are so often forced, even honestly, to surrender altogether, in points of detail at least, on the summons of declared opponents. If *we* know this, think you that Mr. Newman knows it not? Think you that a man so deeply read in history, and who has analysed in so one-sided, but yet so profound a manner, the course of the stream of human affairs from age to age, is ignorant of what every school-boy knows, that the philosophers of a creed are seldom its successful politicians?

---

[2] John Henry Newman (1801–90), another leader, like Pusey, of the High Church or Anglo-Catholic movement; that is, until 1845, when he left the Church of England for the Church of Rome.

[3] Charles James Blomfield (Bishop of London); Henry Philpotts (Bishop of Exeter).

It would do you credit, sir, to desist from these incessant attacks upon the disinterestedness of the Oxford theologians, or to reserve them until you find the Puseyites violating the doctrines of their own creed, by disobeying the authority, canonically exercised, of their ecclesiastical superiors. Such imputations of insincerity are applied with a very bad grace to a party from whom, whatever may be said against the unreasonableness or the real Christianity of many of their doctrines, this acknowledgment cannot be withheld, that instead of being insincere members of the church, they are the only party in it who attempt, or even pretend to attempt, to be perfectly sincere. I assert this without qualification as one of the greatest, or rather as the very greatest of the peculiarities which, in my opinion, entitle this school to be warmly welcomed among us. They are the first persons in the Church of England who for more than a century past have conscientiously and rigidly endeavoured to live up to what they nominally profess—to obey the regulations of that church of which they call themselves members. Even Philo-Puseyite speaks of their "predilection for ceremonies, and vestments, and fastings, and vigils, and saint's days," as something "revolting." But is it forgotten that these things are actual ordinances of the Church of England, and that the Puseyites are simply acting out the written code of their religion? If these things are absurdities, with whom lies the fault? They were not placed in the Rubric[4] by the Puseyites. The charge of insincerity brought against this party for remaining in the church without assenting, or while assenting only in a latitudinarian sense, to the articles, may be much more fairly retorted upon those who, without considering, as the Puseyites do, adherence to the church to be the paramount duty of a Christian, nevertheless remain in it with a tacit reservation that they are to conform to just as many of its rules and authoritative precepts as to them appear reasonable. Let the opposite party, then, bestir themselves to cause such of the ceremonies and such of the religious exercises prescribed by the church as they disapprove of, to be abrogated in the lawful manner, by canonical authority. But until this is done, I confess I honour far more those who act up to what is professed by all, than those who take one part of it and leave another, as suits themselves.

It is not, Sir, by continuing to profess opinions and silently forbearing to act upon them, that either religious or any other prevailing doctrines are to be freed from whatever of irrational or pernicious they may contain. It is too true that this is the ordinary course of changes of opinion. It is a disgusting, but sometimes inevitable era of transition between the pristine vigour and final downfall of creeds or doctrines, originally too deeply rooted in the soil to admit of being eradicated unless they have first reached an advanced stage of corruption and decomposition. In religion, and also in politics, the whole

[4] Directions in a liturgical book.

eighteenth century was a period of this kind. But that is a happy day for renovated humanity, when first a sincere man, indignant at the more and more complete severance of profession from practice, stands up as a fulfiller, in his own person, and a vindicator to the world, of the solemn duty of *doing* the whole of that which he daily professes that he ought to do. By carrying out this principle, and even because he carries it out to its last and absurdest consequences, he challenges and compels inquiry into the grounds of the belief itself and the degree in which it is or is not still adopted to be the rule of conduct for humanity in its altered state; and by the very vigour with which he asserts the false parts of his creed, he, by a reaction as certain as it is salutary, calls forth into corresponding activity and energy those opposite truths, in the minds of other people, which are the suitable means of expelling the false opinions without prejudice to the just views with which they are always, but not inseparably interwoven: thus giving to the world over again that without which its whole scheme would be an abortion and a failure—notions of duty made to be executed, not to be locked up as too good for use, or worn for outside show.

I must not, sir, encroach further on your space; but if you should deem this letter worthy of insertion, I may perhaps return to the subject, and lay before you in a more particular manner the grounds on which I contend that Puseyism is one of the most important and interesting phenomena which has appeared above the horizon of English speculation for many years past.

HISTORICUS

b. "On French Restrictions on the Press," *The Spectator*, 19 August 1848.

THE decree against the press, just passed almost with unanimity by the National Assembly of France, is one of the most monstrous outrages on the idea of freedom of discussion ever committed by the legislature of a country pretending to be free. It is the very law of Louis Philippe[1]—the September law, once so indignantly denounced—with scarcely any alteration but the substitution of the word "Republic" for "Monarchy."

This precious specimen of Liberal legislation declares punishable by fine and imprisonment all attacks on "the rights and authority of the National Assembly—on the rights and authority which the members of the Executive derive from the decrees of the Assembly—on the Republican institutions and the Constitution—on the principle of the sovereignty of the people and of universal suffrage—on the liberty of worship, the principle of property,

[1] King of France, 1830–48.

and the rights of family"; besides which, it ordains similar punishments for "exciting hatred and contempt towards the Government of the Republic," and for "public outrage committed (in their public character) against one or more members of the National Assembly, or against a Minister of any religion paid by the State."

This list of subjects on which discussion is prohibited, or permitted only on one side, includes all the great political and social questions of the age. If only one set of opinions is to be permitted on any matter which involves the right of property, the rights or obligations of family, the question of Republicanism, of universal suffrage, even the particular constitution which the Assembly may hereafter adopt, or the rightfulness of abolishing that constitution—what are the subjects, worth discussing, on which freedom of political discussion is to exist? "The acts of the Executive," says the decree. "The present provision is not to affect the right of discussion and censure on the acts of the Executive and of the Ministers." A most liberal concession, truly! The law is worse, with only this reservation in favour of freedom, than if there were no reservation at all; for the most tyrannical court of justice which could now exist in civilized Europe would reserve more than this. It is not declared that even the *actions* of the Legislature may be censured, but only those of the Executive; and with regard to laws or institutions, no liberty of censure is reserved at all. There was a wretched pretence by one or two of the speakers, that no restraint was intended on the "freedom of philosophical discussion"—that nothing was to be forbidden but incitements to hatred and contempt. But the decree says nothing of the kind. The decree prohibits "any attack." The distinction is good for nothing, even if it were made. To say that attacks are permitted, but not incitements to hatred and contempt, would be to say that discussion shall be lawful on condition that it be cold, dry, and unimpressive; that the dull and the indifferent shall be allowed to express opinions, but that persons of genius and feeling must hold their peace. Under such laws, it has been truly said in one of the French journals, Rousseau's discourse[2] on Inequality never could have been published. Nor could any great writings of great reformers, religious or political, have seen the light if such laws had existed and been obeyed.

How long shall we continue to see the regard for freedom of opinion, which all parties profess while they are on the oppressed side, thrown off by them all as soon as they are in the majority? How much longer must we wait for an example, anywhere in Europe, of a ruler or a ruling party who really desire fair play for any opinions contrary to their own? Is it not shameful that no sooner has a reforming party accomplished as much change in the

[2] Jean-Jacques Rousseau (1712–78), Swiss-French political philosopher, published *Discours sur l'origine de l'inégalité des hommes* in 1754.

institutions of the country as itself deems desirable, than it proceeds to decree that every person shall be fined or imprisoned, who proposes either to go a single step further or a step back? We are aware of the allowances to be made for men lately engaged in a desperate and at one time a doubtful contest against a determined attempt at insurrection; and we know too that this decree is avowedly a temporary measure, to be hereafter superseded by more deliberate legislation. But we lament to say, that in the tone assumed, and the doctrines professed by the speakers, we see no ground of assurance that the permanent measure will be at all different, in spirit and principle, from the transitional one.

It is not, however, for English Conservatives, either Whig or Tory, to indulge any self-complacent triumph over French Republicans. The new act of the French Assembly does not make the laws of France on the freedom of the press worse than those of England have always been. The freedom of the press, in England, is entirely an affair of opinion and custom, not of law. It exists because the laws are not enforced. The law of political libel, as laid down in all the books, is as inconsistent with free discussion as the laws of Russia. There is no censure of any established institution or constituted authority which is not an offence by law. And within these few months it has been seen how eagerly the English Parliament, under the influence of a far less degree of panic, have rushed to make the laws against what was deemed seditious speaking or writing more stringent than before.

A government cannot be blamed for defending itself against insurrection. But it deserves the severest blame if to prevent insurrection it prevents the promulgation of opinion. If it does so, it actually justifies insurrection in those to whom it denies the use of peaceful means to make their opinions prevail. Hitherto the French Government has been altogether in the right against all attempts to overthrow it. But by what right can the Assembly now reprobate any future attempt, either by Monarchists or Socialists, to rise in arms against the Government? It denies them free discussion. It says they shall not be suffered to bring their opinions to the touchstone of the public reason and conscience. It refuses them the chance which every sincere opinion can justly claim, of triumphing in a fair field. It fights them with weapons which can as easily be used to put down the most valuable truth as the most pernicious error. It tells them that they must prevail by violence before they shall be allowed to contend by argument. Who can blame persons who are deeply convinced of the truth and importance of their opinions, for asserting them by force, when that is the only means left them of obtaining even a hearing? When their mouths are *gagged*, can they be reproached for using their arms?

Appendix B:
Comments by Mill about *On Liberty*

1. Letter of 15 January 1855 to Harriet Mill, from Rome.

O N my way here cogitating thereon [writing projects] I came back to an idea we have talked about & thought that the best thing to write & publish at present would be a volume on Liberty.[1]

So many things might be brought into it & nothing seems to me more needed—it is a growing need too, for opinion tends to encroach more & more on liberty, & almost all the projects of social reformers in these days are really *liberticide*—Comte,[2] particularly so. I wish I had brought with me here the paper on Liberty that I wrote for our volume of Essays—perhaps my dearest will kindly read it through & tell me whether it will do as the foundation of one part of the volume in question—

---

[1] "I had first planned and written it as a short essay in 1854. It was in mounting the steps of the Capitol, in January, 1855, that the thought first arose of converting it into a volume...." *Autobiography*, chap. vii.

[2] Auguste Comte, the French philosopher (and founder of sociology). See Mill's remarks on his *Système de politique positive* in chap. vi of the *Autobiography*.

2. Letter of 16 February 1855 to Harriet Mill, from Naples.

T HE more I think of the plan of a volume on Liberty, the more likely it seems to me that it will be read & make a sensation. The title itself with any known name to it would sell an edition. We must cram into it as much as possible of what we wish not to leave unsaid.

3. Letter of 30 June 1857 to Pasquale Villari,[1] from London.

J 'AI fait dernièrement un petit livre qui paraîtra l'hiver prochain et dont je me ferai un plaisir de vous offrir un exemplaire, si toutefois son titre 'De la Liberté' comporte son entrée en Toscane.[2] Il ne s'agit pas cependant de liberté politique dans ce livre, autant que de liberté social, morale, et religieuse.

[1] Pasquale Villari (1826–1917), Italian historian and statesman.
[2] Tuscany had at this time strict censorship of liberal writing.

4. Letter of 5 October 1857 to Theodor Gomperz.[1]

I have nearly finished an Essay on "Liberty" which I hope to publish next winter. As the Liberty it treats of is moral and intellectual rather than political, it is not so much needed in Germany as it is here.

[1] Theodor Gomperz (1832–1912), Austrian philosopher and philologist, Mill's German translator.

5. Letter of 9 March 1858 to Pasquale Villari, from London.

J'ESPÉRAIS vous offrir depuis longtemps mon petit livre sur la liberté, mais plusieurs raisons m'ont décidé à ne pas fair imprimer cet hiver. Au reste, il n'a guère que pour l'Angleterre. Il traite de la liberté morale et intellectuelle, en quoi les nations du Continent sont autant au dessus de l'Angleterre qu'elles lui sont inferieures quant à la liberté politique.

6. Letter of 30 November 1858 to John William Parker,[1] from Blackheath Park.

YOU can have my little book "On Liberty" for publication this season [it would be published in February 1859]. The manuscript is ready; but you will probably desire to look through it, or to have it looked through by some one in whom you confide, as there are some things in it which may give offence to prejudices.

[1] John William Parker (1792–1870) had published Mill's *Logic* in 1843 and the *Political Economy* in 1848.

Post Publication

7. Letter of February [?] 1859 to G. J. Holyoake.[1]

[In 1859 Mill sent Holyoake a copy of *On Liberty*, asking him not to review it until other reviewers had done so.]

I T is likely enough to be called an infidel book in any case; but I would rather that people were not *prompted* to call it so.

[1] George Jacob Holyoake (1817–1906) was a well-known atheist or "freethinker."

8. Letter of 4 March 1859 to Herbert Spencer,[1] from Blackheath.

I fully expected, both that you would go heartily with me in the main object of the little book on Liberty, and also that you would think it does not go far enough. Any difference that there can be between us in the matter can only, however, be on points of detail, not of principle. There are none of your writings which I admire more than your "Over-Legislation."[2]

[1] Herbert Spencer (1820–1903), the philosopher.
[2] See *Westminster Review*, n.s. 4 (July 1853): 51–84.

9. Letter of 31 March 1859 to T. Gomperz, from Blackheath.

T HE book has had much more success, and has made a greater impression, than I had the smallest expectation of.

10. Letter of 6 August 1859 to Alexander Bain,[1] from St. Véran.

T HE "Liberty" has produced an effect on you which it was never intended to produce if it has made you think that we ought not to attempt to convert the world. I meant nothing of the kind, & hold that we ought to convert all we can. We *must* be satisfied with keeping alive the sacred fire in a few minds when we are unable to do more—but the notion of an intellectual aristocracy of *lumières*[2] while the rest of the world remains in darkness fulfills none of my aspirations—& the effect I aim at by the book is, on the contrary, to make the many more accessible to all truth by making them more open minded. But perhaps you were only thinking of the question of religion. On that, certainly I am not anxious to bring over any but really superior intellects & characters to the whole of my own opinions—in the case of all others I would much rather, as things now are, try to improve their religion than to destroy it.

[1] Alexander Bain (1818–1903), philosopher, first biographer of Mill.
[2] [*lumières*] enlightened ones.

11. Letter of 15 October 1859 to Alexander Bain, from St. Véran.

HAVE you seen any of the recent reviews of the Liberty? That in the Dublin Univ Mag,[1] for instance, & the series of letters in the Engl. Churchman?[2] People are beginning to find out that the doctrines of the book are more opposed to their old opinions & feelings than they at first saw, & are taking the alarm accordingly & rallying for a fight. But they have in general dealt candidly with me, & not too violently. As was to be expected they claim for Xtian morality all the things which I say are not in it, which is just what I wanted to provoke them to do. The article in the National Rev.[3] on my writings generally is worth reading. It seems to be by Martineau[4] & I am obliged to him for it, since it is favourable to the utmost extent consistent with the writer's opinions & decidedly tends to increase rather than diminish the influence which he says is already so great. I really had no idea of being so influential a person as my critics tell me I am.

[1] "Christian Ethics and John Stuart Mill," *Dublin University Magazine* 54 (October 1859): 387–410.
[2] Eleven articles appeared, signed R.P.: Sept. 15, 22, 29; October 6, 13, 20, 27; Nov. 3, 10, 24, 31; Dec. 1.
[3] "John Stuart Mill," a review of Mill's *Dissertations and Discussions*, by James Martineau, in *National Review* 9 (October 1859): 474–508.
[4] Rev. James Martineau (1805–1900), Unitarian divine and philosopher.

12. The writing of *On Liberty* as described in Mill's *Autobiography*.

DURING the two years which immediately preceded the cessation of my official life, my wife and I were working together at the "Liberty."

I had first planned and written it as a short essay in 1854. It was in mounting the steps of the Capitol, in January, 1855, that the thought first arose of converting it into a volume. None of my writings have been either so carefully composed, or so sedulously corrected as this. After it had been written as usual twice over, we kept it by us, bringing it out from time to time, and going through it *de novo*[1] reading, weighing, and criticising every sentence. Its final revision was to have been a work of the winter of 1858–9, the first after my retirement, which we had arranged to pass in the South of Europe. That hope and every other were frustrated by the most unexpected and bitter calamity of her death—at Avignon…from a sudden attack of pulmonary congestion.…After my irreparable loss, one of my earliest cares was to print and publish the treatise, so much of which was the work of her whom I had lost, and consecrate it to her memory. I have made no alteration or addition to it, nor shall I ever. Though it wants the last touch of her hand, no substitute for that touch shall ever be attempted by mine.

The "Liberty" was more directly and literally our joint production than anything else which bears my name, for there was not a sentence of it which was not several times gone through by us together, turned over in many ways, and carefully weeded of any faults, either in thought or expression, that we detected in it. It is in consequence of this that, although it never underwent her final revision, it far surpasses, as a mere specimen of composition, anything which has proceeded from me either before or since. With regard to the thoughts, it is difficult to identify any particular part or element as being more hers than all the rest.…

The "Liberty" is likely to survive longer than anything else that I have written (with the possible exception of the "Logic"), because the conjunction of her mind with mine has rendered it a kind of philosophic text-book of a single truth…: the importance, to man and society, of a large variety in types of character, and of giving full freedom to human nature to expand itself in innumerable and conflicting directions. Nothing can better show how deep are the foundations of this truth, than the great impression made by the exposition of it at a time which, to superficial observation, did not seem to stand much in need of such a lesson. The fears we expressed, lest the inevitable growth of social equality and of the government of public opinion, should impose on mankind an oppressive yoke of uniformity in opinion and practice, might easily have appeared chimerical to those who looked more at present facts than at tendencies; for the gradual revolution that is taking place in society and institutions has, thus far, been decidedly favourable to the development of new opinions, and has procured for them a much more

---

[1] [*de novo*] anew.

unprejudiced hearing than they previously met with. But this is a feature belonging to periods of transition, when old notions and feelings have been unsettled, and no new doctrines have yet succeeded to their ascendancy. At such times people of any mental activity, having given up their old beliefs, and not feeling quite sure that those they still retain can stand unmodified, listen eagerly to new opinions. But this state of things is necessarily transitory: some particular body of doctrine in time rallies the majority round it, organizes social institutions and modes of action conformably to itself, education impresses this new creed upon the new generations without the mental processes that have led to it, and by degrees it acquires the very same power of compression, so long exercised by the creeds of which it had taken the place. Whether this noxious power will be exercised, depends on whether mankind have by that time become aware that it cannot be exercised without stunting and dwarfing human nature. It is then that the teachings of the "Liberty" will have their greatest value. And it is to be feared that they will retain that value a long time.

Appendix C:
Comments by Contemporaries about
On Liberty and Mill

1. Caroline Fox (1819–71), diarist, from prominent Quaker family. *Memories of Old Friends* (Philadelphia: Lippincott, 1882).

Letters of 25 November and 23 December 1859 to E. T. Carne.

Penjerrick, November 25. [...] I am reading that terrible book of John Mill's on Liberty, so clear, and calm, and cold: he lays it on one as a tremendous duty to get one's self well contradicted, and admit always a devil's advocate into the presence of your dearest, most sacred truths, as they are apt to grow windy and worthless without such tests, if indeed they can stand the shock of argument at all. He looks through you like a basilisk, relentless as Fate. We knew him well at one time, and owe him very much: I fear his remorseless logic has led him far since then. This book is dedicated to his wife's memory in a few most touching words. He is in many senses isolated, and must sometimes shiver with the cold.

Falmouth, December 23.—No, my dear, I don't agree with Mill, though I too should be very glad to have some of my "ugly opinions" corrected, however painful the process; but Mill makes me shiver, his blade is so keen and so unhesitating. I think there is much force in his criticism on the mental training provided for the community; the battles are fought *for* us, the objections to received views and the refutations of the same all provided for us, instead of ourselves being strengthened and armed for the combat [...]

2. Thomas Carlyle (1795–1881), historian and social critic. [Early friend of Mill's but later an adversary.]

a. Thomas Carlyle, as reported by Henry Larkin, in "Carlyle and Mrs. Carlyle: A Ten Years' Reminiscence," *British Quarterly Review* (July 1881).

ONE morning, when I entered his study, I found him as usual sitting at his table, but evidently in a condition of great suppressed irritability, with Mill's *Liberty* lying before him, which someone, perhaps Mill himself, had sent him. I believe the book had recently been published, but I cannot say positively. Certainly I had until then never seen it, or heard of it.

After I had discharged my trifling business, he rose angrily from the table with the book in his hand, and gave vent to such a torrent of anathema, glancing at Christianity itself, as filled me with pain and amazement. He addressed himself directly to me, almost as if *I* had written the book, or was in some way mixed up with it in his mind. I felt terribly hurt; but what could I say against such a wide-rushing torrent of invective?...

I know the book well enough now,...and I will only say that, putting myself honestly in Carlyle's place, I do not wonder that his indignation was beyond endurance. It must have been to him, in the incisiveness of its attack and the taking popularity of its style, like a vision of the great red dragon standing triumphant before him, ready to devour the fruit of his soul's travail as soon as it was born.

b. Thomas Carlyle, as reported by Alexander Carlyle, ed. *New Letters of Thomas Carlyle* II, 196: London, 1904.

AS if it were a sin to control, or coerce into better methods, human swine in any way;...Ach Gott im Himmel!

3. Thomas Hardy (1840–1928), poet and novelist.

a. Letter printed 21 May 1906 to London *Times* describing incident of 1865.

IT was a day in 1865, about three in the afternoon, during Mill's candidature for Westminster. The hustings had been erected in Covent Garden,...and when I—a young man living in London—drew near the spot, Mill was speaking. The appearance of the author of the treatise *On Liberty* (which we students of that date knew almost by heart) was so different from the look of persons who usually address crowds in the open air that it held the attention of people for whom such a gathering in itself had little interest. Yet it was, primarily, that of a man out of place. The religious sincerity of his speech was jarred on by his environment—a group on the hustings who, with few exceptions, did not care to understand him fully, and a crowd below who could not. He stood bareheaded, and his vast pale brow, so thin-skinned as to show the blue veins, sloped back like a stretching upland. ...The picture of him as personified earnestness surrounded for the most part by careless curiosity derived an added piquancy—if it can be called such—from the fact that the cameo clearness of his face chanced to be in relief against the blue shadow of a church which, on its transcendental side, his doctrines antagonized. But it would not be right to say that the throng was absolutely unimpressed by his words; it felt that they were weighty, though it did not quite know why.

b. From *Jude the Obscure* (1895). Part Fourth, chapter iii.

Phillotson writhed.

Sue continued: "She, or he, 'who lets the world, or his own portion of it, choose his plan for him, has no need of any other faculty than the ape-like one of imitation.'" "J. S. Mill's words, those are. I have been reading it up. Why can't you act upon them? I wish to, always."

"What do I care about J. S. Mill!" moaned he, "I only want to lead a quiet life!"

4. John Ruskin (1819–1900), critic of art, architecture, society, politics, economics.

a. Letter to Mill's election committee in 1865. (Printed in Bruce L. Kinzer, Ann P. Robson, and John M. Robson, *A Moralist In and Out of Parliament* [Toronto: University of Toronto Press, 1992] 40.)

GENTLEMEN,

I cannot be of the least use in any electioneering work, but you may use my name, as that of one who would very heartily rejoice in Mr Mill's success—provided you throw no reponsibility on me—

I am, Gentlemen
Your faithful Servt.
J. Ruskin

b. Letter of 1869 to Charles Norton, in *Works of John Ruskin*, ed., E.T. Cook and A. Wedderburn (London: George Allen, 1903–12) XXXVI, 590.

WHEN I accuse Mill of being the root of nearly all immediate evil among us in England, I am in earnest—the man being looked up to as "the greatest thinker" when he is in truth an utterly shallow and wretched segment of a human creature, incapable of understanding *Anything* in the ultimate conditions of it, and countenancing with an unhappy fortune whatever is fatallest in the popular error of English mind.

c. *Modern Painters*, vol. V (1860). *Works of Ruskin*, VII, 229n.

ART has many uses and many pleasantnesses; but of all its services, none are higher than its setting forth, by a visible and enduring image, the nature of all true authority and freedom;—Authority which defines and directs the action of benevolent law; and Freedom which consists in deep and soft consent of the individual.[1]

[1] "Individual," that is to say, distinct and separate in character, though joined in purpose. I might have enlarged on this head, but that all I should care to say has been already said admirably by Mr. J. S. Mill in his essay on *Liberty.* (Ruskin's note.)

d. *Queen of the Air*, *Works of Ruskin*, XIX, 127.

THERE is much that is true in the part of Mr. Mill's essay on Liberty which treats of freedom of thought; some important truths are there beautifully expressed, but many, quite vital, are omitted; and the balance, therefore, is wrongly struck.

5. Matthew Arnold (1822–88), poet and critic. "Marcus Aurelius," in *Lectures and Essays in Criticism*, ed. R. H. Super (Ann Arbor: University of Michigan Press, 1962) 133, 136, 145.

MR. MILL says, in his book on Liberty, that "Christian morality is in great part merely a protest against paganism; its ideal is negative rather than positive, passive rather than active." He says that, in certain most important respects, "it falls far below the best morality of the ancients." Now, the object of systems of morality is to take possession of human life, to save it from being abandoned to passion or allowed to drift at hazard, to give it happiness by establishing it in the practice of virtue; and this object they seek to attain by prescribing to human life fixed principles of action, fixed rules of conduct. In its uninspired as well as in its inspired moments, in its days of languor and gloom as well as in its days of sunshine and energy, human life has thus always a clue to follow, and may always be making way toward its goal. Christian morality has not failed to supply to human life aids of this sort. It has supplied them far more abundantly than many of its critics imagine....So with Christian morality in general: its distinction is not that it propounds the maxim, "Thou shalt love God and thy neighbour," with more development, closer reasoning, truer sincerity, than other moral systems; it is that it propounds this maxim with an inspiration which wonderfully catches the hearer and makes him act upon it. It is because Mr. Mill has attained to the perception of truths of this nature, that he is,— instead of being, like the school from which he proceeds, doomed to sterility,—a writer of distinguished mark and influence, a writer deserving all attention and respect; it is (I must be pardoned for saying) because he is not sufficiently leavened with them, that he falls just short of being a great writer....A Roman of Marcus Aurelius'[1] time and position could not well see the Christians except through the mist of these prejudices. Seen through such a mist the Christians appeared with a thousand faults not their own; but it has not been sufficiently remarked that faults really their own many of them assuredly appeared with besides, faults especially likely to strike such an observer as Marcus Aurelius, and to confirm him in the prejudices of his race, station, and rearing. We look back upon Christianity after it has proved what a future it bore within it, and for us the sole representatives of its early struggles are the pure and devoted spirits through whom it proved this; Marcus Aurelius saw it with its future yet unshown, and with the tares among its professed progeny not less conspicuous than the wheat. Who can doubt that among the professing Christians of the second century, as among the professing Christians of the nineteenth, there was plenty of folly, plenty of rabid nonsense, plenty of gross fanaticism?...Who will venture to affirm that, by the alliance of Christianity with the virtue and intelligence of men like the Antonines,—of the best product of Greek and Roman civilisation, while Greek and Roman civilisation had yet life and power,—Christianity and the world, as well as the Antonines themselves, would not have been gainers? That alliance was not to be. The Antonines lived and died with an utter misconception of Christianity; Christianity grew up in the Catacombs,[2] not on the Palatine.[3] And Marcus Aurelius incurs no moral reproach by having authorised the punishment of the Christians; he does not thereby become in the least what we mean by a *persecutor*.

[1] Marcus Aurelius Antoninus (121–180 CE), Roman emperor and Stoic philosopher.
[2] A series of underground chambers or tunnels with recesses for graves.
[3] Chief of the seven hills of Rome.

6. George Eliot (1819–80), novelist and essayist. "The Modern Hep! Hep! Hep!" in *Impressions of Theophrastus Such* (1879).

A MODERN book on Liberty has maintained that from the freedom of • • • individual men to persist in idiosyncracies the world may be enriched. Why should we not apply this argument to the idiosyncrasy of a nation, and pause in our haste to hoot it down? There is still a great function for the steadfastness of the Jew: not that he should shut out the utmost illumination which knowledge can throw on his national history, but that he should cherish the store of inheritance which that history has left him. Every Jew should be conscious that he is one of a multitude possessing common objects of piety, in the immortal achievements and immortal sorrows of ancestors who have transmitted to them a physical and mental type strong enough, eminent enough in faculties, pregnant enough with peculiar promise, to constitute a new beneficent individuality among the nations, and, by confuting the traditions of scorn, nobly avenge the wrongs done to their fathers.

Appendix D:
Contemporary Reviews and Critiques

1. *Athenaeum* 1635 (26 February 1859), 281–82.

M R. MILL appears once more before the world after a period of anxiety followed by sorrow. This work is dedicated to the memory of the wife whom he has lost: to her he attributes all the inspiration, and part of the authorship, of all that is best in his writings of many years past.

The subject of the work is *Liberty*: not in the philosophical sense, not in the political sense, but in the social sense. Mr. Mill treats of the conduct of society, the whole, towards its individual parts. He lays down his principle; he enters upon the question of the liberty of thought and discussion; he treats of the value of that individuality which can only exist when the forest allows room for its trees to grow; and he then endeavours to fix the limits of the authority of society over the individual. Nothing more definite than the subject or than the partitions: but the details are rather too much of the essay cast to suit the neatness of the title and the sharpness of the divisions. It would be a great improvement if little side-notes were attached to the paragraphs.

Of the style and the matter, we need only say that it is John Mill all over: and those who do not read large works on logic and political economy, and those—no small number—who cannot realize the individual character of the writer of a review article, even when they know his name, are here presented with a small work, on a subject of universal interest, with the author's characteristics very strongly impressed.

Mr. Mill makes it his principle that the sole end for which mankind are warranted, individually or collectively, in interfering with the liberty of action of any of their number, is *self-protection*. We doubt if any one, in modern times, will venture to dispute the principle. Some will take it as their guiding rule *on principle*: others will aver that, whatever other principles they may also allow to act, there is no proper case of application in which this principle does not *also* apply. Thus those who still think that the honour of God is to be upheld, meaning that their own religious opinions are to be enforced by the State, also maintain that such upholding is necessary to the protection of society.

Of what use then is a principle which everybody grants, and which anybody can turn as he pleases. Of very great use indeed: because it is a true principle and all truths are useful; because it is a sufficient principle, and will do all that is wanted when properly used. That it may be nullified by any one who pleases is no more than must be said of every principle which is to act by conscience, and is to be the rule of the community only so far as it is the sum total of the convictions of the units which make up that community. Nothing is more common than confusion between a rule of law, the penalties of which are to be enforced upon external evidence, and a rule of morals, which is to have its application settled, as it is aptly said, in *foro conscientiae*.[1]

So then, a person will exclaim, I have only to say I believe it to be for the protection of society, and I may do anything that law will let me do. Not a doubt about it—because you may do all that law will let you do without saying anything to anybody: but to whom are you to say it? To your own inner self, to which every rule must appeal that cannot be heard before the Queen at Westminster. If you like to say to yourself, Now, my dear fellow, let you and I lie to each other, you can do it. But the truth is, we believe, that people in general stand more in awe of themselves than they know of: they seldom cheat themselves wilfully. Nor need they attempt such fraud, while there are so many easy ways of putting on an inner mask.

Mr. Mill's book is all the more likely to be useful, from the very vagueness of the rule which he is obliged to lay down. Either this or something as vague must be the rule: and nothing but calm discussion, such as ranges opinions against each other without displeasing any prejudice short of rabid feeling, can fix the rule in the minds of men. And Mr. Mill's mode of arguing is pre-eminently of this character. He is always in good humour with the bodies and souls of those whose opinions he condemns: and when, as happens not seldom, he attacks established notions in a manner well calculated to shock those who cannot bear opposition to their fundamental tenets, he never makes the reader feel that himself is looked at. We are much in want, on the subject of society, of that good teaching, meaning that self-teaching, which arises from discussion of the opinions of powerfully thinking men. We are living at a time in which law is invoked on a score of matters which no law can reach.

[1] [*foro conscientiae*] in the court of conscience.

2. *Saturday Review* 7 (19 February 1859), 213–4. [This was the second notice of Mill's book published by *Saturday Review*.]

No one will accuse us of an undue partiality for Calvinism, but we think Mr. Mill misapprehends its whole scope. We will not quarrel about the word, which appears to us to be used somewhat vaguely; but we say that the belief that to obey God's will in every action of life is the highest aim of human existence, far from being a slavish one, is the noblest conception of life that any mortal creature can form. So far from crushing the faculties and susceptibilities, it is the best of all means of developing them to the highest pitch of excellence and glory of which they are capable. No one will accuse Mr. Mill of believing that the desirable position for man is that of living exactly as his inclinations prompt him from time to time, without reference to any general principle whatever. A man who lives to develope his own faculties, or to benefit his race or nation, subordinates his temporary inclinations to those ends and raises and purifies his character by doing so. Self-control is, indeed, the highest and most distinctly human function of life, and differs as widely as possible from a slavish mechanical submission to superior force. Willing obedience enforced on oneself at all risks, and in the face of any amount of dislike, is the greatest of all agents in ennobling and developing the character, whether it is rendered to a principle or to a person; for it implies action, and action of the most unremitting and various kinds. Is a dog a worse dog for obeying a good master? Is a wife the less womanly for obeying a good husband? If not, is man less manly in obeying God? The iron does not obey the blacksmith, nor does a slave under the fear of the lash, in the proper sense of the word, obey his master. He rebels against him whilst he yields to him. What all Christians understand by obeying God's will is, entering into and adopting God's plans and purposes as the rule of life, and acting up to them in every particular. "Love is the fulfilling of the law." Mere acquiescence and submission is quite another thing. Almost all Christians, at least in Western Europe, have always understood the plan of God respecting them, which they were thus to obey, to involve the diligent cultivation of various parts of their nature; and, in point of fact, the extreme vivacity and individuality of much of the history of modern Europe are derived from this very obedience which appears to Mr. Mill so slavish. The Crusaders were trying to obey God when they invaded Palestine; and so were many of the Popes when they asserted, and of the feudal kings when they denied, the right of the Church to temporal supremacy. Luther, Cromwell, Queen Elizabeth, and many others, considered obedience to God as the mainspring of their lives. How far they rightly apprehended God's will is quite another question; but it is too plain for argument that obedience to God was in them an active and not a passive, a developing, and not a crushing sentiment. Indeed, the very parts of history in which great men were greatest, and in which individual energy was most highly developed, are just those periods at which the sentiment of obeying God was most powerful. Calvinism is notoriously the creed of the most vigorous and least submissive nations in the world. A theory must be strangely wrong which proves that the Scotch in the seventeenth century ought to have been a slavish pusillanimous people, with no marked characters amongst them. It is of the essence of Calvinism, as Mr. Mill uses the word, to recognise special talents and faculties as good and perfect gifts given by God to be used and honoured by the use accordingly. Surely such a belief supplies the most effective means for developing individuality. It is only when it is perverted that it can crush the mind. That human nature is corrupt—i.e., that men have a natural tendency to do wrong, or (which is the same thing) a natural incapacity to do right—is a fact which every system of morality must recognise in some form or other. That there is any element of human nature which must be radically exterminated is no part of what Mr. Mill calls the Calvinistic doctrine. We full admit that Calvinists, as well as other people, have often entertained very wrong notions as to what God's will is, and that they have frequently depicted it in such a light as to make it almost indistinguishable from the will of the Devil. Of course, to obey such a will as that is a dreadful thing; but even in that case, the result would be to develope the character (though in a very unpleasant direction), and not to crush it. A man who tyrannizes over himself, crushes his own affections, and destroys his own sensibility because he believes it to be God's will that he should do so, has done what is very wrong and very foolish, and has experienced what may almost be called blasphemous feelings; but when all is done, he has developed himself in a certain direction. His will is strengthened and not destroyed. He has a fair chance of becoming a sort of devil, but is in very little danger of being a mere commonplace man. We have little doubt that, if it were possible to effect a detailed comparison between families in which what Mr. Mill describes as "Calvinism" does and does not prevail, it would be found that, *Caeteris paribus,*[1] the former had a larger share of originality of character than the latter. If we are right in considering the principle of obedience to be an active and not a passive one, this might have been expected.

The real sources of the prevalence of the weak, slight, ineffectual type of character which is such a grievance to Mr. Mill, appear to us to be quite unrelated to religious principle. Small French shopkeepers are, to say the least, as feeble a folk as any class of Englishmen, and their worst enemies

---

[1] [*Caeteris paribus*] Other things being equal.

would not accuse them of having been degraded by Calvinism. The real cause, or at least one great cause, is undoubtedly to be found in the prevalence of small prosaic occupations, which engross the attention without developing the intellectual or moral powers of those who pursue them. How can he be wise whose talk is of oxen? And if oxen, which are at any rate living creatures, with dispositions, wills, health, and other individual peculiarities, do not afford sufficient occupation to the mind to develop its higher powers, how can the sale of pastry, the concoction of hair-dyes and perfumes, and a hundred other petty occupations of the same sort, with their small vicissitudes and trifling successes, make men and women of those who pass their life in them? When we remember that the class occupied in these trivial pursuits is at present one of the most numerous, most increasing, and most influential in the country—that men who represent its level of education and knowledge make its inclinations, the weakly propensities which would be its passions if it had any, and the minutiae of its daily life, the subjects of photographic descriptions—and that literature of this kind, which never rises above grotesqueness, and never touches the great interests of life in any other temper than that of Thersites,[2] is the principal food of what many people call their minds—we need not wonder that herds of wretched dwarfs are growing up amongst us who are the natural prey of intolerant bigots, and the natural enemies of all that looks unusual to narrow minds coddled into imbecility by every influence which can convert the strong wine of our native English character into a wretched mixture less unworthy of the title of *eau sucrée*[3] than of any other.

[2] An ugly, abusive Greek soldier killed by Achilles in the Trojan War.
[3] [*eau sucrée*] sugared water.

3. *The Rambler*, 59 (May-November 1859), 62–75, 376–85. By Thomas Arnold, Jr.

[Thomas Arnold (1823–1900), son of Dr. Thomas Arnold, headmaster of Rugby, and younger brother of Matthew Arnold. Forsaking the liberal Protestantism of his famous father, he became a Roman Catholic in 1856. Here he appears in the Catholic journal, *The Rambler*.]

Mill on Liberty

ANY book of Mr. Mill's which professes to lay down fixed principles, applicable to important questions of social and individual ethics, deserves to be as carefully studied by those who possess known landmarks and unalterable methods for the guidance of life and the discipline of the soul, as by those to whom all questions of the kind are still open. The Catholic faith places a man in the best position for forming a sound ethical code, and extending it to new cases and exigencies as they arise: but it does not itself explicitly include such a code.…

Perhaps there is no single moral question upon which a greater medley of opinions is afloat among Catholics than that of individual liberty. This by itself shows the disputable nature of the whole subject; for upon articles of faith it is notorious that there is no such discordance. Yet the data possessed by a Catholic places him in a peculiarly favourable position for solving difficulties. But to recommend his views to others, he must neither spare the labour of thought nor shrink from the arena of discussion.

The occasion of Mr. Mill's Essay is to be found in the relation of the rationalist party in England to the prevailing state of opinion. As far as external indications go, rationalism in England is less influential, less progressive, than it was twenty years ago. In these last years, such wild outbursts of spiritual rebellion as the *Nemesis of Faith*[1] no longer rise to startle the religious world from its propriety. Fifteen years back, the popular book on cosmogony and geology was the *Vestiges of the Natural History of the Creation*[2]; now it is the *Testimony of the Rocks*[3]. Among the Reviews of that school, some, like the *Prospective*, have vanished altogether; others, like the *Westminster*, contrive to exist, but with a stationary circulation, and less than

---

[1] *Nemesis of Faith* (1849), by James Anthony Froude (1818–94), English historian and biographer.
[2] *Vestiges of the Natural History of the Creation* (1844), by Robert Chambers (1802–71).
[3] *Testimony of the Rocks; or Geology in its Bearings on Two Theologies* (1857), by Hugh Miller (1802–56).

the old pugnacity. The *Examiner* has dropped its racy diatribes upon Anglican Bishops, finding probably that they would not suit the soberer tastes of its present public. In 1834 the Church Establishment appeared to be tottering under the blows of a legion of enemies; in 1859 it seems to be as secure against a crash as the Bank; and yet in spite of these appearances, it is certain that rationalism is not less, but probably more widely spread. The thinking, reasoning persons in a nation must always form a small minority; and when the mediocre majority are attached to orthodox opinions, or what they deem such, while the social fabric is steady and the social bond strong, the dissenting or rationalist opinions can only find favour among the thinking minority. Now in England it is probable that a considerably larger proportion of this small class belongs to the rationalist camp at the present day than twenty years ago....

Against this disposition of the majority to encroach upon the freedom of thought and action of dissenting minorities, Mr. Mill, on the side of the rationalists, has skilfully chosen his ground. In some ways, the yoke of the dominant system is more oppressive to rationalists than to Catholics. We are, indeed, liable to be treated with unjust suspicion, to have our children proselytised, and to experience in the court of law and in the boardroom the intolerance of the half-educated masses; but, at any rate, we are not now persecuted into conformity. But rationalists, having no external organisation, are left under the full pressure of the popular system in many things where it is most irksome. They may think that marriage should be a revocable contract; yet public opinion renders a marriage before a registrar ordinarily inadmissible. They may consider baptism an idle ceremony; yet few of them will brave social opinion so far as to deprive their children of it. Thus opinion exacts a conformity to the usages of the popular religion, which rationalists cannot but feel to be humiliating. In order to mitigate this rigour of opinion, Mr. Mill correctly judged that a direct attack upon the received system would not advance his object. But he took up the cry which the received system loudly utters, and prefixing the name of Liberty to his essay, he claimed for the thing its full application in the domain of law and of opinion....

To the doctrine of human freedom, thus explained, I am disposed to give a decided general adherence. That doctrine is, that the liberty of thought and of its expression should be entire; and that the liberty of tastes and modes of living should be only limited by the single condition, that the rights and interests of others be respected. By liberty, I mean absence of accountability of any *temporal* authority; and, with Mr. Mill, I understand by the subjects of this liberty persons of full age and of sound mind. And my thesis is this, that although, in bygone states of society, the employment of coercion in order to bring recusants to conformity may have been occasionally defensible, as producing, on the whole, more good than evil, the circumstances of modern society are such as to render the use of such coercion inexpedient and reprehensible, because certain to produce more evil than good.

It is objected that such a doctrine is suitable enough to the circumstances of a Catholic minority in England, but that no English Catholic would advocate its application to the case of the Catholic majority in Austria, or France, or Spain, or adapt to the latitude of Vienna the rule which he approved for the latitude of London. I answer, that I make no mental reservations. Having faith in my thesis, I am prepared beforehand for the extension of the principle laid down to every variety of circumstances. Mr. Mill himself, in defining the range of his doctrine, "leaves out of consideration those backward states of society in which the race itself may be considered as in its 'nonage'." "Liberty," he says, "as a principle, has no application to any state of things anterior to the time when mankind have become capable of being improved by free and equal discussion. When the wisdom of the governors is far in advance of the wisdom of the governed, and the means do not exist, by the communication and comparison of ideas, of equalising the two, it is desirable and right that the subjects should be coerced, if necessary, to their own good." In the employment of coercion; whether directly or by penalties attached to non-compliance, to bring men to the true faith, I believe that the test of lawfulness is success. To exact the hollow profession of the truth, while the heart internally rebels, so far from being a success, is a more disastrous failure than acquiescence in open recusancy. Coercion *succeeds* only when it produces higher moral results to the persons coerced than were attained under toleration; only when they, or at least the majority of them, are brought to admit the expediency of the coercion, and are visibly benefited in their moral nature by having embraced the true and discarded the false opinion. To such success I conceive three concurrent conditions are requisite:

First, that the persons coerced should not be persons of full-developed intellect, but in that immature mental state, akin to the case of children, which justifies, in Mr. Mill's own opinion, the use of despotic means to effect their improvement.

Secondly, that there should exist a body of teachers on the side of that true faith to which men are to be coerced, sufficiently wise, zealous, and virtuous, and also sufficiently numerous, to ensure that the true doctrine shall be exhibited in its proper light to the persons coerced; that they shall be led to see its intrinsic superiority to the falsehood which they had formerly embraced, and, partly through that insight, partly through the moral elevation caused by contact with the wise and good, attain to a higher and more developed state of being than they had formerly known.

Thirdly, that there should not exist, in the neighbourhood of the scene of coercion, a civilised community or communities of persons, who, having themselves repudiated the true doctrine, will sympathise with those who are being coerced to accept it—will encourage them to make resistance, active or passive, to the coercive measures employed, and will nourish in them a feeling of ill-usage, and of suffering unjustly in a good cause, if the resistance is unsuccessful.

Only when these three conditions meet can coercion be really successful, and therefore legitimate.... Certain particular propositions contained in Mr. Mill's Essay have now to be examined.

The line of argument followed in the first part of this article tends, though by a different road, to the same general conclusion with that of the Essay, namely, that the *liberty* of thought and discussion should be entire. For it need hardly be said that if the lawfulness, at the present day, of coercion to the true faith be denied, the lawfulness of any coercion from it is denied *à fortiori*[4]. That, indeed, could not at any time have been legitimate, according to the premises laid down, since the third condition of success could by no possibility be fulfilled in the case of the coercion of Catholics by Protestants. No Lutheran or Anglican, however convinced he might be of the truth of his own opinions, could deny the existence of a large external body, ready to extend its sympathy to any Catholics whom he might attempt to coerce, and to encourage them in at least moral resistance. Protestant coercion cannot, therefore, by the nature of things, attain to more than *political* success. But to maintain that discussion ought to be perfectly *free*, is quite a different proposition from maintaining, as Mr. Mill does, that it is essentially necessary to the profitable holding of any truth. Mr. Mill speaks as if human improvement were entirely dependent on the culture of the ratiocinative faculties. In his view, an opinion is profitless to the holder if believed merely because others believe it; unless we know the adversary's case, we do not properly and efficaciously know our own. This would be true, if it were granted that whatever opinions a person may hold are either false or but partially true; for then discussion would either bring out the falsehood, so inducing us to renounce it,—a decided gain,—or it would make us appreciate and mentally appropriate the complemental truth, which would be also a gain. But assume that the opinion is entirely true, and also that it relates to matters in which the deepest and most vital interests of the soul of man are concerned. The utmost that the exercise of the ratiocinative faculties can now effect, will be to induce the conviction that the balance of probability lies on the side of the opinion. For, from the nature of the case, since the

[4] [*à fortiori*] with stronger reason.

opinion relates to matters removed from the criticism of the senses, or of any faculty judging according to sense, physical or scientific certainty of the truth of the opinion is unattainable. Take as an obvious instance the opinion of the immortality of the soul. But now, if the ratiocinative faculties be not appealed to, is the opinion therefore necessarily a sterile encumbrance on the mind, and a clog on its free working? Evidently not. There are other faculties,—the contemplative, the illustrative, the imaginative faculties, to say nothing of the sentiments and emotions,—which may be freely and largely exercised, while all the while the absolute truth of the opinion is assumed; and it cannot be denied that the exercise of these, no less than of the ratiocinative faculty, is calculated to deepen and enlarge the mind. Any one who understands what is meant by religious meditation will see at a glance the truth of what is here asserted, that a man's belief, though its grounds be not questioned, may be to him a vital and invaluable possession. He who, without questioning, has *realised* his opinion, holds it at last, not because it is the custom, not because others hold it, but because he has made it his own, and feels it by the testimony of his own consciousness to be true. Meditation upon it has brought out relations, before unperceived, with other truths; has presented it under various images, and illustrated it by various analogies; has seen it hold water under a wide range of circumstances, and tested its purifying and elevating influence upon many various natures.... When [Mill] speaks of the necessity of perpetually discussing all received opinions, it is evident that his secret meaning is, that those opinions are in a great measure *false*, and that unembarrassed and fearless discussion would disclose their falsehood. For if they were wholly or mainly *true*, he could not but allow that constant meditation upon them, rather than constant discussion of their grounds, should be recommended as the best means of again penetrating life and character with their spirit....

Again, to maintain that in the present state of society it is desirable that every man should be free to form and express what opinions he pleases, is a totally different thing from maintaining that opinions have no moral colour,—that whatever a man *has a right* to think and express (relatively to society) he is *right* in thinking and expressing relatively to God and conscience. Mr. Mill seems to imply this doctrine of the moral neutrality of opinions in several passages of the Essay; nor, indeed, is he inconsistent in so doing, since he is an avowed upholder of the doctrine of philosophical necessity. In the second volume of his *System of Logic* he says: "The doctrine called philosophical necessity is simply this: given the motives present to an individual's mind, and given likewise the character and disposition of the individual, the manner in which he will act may be unerringly inferred; that if we knew the person thoroughly, and knew all the inducements which are acting on him, we could foretell his conduct with as much certainty as we can predict any physical event." To this doctrine Mr. Mill expresses his adherence. But if it be assented to, it is evident that there is no place for culpability to come in, either in character, action, or opinion. For "character and disposition" are partly born with us, partly formed by the mutual action and reaction between ourselves and the external world; "motives" are mainly supplied to us by our passions and desires. At the beginning of action, therefore, the contact of motive (which is of physical origin, and therefore not culpable) with the character (for which, as it was born with us, we are not then morally responsible) produces, according to this doctrine, inevitable results in conduct. This inevitable conduct inevitably tends to mould the character into a certain form; and so the process goes on; and as this doctrine of necessity denies the self-determining power of the will, there is no place, from the beginning to the end of a life's actions, in which to insinuate any thing like culpability or moral turpitude. Opinions will of course, follow the same rule. But those who believe in free-will in the sense in which the Church teaches it, in the sense in which Coleridge explains it in the *Aids to Reflection*[5], as a spiritual super-sensuous force in man, as a self-determining power, the existence of which justifies the solemn ceremonial of human justice, and authenticates the doctrine of a final judgment,—can never admit that man is not responsible for the regulation of his passions....

The practical inconsistency which prevails among Christians, and which furnishes the ground for Mr. Mill's strictures, arises from this,—that many, who are thoroughly addicted to the pursuit of temporal good, *pretend* nevertheless to walk in conformity to this Christian morality, and to need no other ethical rules than those which the Gospel furnishes. It is as if Dives, in the midst of his moneygetting, were to affect the detachment and mortification of Lazarus.[6] It is indisputably true, as Mr. Mill says, that the Koran contains excellent moral precepts which are not found in the New Testament; he might have added that Aristotle has yet more excellent maxims than the Koran. But what is the reason? These maxims are all fitted to aid man in arriving at his *natural* ideal, namely, "the harmonious development of all his powers to a complete and consistent whole." As reason is capable of discovering this ideal, so it is capable of ascertaining the ethical principles which subserve to its attainment. The morality of the temporal life, in all its parts,—that of the public assembly, that of the bar, that of the counter, or that of the farm,—is capable of being ascertained by human reason unaided by revelation, and for a large part of it has been so ascertained. So far, then,

[5] *Aids to Reflection* (1825), by S. T. Coleridge (1772–1834).
[6] Dives is the traditional name of the unnamed rich man of the parable involving the rich man and the diseased beggar Lazarus in *Luke* 16.19–31.

as an individual is bound, or inclined, to bear a part in the world's work,—
so far as he cannot, or will not, give himself up wholly to God,—so far it is
his duty to guide himself by the best and wisest ethical rules which he can
find, from whatever source derived, applicable to that particular department
of the temporal life in which his station is. The higher Christian morality
which he possesses will often enable, nay compel, him to *revise* ethical
judgments which have been arrived at independently of religion; but it will
not serve him, in these worldly matters, as an exclusive code.

But when Mr. Mill speaks of the Christian morality as being, "not the
work of Christ or the Apostles," but gradually built up by the Catholic Church
of the first five centuries,—when, again, he speaks of its having "received
additions in the middle ages" which the Protestant sects merely cut off,
substituting fresh additions of their own,—one cannot but wonder at so
strange a distortion of the facts. That the leading principles of the Christian
morality, as above defined, were taught by our Lord and His apostles, is so
palpably true, is so easily established by a multitude of texts, that it were
waste of words to go about to prove it; that the same principles were taught
by the Catholic Church of the first five centuries is also notorious; it is
equally certain that these are the main principles of Catholic morality at the
present day. Mr. Mill ought to inform us what were the additional principles
invented in the middle ages. Some such might be found, perhaps, by culling
extracts from mediaeval writers, after the fashion of Mosheim's citations from
St. Eligius (see Newman on *Popular Protestantism*[7]), but certainly in no other
way. The separated bodies have, indeed, either impaired these original
principles, or joined to them, as Mr. Mill says, "additions adapted to the
character and tendencies" of each. By setting up the State as the supreme
power in the Church, the Anglican body has impaired the testimony of its
members to the first principle; many of them have had already, and will
have again, to choose between the edict of Caesar and the command of God;
while their position as a separate body disposes them, in the case of collision,
to prefer the former to the latter. The Methodists have added to the morality
of Christ a kind of morbid self-inspection, which is perpetually asking itself
the questions, "Am I right with God or not? is my inward state satisfactory?
shall I be saved, or shall I be lost?" The Antinomian sects have, to say nothing
of what they have added, abandoned the second and third principles,—purity
and the regulation of the passions. Lastly, all have, in different ways and
degrees, abandoned the principle of humility, and added various kinds and

---

[7] Probably a reference to *Ecclesiastical History: Ancient and Modern*, by Johann L. Mosheim
(1694?–1755). John Henry Newman (1801–90), leader of the Anglo-Catholic movement
until his conversion to Roman Catholicism in 1845, wrote no work called *Popular
Protestantism*.

forms of pride. Dryden, it will be remembered, challenged Stillingfleet to name a single Protestant work on humility; and when his adversary produced one, it proved to be in the main a translation from a Catholic treatise.

The last chapter consists of "applications" of the general doctrine of the Essay, one of which only can here be noticed. Although not strictly belonging to the subject of the Essay, which is social liberty, not political enfranchisement, Mr. Mill has handled in this chapter the question as to the limits of the interference of government in the business of society. There is often a misuse of words here which leads to confusion of thought. English popular writers, when they hold up England as a pattern of political liberty to foreign nations, generally mean that we have a right to vote for a member of parliament, which they have not; a right to tax ourselves for local purposes, which they have not; together with many other privileges of the same kind. On the other hand, there are those who, revolted by the self-satisfied air with which these privileges are paraded, and detecting an ambiguity in the terms used, are apt to speak slightingly of these supposed advantages. These persons say, "Why attach the name of liberty to functions which we are by no means impatient to exercise? If government officials will undertake the laying of our water-pipes, and the cleaning and lighting of our streets, we shall thank them for relieving us of a task which the wider knowledge and experience they can command enables them probably to execute better than ourselves. Certainly we shall not regard their interference as an invasion of our liberty. Nor, again do we think it essential to our liberty that we should have a voice *valeat quantum*[8] in the election of the members of the Legislature, in preference to any other mode of appointment. Continental experience proves that towns can be made beautiful and healthy as well, perhaps better, by a centralised than a localised administration. Nor does our vaunted parliamentary machine always work smoothly or profitably; it economises neither time nor money. What we understand by liberty is exactly what Mr. Mill understands by it, namely, the power of managing our own life as we please; of reading what books we like; of unhampered locomotion; of cultivating and developing our own and our children's minds by the methods we think best, provided we do not trench upon the rights of others. If we think an institution wrong,—slavery, for instance,—we desire the liberty of publishing our thoughts without being tarred and feathered; if we prefer one style of religious worship to another, we would prefer to be free to practise it without constraint either from a government or from a mob. The charter of our civic rights may include all the fine openings for fussy self-importance that you describe, and perhaps many more; yet without the species of liberty

---

[8] [*valeat quantum*] for what it is worth.

we have insisted upon, we shall not be free in any sense that seems to us worth caring for."

A tendency to such reasoning as this is often perceivable on the part of the Catholic minority in England, and not unnaturally so. Local self-government and the representative system do not work favourably for English Catholics. Although they form more than one-twentieth of the population, they can command only one six hundred and fifty-fourth part of the parliamentary representation, and even that happens through a fortunate accident. The same is the case, as a general rule, with all municipal offices. Every where in England Catholics are in a minority; and minorities, being unrepresented under the present *regime*, cannot get their man elected, nor cause their voice to be more than imperfectly heard. The positive prejudice also which disqualifies Catholics, as such, in the general English mind for posts of honour and trust is still, though with diminished intensity, powerfully operative. It might seem, therefore, at first sight, to be our policy rather to aid in accumulating power in the hands of the government than in the maintenance and extension of the system of local management. Government officials, it may be said, are more or less accessible to reason; they are mostly raised by education above the sway of mere blind prejudice; if we can make out a clear case of hardship to them, they will redress it. But the blind unreasoning bigotry of the bulk of the English middle class is unimpressible and unassailable; to attempt to extract fair concessions from them, when the Pope is in the case, is, as Sir John Fortescue[9] would say, to go "scheryng of hogges," with the old result of "moche cry and little wole."

All this is true; yet still Mr. Mill is probably right when he says, that the more narrowly government interference in local concerns can be circumscribed, the better. First, for the sake of the great principle, that "though individuals may not do the particular thing so well, on the average, as the officers of government, it is nevertheless desirable that it should be done by them rather than by the government, as a means to their own mental education,—a mode of strengthening their active faculties, exercising their judgment, and giving them a familiar knowledge of the subjects with which they are thus left to deal." Secondly, because Catholics have no cause to despair of being able ultimately to work round free institutions more to their advantage than they seem to be at present. Let them show themselves the equals of their Protestant fellow-citizens in public spirit, in intelligence sharpened by education, and in acquired knowledge,—in short, in the whole circle of the civic virtues and qualifications, and they may reckon on not being always excluded from posts of trust. This book itself, the weighty

[9] Sir John Fortescue (1394–1476), English jurist.

maxims of which are destined to leaven very extensively, if we mistake not, the general sentiments of society, will contribute to dissipate the intolerance which defeats their just claims. Thirdly, the precariousness of favours obtained by a minority from a government has to be considered. When we stand with our countrymen man to man, we know where we stand. We may be disliked and suspected at first; but if we can once get a footing, and satisfy them that we personally are a decent sort of people, and that our claims are just, we shall have gained a success which can never afterwards, unless through our own fault, be wrested from us. For all experience shows that rights thus gained are progressive, and that their expansion can only be arrested by external constraint; on the other hand, the concessions which a government has made to a minority in a time of quietness may be revoked in a time of excitement. Are examples needed? Look at the seeming prosperity of English Catholicity under the government of Charles I before the year 1640, and again under James II. In each case the relief afforded by the government was given in defiance and in advance of the general sentiment of the nation, and was soon swept away beneath a torrent of penal inflictions; but to take advantage of more equal laws, and to disarm by sensible and spirited conduct the inveterate prejudices of individuals and of local coteries, is, *pro tanto*[10], to alter the general sentiment itself.

[10] [*pro tanto*] to that extent.

4. *British Quarterly Review* 31 (1860), 173–95.

MILL has expended nearly half his little treatise in vindicating the "Liberty of Thought and Discussion," which we had vainly imagined was pretty well understood and enjoyed among us.

Mr. Mill seems to think otherwise; and as this is the subject to which he has, after all, principally devoted his book...we shall, in this article, confine our criticisms for the most part to the chapter on "Free Thought and Discussion."

Mr. Mill seems to think that there is still a great deal to be done before we can be said fully to enjoy this inestimable right. We cannot agree with him. As far as legal penalties go, we are as free as any people can well be. For any remaining inconveniences which may attend the patron or champion of unpalatable or obnoxious opinions (not from the *hands*, for they are tied, but) from the looks or even tongues of his fellow men, or from any other methods of showing aversion that cannot be recognised or repressed by law without greater social "tyranny" than the law can ever cure, we do not flatter ourselves that Mr. Mill, or any one else, can devise a remedy; further, we doubt whether it would be good for the progress of truth (partly on Mr. Mill's own showing), if exemption from all such opposition could be secured for its champions. This we shall endeavour to make out by-and-bye; meantime, as regards civil liberty, we do not see that Englishmen can learn much from Mr. Mill's long chapter on "Freedom of Thought and Discussion," however useful it might have been if published (supposing it *could* have been published) in Italy, or Spain, or Portugal. Mr. Mill, indeed, hints that even legal exemption from pains and penalties for the expression of opinion, is not quite secured to us; and in illustration alludes to that great "Pooley" case, of which Mr. Buckle attempted to make so much use in a recent number of *Fraser's Magazine*[1], but which proved a fatal *ignis fatuus*[2] to that enterprising gentleman, and finally plunged him into as deep a bog as ever controvertist was smothered in. Mr. Buckle's essay was valuable, however, as a piece of triumphant self-confutation; for it not only showed, in contradiction to Mr. Mill, that Englishmen may use all proper freedom "of discussion," but a great deal more; and that the greatest declaimers for liberty are but too apt to resort to the worst vices of that "social tyranny" against which they protest—abuse and vituperation.... In spite of any such rare instances as that of Pooley, we are still disposed to say that, practically, no great increase of our liberty of "discussion" is possible. As Mr. Coleridge justly argues,

[1] May 1859. Mill discusses the Pooley case in Chapter II of *On Liberty*.
[2] [*ignis fatuus*] will of the wisp; delusive hope.

people are not to be permitted to scribble blasphemy and obscenity on our gates and walls, for the expression of "free thought" or the vindication of a "liberty" that is certainly neither "civil nor religious"; any more than a Christian is to be permitted to dangle a lump of pork before the nose of a Jew along the street by way of expressing his superiority to the Jew's religious prejudices. Such things cannot be allowed by way of vindicating individual liberty; and so, in spite of an occasional great "Pooley" case, it is quite true (and, we think, every day sufficiently confirms it) that there is, practically, in this country the most unfettered freedom of discussion. We heartily wish indeed that every remnant of obsolete law which savours of forcible repression, may be abolished, if only for consistency's sake; but we cannot say that, practically, any serious let or hindrance is given to the most free (if only tolerably decent) discussion of any opinions, however paradoxical or obnoxious. Of this we think we have *more* than fair proof—say in Mr. Buckle's diatribe against Sir J. Coleridge (for that is not decent), and in Mr. Holyoake's lucubrations, for a similar reason; and a *fair* proof in Mr. Mill's own book, and in innumerable others, teeming with paradoxical speculations on all sorts of subjects. Mr. Mill, for example, has certainly given free expression to his opinions respecting the Christian ethics. Yet, we suppose, no one thinks it would be desirable to lay any interdict on the freest expression of such opinions. It is a little inconsistent, indeed, that, while in the very act of proving the liberty of discussion, men should grumble at society as though it had denied it. So far, however, are we from apprehending any harm from Mr. Mill's expression of opinions, that we shall quote them *in extenso*—not for the purpose of confuting them (though we may, perhaps, make an observation on one or two points), but just to show we have no objection to convince our readers by a practical proof that we have not spoken without reason when we said that Mr. Mill cannot consistently complain of want of freedom in avowing his opinions. He is certainly as much at issue, in the following passage, as it is well possible for him to be, with the general feeling of the mass of his countrymen. As to his statements, we have no fear of their making any wrong impression on any who are really well acquainted with the New Testament morality. We trust that Mr. Mill will be duly sensible of the liberality which not only does not seek to "gag" him, but actually gives his opinions a chance of a wider circulation. [The author here quotes Mill's discussion of the incompleteness and onesidedness of Christian morality, as built up by the Catholic Church of the first five centuries.] ...However, to leave the question whether England has the privilege of free thought and discussion so far as exemption from all legal penalties is concerned, let us further consider—and this is the principal object we have in view—whether the sort of social immunity our author would advocate for the champions of unpalatable truths or errors is not an imaginary one; whether, in truth, his principle is not *nugatory*, and whether if it were practicable, it would be beneficial.

That it is possible, as Mr. Mill remarks, for society to exercise a very stringent repressive power in relation to both opinions and practices that are obnoxious to it, without appealing to law at all, is very true; that this power may, by putting the individual under the ban of society, make him feel very uncomfortable, much "as a toad under a harrow," as the saying is, that it may, perhaps, if he be a coward or faint hearted, compel him to a very unwelcome silence and inaction, and lead him "to hide his light under a bushel," is equally true. That this power in society may, in a given case, be exerted very unwisely, and inflict great hardships, may, in fact, be a "tyranny of the majority," is also undoubted. But we do not, we confess, see any direct remedy, supposing each man does only what his undoubted legal rights permit him to do, and the law remains impartially indifferent on both sides, that is, merely compelling all to keep the peace. We see no remedy, we say, except that of enlightening the public on the very questions on which the said power of moral repression is supposed to be inequitably exercised; that is, the persons who hold the obnoxious tenets, or plead for the obnoxious practices, must face all the obloquy, whatever it is, of proclaiming the one, and doing the other—the protests and frowns of society notwithstanding. Society, of course, cannot be compelled to listen with patience to what it had rather not listen to; nor can people be compelled to associate or hold parley, or, if you will, only fair and candid discussion, with men whom it abhors; or to think no worse of them if they chance to hold opinions which, though not punishable by law, the said society deems in the highest degree profligate, impious, or seditious, necessarily leading to vice and immorality.

Mr. Mill, it is evident, would be as averse as any man, to any such vindication of individual liberty as would, in fact, be the slavery of society at large; and, of course, neither Mr. Mill nor anybody else would be so absurd as to plead for anything of the kind. It is, we admit, very proper that every man should be at perfect liberty to speak his opinions and sentiments, whatever they may be; and, in spite of Mr. Mill and Mr. Buckle, we cannot see that this is a liberty which is not pretty well understood and practised among us. But it is at least equally proper that another man should run away from him if he thinks it best to do so, or close his ears, or refuse to have anything to do with him, or warn other people against him, and in a thousand other ways, if he thinks proper, show his displeasure and his aversion.

Now here we confess to a difficulty; and Mr. Mill's principle, by which he would limit the power of society over the individual, seems to us far too vague to be of any real value. Mr. Mill says that no restriction, in the way of moral coercion, on individual liberty, is justifiable except as prompted by "self-protection." But, then, who shall define the limits of what is morally justified by "self-protection?" The vague generality conveys nothing. Let us try it upon a single and simple case; and see whether it can do anything for us. Let us take the case of an atheist, with full power (as we would certainly grant him), of publishing his opinions, and making any proselytes he can. Now every conscientious theist will regard his sentiments as of the most deadly and pernicious character, and recoil from them not only with disgust and fear, but horror and indignation. In the exercise, then, of his undoubted liberty, and what he believes due to self-protection, has he a right to decline the acquaintance of the said atheist? or, though previously a friend, to cut his acquaintance on his becoming such? to refuse him access to his own house, to refuse to meet him at the houses of others? to point him out as a man to be shunned and avoided by his children—his servants—his dependents,—all, in short, over whom he has influence? to refuse to argue with him, if he pleases; or, if he argues, to give vivid and natural expression to his abhorrence of atheistical sentiments? Why, yes; Mr. Mill himself appears to concede all this; for he says:—

> We have a right also, in various ways, to act upon our unfavourable opinion of any one, not to the oppression of his individuality, but in the exercise of ours. We are not bound, for example, to seek his society; we have a right to avoid it (though not to parade the avoidance), for we have a right to choose the society most acceptable to us. We have a right, and it may be our duty to caution others against him, if we think his example or conversation likely to have pernicious effect on those with whom he associates.

But then, if every theist does the above-mentioned kind of things—and we think no one can challenge his moral right to do them with not unreasonable notions of "self-protection"—then, since the atheist is as one to ten thousand in any community, nay, in a much less ratio, he will as effectually be under the "ban" of society, as though sentence of excommunication had been pronounced against him. The full power of "discussion" is still left to him, only he must "discuss" in solitude, or if men listen at all, in defiance of the universal frown and aversion of society; and thus he will be placed under that so-called "tyranny" from which, as it seems to us, Mr. Mill would vainly seek to deliver every apostle of an unwelcome or abhorred dogma. Yet is any one to blame? Is not the conduct of society what naturally flows from its honest view of the nature and consequences of the proscribed doctrine, and in strict consistency with the undoubted legal rights of every individual member thereof? Mr. Mill's principle, therefore, appears to us to be too vague to be of service. The notions of "self-protection" will undoubtedly depend on the degree of intensity with which the opinions proscribed are deemed odious and pernicious; and the stringency of the moral coercion which society, quite involuntarily and necessarily, will employ, will be in proportion.

None will contend, we fancy, that any such modes of limiting the freedom or repressing the exuberance of individual action, as have been above enumerated, can be the legitimate subject of law. Now, if so, whether the action of society be a hardship or not, we see no other way of dealing with it than the one already stated, namely, that the very parties whose opinions and practices, for the present, are obnoxious, shall heroically persist in avowing the one and doing the other, till they convince society (if it *can* be convinced) that the one are true and the other beneficial—or at least harmless: that is, they must, through the usual modes of persevering agitation, succeed in turning the *minority* into a *majority*, by convincing the reigning majority, that it is mistaken. During the process of doing this we see not how the moral "penalty," such as it is, can be evaded. The true mode of laying the spirit of opposition, is by convincing it that the particular tenets or practices that rouse its displeasure, are not worthy of its censure or aversion. But, in order to do this, those who undertake the task of undeceiving the public, and of chaperoning a suspicious opinion into the world, must necessarily encounter all the storm of obloquy which will attend the utterance of what the public is intensely averse to, and the doing what it will unsparingly condemn; and so the position of the patron of supposed error, or heterodoxy, or immorality, will, in the very nature of things, be a very uncomfortable one; and if it be called "persecution," it is such "persecution" as all the Essays on Liberty in the world cannot obviate, being the result of the constitution of human nature itself.

Mr. Mill, if we apprehend him rightly, seems to think that the alleged tyranny of society against obnoxious opinions or practices, can be put down in some other way; by general reasoning, for example, on its being wrong to do anything in the way of restricting the liberty of the individual which is not dictated by "self protection;" by inculcating the duty of listening with candour to anything that everybody has to say for his opinions; by telling us to be always ready obligingly to reopen our own convictions to a renewed sifting on every summons of a new objection, or a renewed statement of an old one; by reminding us of our fallibility, or by exhorting us not to use any of the curt, perhaps discourteous, methods of closing argument when we *think* we have examined enough, and have made up our minds; which last at present is undeniably a great saving of time and patience, but which may be thought, by a pertinacious champion of an imagined novelty, one of the most annoying, as it is certainly one of the most common, ways of restricting his sphere of propagandism. But we apprehend that Mr. Mill's view of the efficacy of any such general exhortations, where men conscientiously believe that truth, important truth, is concerned, is an illusion. The real difficulty is to convert them to the opinion that the opinion which they think immoral, pernicious, fraught with deadly consequences to their children or their country, is one of which they may as calmly discuss the *pros* and *cons*, and let those over whom they have any influence, do the same, as of an opinion about the prospects of the coming harvest, or the practicability of a proposed machine. But this cannot be so long as a man really believes that such and such opinions are of deadly quality. Could we respect him, if, merely on the general ground of his hypothetical fallibility, he were willing to listen to everything that could be urged for them as readily as he would to arguments for the undulatory theory of light, or the possibility of a planet outside Neptune?...

We repeat, that the only effectual method of sheltering an obnoxious speculator from the aversion and contempt of the community at large (from all substantial injury, all "penalties", we suppose the law to secure him) will be found to be that of convincing society of the falsity of its conclusions; and this will not and cannot be done, except as those who think them false shall face all the odium that may be implied in endeavouring to confront and to confute them. That they should have the liberty of asserting as loudly, as clearly, and as frequently as they please, these unpalatable truths (or falsehoods) is conceded.

As long as the public *conscientiously* holds such and such opinions fraught with such and such consequences, you cannot show that they are not fraught with them, except by persevering, in the face of obloquy, in advocating them; the *effects* of conviction cannot be wrought beforehand by bespeaking those effects anterior to it. And now comes a seeming puzzle, which, however, experience easily enables us to answer. If it be said "How is a man to convince or convert those who won't listen?" a sufficient answer would be to ask, "And how shall they listen except some one shall speak? How shall they believe without a preacher?" And if he *does* speak, then of course will come the necessary conflict of feeling to which we have adverted so often. But to the question, "How shall a man convince or convert others if the public in general will not listen?" the proper answer is, "Just as in other cases where the world has been heretofore disabused of errors, and those as inveterate as any that are likely to be dissipated by our modern *illuminati*[3]; that is, by persevering

---

[3] [*illuminati*] persons claiming to be unusually enlightened.

in the assertion of obnoxious opinions." It is the old course, often taken in the face of much greater opposition than any that now threatens the *soi-disant*[4] Reformer; of legal penalties, torture, and death itself, superadded to the most stringent moral repression which contempt and neglect, or the most intense aversion could produce. If a man cannot face even these last, it is pretty dear that he is not predestined to be an Apostle of the Truth.

At all events, it cannot be helped. These obstacles must be faced. For none will say, we presume, that it is "tyranny" to refuse to listen to the "voice of the charmer, charm he never so wisely;" that it is tyranny, if a man is allowed to publish a book, unless men will also read it; that it is tyranny if he be allowed to express what opinions he pleases, so long as people will get out of the sound of his voice; or, if they remain, frown or look displeased, or laugh or hiss, or shrug their shoulders, or persuade their neighbours not to listen. No; if we vindicate the right of a man to say what he pleases, we must also vindicate the right of his neighbour not to listen to him if he pleases, or, listening, to turn away with the natural expressions—natural as long as he remains in the same state of mind—of dislike or indignation. Good breeding, or pity, or even contempt, may sometimes modify or disguise the expression of these feelings; but they will exist and whether expressed or not, we apprehend that the practical difficulties of the would-be Reformer will be much the same, and that no general discussion can mend the matter. To attempt to amend it by enforced suppression of feeling is what we should all deprecate, as killing much more liberty than it would save. But we humbly think that, even the suppression by universal and conventional consent would also kill more freedom than it would save; for it would demand the repression of natural feeling on the part of the many in behalf of the few, and must far more imperil that brusque "individuality" for which Mr. Mill pleads so strongly, than the present state of things.

"Hands off," is fair play, and there we must stop. Meantime, of course, every advocate of a crotchet will be disposed to complain if he may not pour his merciless discourse into your ears, or hold you by the button as long as he pleases; or if, having once inflicted on you the same or similar arguments, he sees you bolting as soon as you hear the inevitable harangue begin, or taking little pains, or none at all, to conceal your aversion and disgust.

If a doctrine be really true, and important, perseverance through evil report and good report will have its reward at last; by little and little animosity and prejudice will be disarmed, advocates gradually enlisted, and favourable conjunctures secured for disseminating the once obnoxious tenet more rapidly. These propitious results, as experience shows, will come at last; but

[4] [*soi-disant*] self-styled.

in the very nature of things they must be waited for, and, in some degree, generally suffered for; it is the inevitable penalty which, for the reasons already given, must be paid, unless men (which would surely be the last calamity that could befall them) were ready to listen to what they deemed the most pernicious doctrines and the most beneficial truths with the same unenviable equilibrium of feeling. He who would convince them that these feelings ought to be reversed must count the cost; if he decline the payment, there is no smooth path, no "royal road" of ease by which he can attain the same end. A man cannot be "nursed and dandled" into a Reformer. This was the old way, and we suspect must ever be the way of spreading either unwelcome truth or unwelcome error in the world. Nor, in truth, can we wish it to be otherwise; though if we wished it ever so much, it could not be otherwise. It is impossible to suppose any one holding with any firmness views, on the maintenance of which he conscientiously believes that the best interests of his country, the virtue, the morality of his children, of his family, in short, of everybody, are involved, consenting to hear them impugned with the same *sangfroid*[5] as he would listen to doubts as to whether or not Jupiter be inhabited,—though even *that*, it seems, from recent experience, requires some patience on the part of controvertists who take the other side! Take, for example, the case of the theist as opposed to the atheist. It is quite certain that any devout theist believes in the existence and intimate presence of a Personality unspeakably more worthy, in his estimation, of veneration and affection, than the dearest earthly friend. He might be quite willing, for what he deemed the truth's sake, to enter into discussion as to whether such a Being exists, though even *that* is painful to him; and it is best done, where it generally is done, in books, and without personal collision. But it can hardly be expected, because it is hardly possible, that he should permit any unnecessary communion with an atheist; it is reasonable that he should keep himself as much as possible out of the atheist's company, and take care that all over whom he has any control should be kept out of it too. Mr. Mill may say, perhaps, that this is very illiberal; we reply that it follows, naturally and necessarily, from the man's views of the moral importance of the doctrine he holds and the pernicious consequences of the contrary doctrine. It is in vain to say, "Yes; but these views of the moral importance of such doctrine have led to legal persecution—to burning men's bodies for the good of their souls"; for it is conceded that the atheist is at liberty to publish doctrines as loudly and as widely as he pleases; we vindicate his full liberty; but we can go no further without impairing the liberty of others. We cannot prevent the natural expressions of aversion which doctrine so obnoxious to the generality of

5 [*sangfroid*] cold blood, composure.

mankind must produce. Be it recollected that a sincere theist would sooner hear his dearest friend calumniated, his father's or his mother's honour assailed, than the existence of that Infinitely Good Being in whom he believes, called in question; above all, lightly and scornfully. If we vindicate him for showing the liveliest feelings of indignation or aversion in the former cases— we mean, of course, within the limits of law—can we blame him in the latter? To suppose a theist quite unmoved in the matter would be to suppose that he was really in a state of scepticism or indifferentism; a state which, as it seems to us, the sort of moral toleration which Mr. Mill's theory requires, necessarily presupposes, or would infallibly lead to....

And so it must be with every other opinion which men conscientiously believe involves the vital interests of society and humanity. So far as the liberty of publishing obnoxious opinions is concerned, there is no question; no legal penalties whatever should be attached to this act. But similar liberty, on the other side, implies that men so publishing must be prepared to face all that opposition on the part of society which Mr. Mill (if we understand some of his representations) would regard as a sort of moral persecution; while yet in other passages, as we have seen, he seems to allow to society the right innocently to do all which really involves it;—so fruitless, because so unpractical, seems to us this discussion.

Mr. Mill argues that the majority should be more willing to give a ready hearing to opinions accounted "heretical," inasmuch as those who hold them, being the minority, are generally a much weaker party. This is a very good reason why they should be permitted to express them to as many as they can induce to listen to them; but no reason at all why, if their doctrines be thought pernicious by the bulk of the community, the moral repression should not be stringently exerted. Numbers have nothing to do with this question; if it has, then a single individual, though holding the most ludicrous and pernicious moral paradox, ought to be heard with most patience and indulgence. This is not an appeal to reason but an *argumentum ad misericordiam* [6]. The degree in which the moral repression, so often spoken of, is exerted, will depend on quite other things; its energy will be simply in proportion to the degree in which doctrines are sincerely deemed—wrongly or not—deleterious to truth and man's well-being; and it must be so unless, as we have said, the community has already become really callous to the importance and significance of the views it professedly holds, and has already resolved on betraying the citadel while nominally manning its walls.

[6] [*argument ad misericordiam*] appeal to pity.

Nor, again, must it be forgotten that the terms on which the parties usually meet are not equal. It is generally but too easy for him who takes the *negative* side to be perfectly tolerant of the opinions of his neighbour, and to be most philosophically calm, that is, indifferent, whether his reasonings are accepted or rejected. "Vacuus viator cantat;"[7] he who believes that all religions are equally false, or none certainly true, is, no doubt, well qualified by his scepticism to hear with edifying impartiality the arguments for any, and in turn to dispute smilingly against all. The thing does not, in his esteem, involve any consequence which should ruffle his feelings, or disturb the serenity of his Pyrrhonism.[8] The same reasons make him comparatively indifferent about proselytism; and though he is, like all human creatures, not quite indifferent on that point, he is usually quite unwilling to run any great hazards of loss of reputation, or "the cold shoulder" from his friends, by indiscreet avowals. Hence it is that infidelity not infrequently exists, as Mr. Mill affirms, among those who are not suspected of it by the world, but perfectly known to be infidels among their intimate friends. A negative creed has always tended to form this Nicodemus[9] sect of disciples—men who come to visit the oracle by night, and are reluctant to visit it by day. This species of moral cowardice is very naturally connected with a creed that cannot easily stir enthusiasm, far less make men willing to be martyrs for it. But if (perfect liberty of speech and expression being granted them) men cannot prevail upon themselves to endure even the moral stigma of preaching unwelcome doctrine, we see not such merit in this negative creed as to make us carpet the rough road by which all triumphant truth has hitherto trudged its way in the world.

But now, let a man believe any religion to be true and divinely revealed, and his whole position is essentially changed.

In like manner the theist and the atheist cannot meet on equal terms. The atheist has no profound emotions stirred by his stolid Fate, or his capricious Chance. It is not a person, but an abstraction, that is in question. But, in the sincere theist's estimation, the atheist's dogmas are necessarily more hard to bear than any amount of personal abuse. It is impossible for the atheist "earnestly to contend" for such a faith as terminates in an abstract "law," from which all idea of a Personal Lawgiver has been somehow eliminated, and he can afford, if need be, to be silent about it; and therefore would generally prefer a diatribe against the hardships of any man's being

---

[7] [*Vacuus cantat coram latrone viator*] The traveler who has an empty purse sings in the face of the robber.

[8] Pyrrhonism. The Greek philosopher Pyrrho (360–270 BCE) is regarded as the father of skepticism.

[9] Nicodemus. A Pharisee and member of the Sanhedrin who defended Jesus against other Pharisees.

thought the worse of for holding such sentiments to a courageous avowal and defence of them—courage which almost all religions, however false, can inspire, but which a negative creed seldom teaches. Hence the pleas for a more easy style of proselytism.

But the test is inevitable; and those who hold sceptical or negative views, if they wish them to prevail, must learn to face the ordeal—it is very moderate in our days—of being at least active missionaries and confessors, and, if need be, moral "martyrs;" that is, so far as the title can be earned by merely allowing their neighbours to exercise the undoubted right of disregarding or despising their claims.

Again;—we can hardly suppose the world at large really acting on some of the principles here laid down, if we suppose them to hold any previous convictions at all; either a general state of doubt must be presupposed to make men thus act, or an incipient treachery to their convictions, which must tend to such a sceptical state. If we understand Mr. Mill, no man has a full right to rest satisfied with his opinions unless he has examined, and is prepared to refute, every objection that can be brought against them. We suspect that even if they recognised any such principle, men would much sooner practise silence on all sides, that is, become indifferent to the truth, rather than live such a life of logical torments. But let us hear Mr. Mill: "However unwillingly a person who has a strong opinion may admit the possibility that his opinion may be false, he ought to be moved by the consideration that, however true it may be, if it is not fully, frequently, and fearlessly discussed, it will be held as a dead dogma, not a living truth."... [The author here quotes Mill's argument that if a man is unable to refute the reasons for an opinion opposite to his own, he has no ground for preferring either opinion.] Query. May not a man be justly a believer in the Copernican theory without knowing a tenth of what *may* be said for the Ptolemaic? Or reject the Mahometan religion, without knowing a twentieth of what is said for it? if not, we fear that, Whether men be atheists or theists, Christians or infidels—in short, hold any opinion or the contrary (out of the mathematics)—there is not a single well-grounded opinion in the world, and never will be.

However, we must be content to deal with the possible; and if men were ever so willing to entertain all objections, lest haply there should be some they had never met with, and could not refute, and so their opinions be vitiated, the necessities of life will not permit this logical Quixotry. Let us suppose a man, for example, fully convinced of the truth of Christianity, after reading one or two (or one, if you please) of the best works for it and against it, is he to renew the examination every time a new theory is started, or an old one better stated? That is, is he to peruse every treatise which promises anything of novelty in the objections, before he is fully warranted to repose upon his conclusions, and act upon them with undoubting confidence? Is he to regard his "rational position," that of "suspension of judgment"? Observe, we do not say that, if he has difficulties, he should not endeavour to settle them; let him do so if he can; but if he has none, or if what he has cannot, he believes, affect the balance of evidence on which he has already once deliberately decided, is he yet to reopen the question to everybody who summons his attention to a new light? If so, he would never have the chance of a stable conviction. The controversy has been carried on for the last eighteen hundred years, and it cannot be said (though the arguments of infidelity have been repeated *ad nauseam*) that some new objections are not found out, and from time to time propounded to the world. May not a man act on the assumption that he has moral certainty until he has actually done far less than examine and refute all the objections that have been discovered even up to this time? If not, we suppose it must fare much the same with every form of infidelity also; for there is no lack of new objections for the infidel to examine! And indeed it must be the same with every form, whether of truth or error, for not one man in a million has leisure or ability to obtain this sort of knowledge of the grounds of his opinions—certainly not in any of the professions, law or physic, for example,—on which, nevertheless, it is imperative that a man should act. The very attempt of men of all opinions thus to verify them would soon lead, in weariness, to the habit of scepticism to which we have so often alluded, and indispose to action in the same proportion; *or* to a condition of universal and intolerable wrangling and contention, which would make the world a positive nuisance, and which would equally impede action by consuming in debate the time which should be given to action.

What, then, we ask, is a man who has fairly examined evidence, and is fully convinced of the justice of his opinions, to do? Must he always be repeating the process when he finds that something has been said which he either had not seen, though said before, or is said now for the first time? Human life is not sufficient for this otiose investigation. If this sort of examination is obligatory, "never ending, still beginning", the condition of the inquirer under this "law of liberty" seems, after all, about as happy as that accorded to us by some of the High Churchmen, who concede the right of "private judgment" in words, but, at the same time, deny the thing. It is a right to *inquire*, they say, but only to come at last to a foregone conclusion. Are you satisfied that *that* is true which they think not so? "Inquire again, dear neophyte," they say. You inquire again, and come back in the same mind. Still the remedy is the same. Meantime, it is pretty plain that the unhappy inquirer will never, in the estimate of his High Church oracle, have inquired enough, till he has inquired himself into the belief of the said oracle. We shrewdly suspect it would be much the same with any one who conceived that it was his duty to listen candidly to every form of novel objection to his views which any opponent could manage to invent. He would rarely be found to have inquired enough, till he had conspicuously signalized his logic and candour by adopting the views of his opponent.

And even if a perfectly prompt and equally courteous hospitality to all sort of opinions could be exercised without implying culpable indifference to them all, many may, even on Mr. Mill's own showing, doubt whether it would be good for Truth to have this fair-weather passage through the world. Mr. Mill contends that, as a general fact, all dogmas are the most vigorous when militant—while they are being fought for; and that as soon as the truth is established, and at last universally acquiesced in, that moment it is apt to be forgotten. [Here the reviewer quotes Mill's argument that the living power of a doctrine begins to decline as soon as it has gained ascendancy over other doctrines.] From these sentiments, taken in their literality, one would imagine that it was best that truth should never be established at all; that, like the fox, it was worth nothing but to be chased; made, not to be eaten, but to be hunted. For, according to this doctrine, at least those who contend for a truth are in earnest about it, while, once hunted down, friends and foes give it the slip altogether....

But, whether the extreme inference is more in consistency with Mr. Mill's general principles, or his disclaimer of it, we cannot now stay to inquire. Meantime, experience at least teaches thus much; that the actual establishment of any unwelcome dogma is not to be effected without much struggle and contention, and that, while compelled to fight for a footing, and to face at least the moderate obstacle which is implied in the expressed aversion of those who do not sympathize with it, it is apt to gather strength because really earnest emotion is involved in the matter. It would not, therefore, be well that any patron of a novelty should have that luxurious and easy course, which the complete ascendancy of the principles of this Essay would secure for him. He would certainly stand a poor chance if the principles of that same Essay be true; since it seems that it is only while in some degree "militant" that any novel truth—or falsity—can gather omens of success.

Mr. Mill pleads thus strongly on behalf of those whose "reticence," as regards certain opinions, is the effect of their timidity—a fear of a too stringent public opinion. He tells us

Our merely social intolerance kills no one, roots out no opinions, but induces men to disguise them, or to abstain from any active effort for their diffusion. With us heretical opinions do not perceptibly gain, or even lose, ground in each decade or generation; they never blaze out far and wide, but continue to smoulder, in the narrow circles of thinking and studious persons, among whom they originate, without ever lighting up the general affairs of mankind with either a true or a deceptive light. And thus is kept up a state of things very satisfactory to some minds, because, without the unpleasant process of fining or imprisoning anybody, it maintains all prevailing opinions outwardly undisturbed, while it does not absolutely interdict the exercise of reason by dissentients afflicted with the malady of thought. A convenient plan for having peace in the intellectual world, and keeping all things going on therein very much as they do already. But the price paid for this sort of intellectual pacification is the sacrifice of the entire moral courage of the human mind.

The last sentence is certainly a singular paradox. It is a new thought that "moral courage" is *sacrificed* by the circumstances which test its presence or show that it does *not* exist, and that it will exist and be manifested so soon as there is no occasion for it! The state of things which demands a little moral pluck—and it is very little that is asked in the present day—may be bad or good; but assuredly it is not answerable for *extinguishing* the courage which will only be brave when there is nothing to be faced. It may reveal the cowardice of the "heretics" who dare not speak, but certainly does not quench their zeal; for that, *ex hypothesi*[10], must be non-existent....

There is one speculation of Mr. Mill on which we must say a few words. However plausible in general, its application to our own day seems more than questionable; contradicted, in fact, in the most emphatic manner by all the phenomena around us. He says that high civilization tends in a certain degree to make men all alike—to repress unduly the manifestations of individuality and spontaneity, and to operate prejudicially by inducing men to stifle their genuine sentiments and convictions, and to think and act just as the majority about them are thinking and acting; in other words, to yield to what some would perhaps call the "tyranny of society." We should indeed demur to call it by such a name; we should rather visit it on the *individual*, and say the tendency originated in mere indolent love of quiet or in moral cowardice. But as to the *fact*, that there is generally some such tendency in high civilization, we should not care to deny it. And we may remark, that if anything could *increase* it, it would be a too solicitous courtesy in listening to the expression of all sorts of sentiments—even those most abhorrent from

[10] [*ex hypothesi*] by hypothesis.

our deepest convictions of truth. It is one of the characteristics of the high conventional regard for the feelings of others engendered by much social refinement, that men only too often *suppress* what they deem unpalatable truths. Let there be no opinions so unpalatable that everybody will not be perfectly at his ease in listening to and expressing them, and it could only be by the prevalence of a general indifferentism. If there could be an unreserved expression without giving offence to others of any and of all kinds of opinions (though it is just as likely that people would hold their tongues from the same indifferentism), it could only be because society had already arrived at the *ne plus ultra*[11] of the alleged ill effects of a high civilization; could listen with equal and imperturbable calmness in the spirit of the required mental freedom, only because it was indifferent to all opinions, and because strong "*individualism*" had ceased to exist. The result of *this* kind of freedom would be mainly favourable to every species of scepticism. Whether the sceptic succeeded in imposing silence on all such subjects, or induced society in general to listen to the unrestrained expression of opinion without any wincing or vehement reclamation, the business of the propagandist of scepticism would be equally well done.

But, whatever may be the general effect of a high civilization, with its multitudinous conventional restraints, in repressing an exuberant "individuality" (and we are fully disposed to think that the general effect is as Mr. Mill states it), there does seem something droll in the notion that these repressive tendencies are at all a feature of the present day. On the contrary, we should say that never, since the world began, so far as history informs us, has there been an epoch distinguished by a greater *flush* of all sorts of opinions, even the most reckless and absurd. We can hardly see the "green ground" in Truth's meadow for the dandelions, thistles, and poppies that have sprung up in it. Never has there been a period in which men have either given expression to a greater number of speculative monstrosities, or avowed them with greater freedom or more enviable superiority to modesty and shame. Why, there is hardly an extravagance, in either political or theological speculation, from the extremes of Communism to Despotism, from the extremes of Atheism and Pantheism to Mormonism—no folly of pseudo-philosophy, from Table-turning and Spirit-rapping to Biology and Clairvoyance, that has not graced our era. The present age, in Germany and in England, exhibits a perfect Babel of opinions. As *we* read the present day, every eccentricity of speculation seems obtruded on the world without a thought of patient investigation, or any attempt to ascertain whether it is worth while to plague the world with it at all; every man has a "psalm,"

---

[11] [*ne plus ultra*] acme, culmination.

every man a "doctrine," of his own, and incontinently sings the one and says the other in the ears of the unfortunate public. It is, in truth, a very Pentecost[12] of the spirit of speculative error, with the correspondent "gift of tongues." We do think that for the present, "individualism," at least in the direction of *speculation*, inflicts far more on society than society inflicts on it.

---

[12] As this writer uses the term, a festival of the Christian Church occurring on the seventh Sunday after Easter, to celebrate the descent of the Holy Ghost upon the disciples.

5. *Bentley's Quarterly Review* 2 (1860), 434–73. By R. W. Church.

[Richard William Church (1815–1890) was a clergyman and prominent church historian. At Oxford he fell under the influence of John Henry Newman, leader of the Anglo-Catholic movement, but did not follow Newman to Rome in 1845. He became Dean of St. Paul's in 1871.]

Mill on Liberty

E VERY one who feels interest in truth, and who tries to "enlighten his practice by philosophical meditation," must feel thankful when a bold and powerful thinker like Mr. J. S. Mill takes in hand one of those latent but embarrassing difficulties, which few think of putting into words, but which underlie whole tracts of discussion, and are for ever coming up in the commonest questions of practical life. We run against them, or they against us, at any moment: but because they are so common, and we feel sure that they must occur to every one round us—and yet no one seems to think them worth special notice—we fancy them too trivial to be made the distinct subject of our thoughts, and allow the feeling of the difficulty to haunt us obscurely, and often to inflict an indefinite but serious sense of dull worry. One of these usually unanalyzed difficulties is the question, which most people must have practically encountered some time or another, of the influence to be exercised by any means short of or beyond direct argument, on other people. In the present Essay, Mr. Mill undertakes to discuss this question, or, as he states it in its broadest terms, "the nature and limits of the power which can be legitimately exercised by society on the individual."

The value of such an attempt is not to be measured simply by the conclusions arrived at. A man must be very sanguine who should expect to see a question, which he must have found for ever recurring in human history and pervading his own experience, closed and settled, even by a thinker like Mr. Mill. Only very young speculators, who, in their earliest attempts at thought, turn in their simplicity to logic, or to Locke on the "Conduct of the Understanding," for an infallible specific which shall insure their thinking and reasoning right, believe that such final solutions are anywhere to be looked for. At any rate, only those who are very easily satisfied, or are very servile admirers, will admit that it has been arrived at in Mr. Mill's Essay. The gain is in the treatment of such a subject at all by one so competent to handle it. The distinctness, the daring, the vigour of the discussion, the novelty which it throws round what is old and trite, the reality into which it quickens what is inert and torpid, even the peril and menace which it not obscurely discloses to convictions which may be matters of life and death to us, act as a tonic to the mind, and awaken, exercise, and brace it, even if they do not, as they well may, elevate the heart and widen the range of its ordinary contemplations. The reading of a book like this ought to be an event in a man's mental history. It is a challenge to him to analyze much that is vague and confused in his thoughts and current notions; and it is at the same time a help and guide in the process, by presenting the problem itself as conceived by a mind of greater than average reach and clearness. The discussion is important, too, in other ways, whether or not we are convinced by its argument, or even whether we can get any satisfactory and consistent answer to the question at all; for it shows us the term to which difficulty and inquiry have reached on the subject, on what scale the debate has to be carried on, and under what conditions; and, possibly, within what limits an approximately sufficient truth may be hoped for at present. It is both interesting and important as a measure of the grasp and strength of one of the foremost thinkers of his time. And perhaps its use is not the least, if it teaches us something more vividly of the real power or inability of the human mind to penetrate and master the complicated elements of our social state, and of its success in bringing them into a harmony, which we can feel to be both philosophically complete and also answering to the fact.

The subject of social liberty may be said to belong by special appropriateness to Mr. Mill, and to have a natural claim on him for a thorough sifting. Mr. Mill, as everyone knows, regards democracy as the inevitable and beneficial result to which society is everywhere tending. In this he is not singular; but he differs from the majority of those who think with him, in the great clearness with which he discerns the probability, and in the extreme uneasiness with which he regards it, that as the dangers of political oppression of the many by the few disappear, the dangers of social oppression of the few by the many will increase. The foresight of this result does not, indeed, in any degree shake his full faith in the democratic principle; but it presents a serious abatement of the benefit which he hopes from it, and he loses no opportunity to show his ever-present sense of the danger, and of the necessity of providing means to counteract it. No one can have looked through the collection recently published of his review articles, extending over a considerable period, without observing how early he became alive to the substantial magnitude of the peril to individual freedom which seems to wait of necessity on the triumph of the power of the majority, and how continually this menace recurs to his mind, as the dark shadow attending on it, and as the heavy price to be paid for it. It is true, he notices with a sarcasm Sir Robert Peel's[1] use of De Tocqueville's phrase, "the tyranny of the majority." But into no man's mind has the import of the phrase sunk more deeply than into his own, and no one's words sound more impressive to us, in bidding us watch its nascent influence and be prepared against its more formidable growths. But hitherto his allusions to the subject, though full of meaning, have been incidental; and so serious a matter required to be treated by itself. The question as relating to the great concomitant drawback to a progress, otherwise as promising as it is certain, deserved special examination from one to whom, both as a philosopher and as a practical man, the acceleration of that progress had been the object of life. What Mr. Mill has written on the political tendencies and prospects of these times would not be complete without a full discussion of the most menacing tendency of future democracy; one which, if predominant, would kill all improvement even more surely and relentlessly than the old-fashioned tyrannies. The Essay on Liberty may be regarded as a democrat's protest against the claim of the masses, sure to be advanced, in proportion as they grow stronger, to impose their opinion and will without appeal, and to beat down and trample out all self assertion and independence in minorities and individuals. One who hopes everything from popular ascendancy also fears it, and tries beforehand to establish in the opinion of society some well-recognized line round private life and private freedom, before the foreseen power of democracy arrives, to invade and confound all limits by blind usurpations to which there can be no resistance, and by a wayward but inexorable interference from which there will be no escape.

But Mr. Mill's aim is not wholly prospective. He thinks that the control of society over individual opinion and action is at present far too stringent; that it is illegitimate and exorbitant in its pretensions and mischievous in its effects. And as he is markedly distinguished from the common run of representatives of liberal doctrines in another point besides the one just alluded to, that is, in thinking very meanly of the men, the society, and the opinions of this generation, and in holding cheap the measure of improvement to which it has reached, he finds the yoke all the more intolerable. His Essay is directed not only to provide against anticipated dangers, but to abate what he feels to be an existing evil. Having but little respect for the opinions which hold sway over present society, and which it sanctions and arms with its influence, he is anxious at once to cut from under them the ground on which their power over the separate units of society rests. The path of thought and truth and individual development is, he holds, miserably encumbered with ignoble entanglements, with maiming and crippling snares, with arbitrary and cruel restrictions, arising out of the interferences of society and the deference or the fear which it inspires. It is the purpose of his Essay

---

[1] Robert Peel (1788–1850), Tory politician who had been prime minister of Great Britain from 1834–35 and 1841–46.

to reduce within much narrower limits these customary and hitherto recognized rights of interference, as he finds them exercised now; and to lay down a rule for the jurisdiction of society over the individual, grounded on a clear and definite principle; lightening the weight with which society presses on its members, and destroying the prerogative by which its accidentally prevailing opinions impose themselves with irritating or degrading peremptoriness on those who wish to have, or ought to have, opinions of their own....

Whether we are better or worse, whether we have more or less character, than other times, we really cannot tell: it seems to us a fruitless and insoluble question. But we can ascertain something positive of what is going on round us; and on this ground it seems to us that we recognize in Mr. Mill's picture but a partially true representation of what is. Custom is very powerful, but not omnipotent. The current which runs through society is neither so uniform nor so irresistible as he makes it. On the contrary, the face of society appears seamed and traversed in all directions by a vast number of currents, different in their course, strength, and tendencies, pressing on one another or violently conflicting; accelerating, diverting, retarding, with endlessly varying results from day to day; and, as in the sea and the atmosphere, each strong current infallibly provoking its balancing counter-current. Such a state of things is consistent with much respect for custom, but it is inconceivable without also a large amount of activity of mind and resistance to custom. We cannot help feeling that if in these later days we have seen many lamentable exhibitions of stupidity, selfishness, and lowness of mind and feeling, we have also witnessed scenes, and on no narrow scale, which for the wisdom, manliness, and self-devotion displayed in them, ought to have exempted the time from the unqualified charge of "rejecting the stuff of which heroes are made." At least they have done this: they have produced in the public mind, and in the literature which reflects, and by reflecting confirms, its impressions, a singularly hearty—many people think a one-sided—recognition of the worth of the bold, enterprising, self-reliant qualities of character. And in the domain of mind, a representation is surely not an adequate one which leaves behind the impression of a prevailing servility and submission to intimidation. To take one point, and that an important test—has criticism, the criticism which is most sought for and listened to, made no advance, in largeness, in fairness, in temperateness, in the manifestly sincere effort to discharge a judicial office in a judicial spirit? Is not the criticism which now finds favour, and is regarded as answering to its true ideal, one which shows the sense of responsibility, which conscientiously endeavours to appreciate the strength of an adverse case, which is not afraid of a fair statement on both sides, which admits instead of slurring over difficulties, which aims at expressing its own real thoughts modestly but with independent firmness? Are the past periods of history, or the marked characters which appear in them, examined and judged simply by our received beliefs about them, and by our own standard and ideas? or has the tendency set in with indubitable force, to re-open, where any call appeared; the most settled historical traditions, to search for and weigh with the utmost care all new evidence, to admit a reversal of the strongest prepossessions, to do the fullest justice and render the heartiest sympathy to men and times not only most different, but in spirit and rules of action most opposite to our own? A generation which has produced, and which has listened attentively to Mr. Carlyle, Mr. Froude,[2] and Mr. Buckle, cannot be charged with shrinking blindly from independence of thought. Again, we have had some keen controversies. For some of them, Mr. Mill cannot be expected to feel much respect or interest; they probably appear to him as sad wastes of life and time, lamentable aberrations of mental power, which might have been more healthily and hopefully employed. But at least they are evidence against that stagnant condition of thought which he thinks so fatal and so characteristic of this time. There has been shown in them, that which he cannot find, a disposition to ask for reasons for what had been taken for granted, a refusal to be led by powerful popular prejudices, a readiness to accept and defend, on examination and supposed evidence, positions at once highly unpopular, and regarded as absolutely indefensible. At least there was some boldness and independence of mind in the course which, in Popery-hating England, has led so many educated Englishmen of our day, freely and on conviction, towards Rome or Romish ideas, to the utter sacrifice, in many cases, of that which Englishmen of any intellect value most, position and influence among their countrymen....

No one can undervalue the strength and clearness with which Mr. Mill has stated the argument for liberty of thought in its largest sense. If it leads to the unpleasant consequence, that society may do and is doing too much for what we hold to be truth in religion and morality, its ground, at least, in the fallibility of man is but too undeniable to any one who reflects either on himself or others. Opinions, says Mr. Mill, must neither be proscribed nor protected, because we none of us can be certain for others, however we may practically be for ourselves, that we are right: opinions must be left to find their level, persons must be left to make them out for themselves, because there is no public and universal test of certainty to which men can appeal against their opponents; and each man can but fall back, as the last resort, on his own reason. The elaborate and exhaustive reasoning with which Mr. Mill pursues this line of thought is good, as regards those who have the

---

[2] James Anthony Froude (1818–94), historian and biographer.

power, and on whom therefore falls the responsibility, of forming opinions. As between them, one man's reason must be held as good as another's, and the only possible way in which one opinion can fairly prevail over another is by balance of argument, which balance may be reversed to-morrow. All who appeal to reason must accept the known conditions of reason, must abide the consequences of their appeal, must admit the possibility of their being wrong, the possibility in theory, however it may seem not worth taking account of practically, of their strongest and most important convictions turning out unfounded. There are difficulties attending on this aspect of the case, even as regards those who do and can reason, which we should have liked to see noticed by Mr. Mill; not the least of them being, how that cautious consciousness of the conflict of probabilities which is forced on us by reason, is to be reconciled with the unhesitating will and earnestness which is the prime element of all high and successful action. But however the case may be to those who can think, what about those, who not only do not, but in honest truth cannot think?

If there are schools of opinion, which in treating practically of the conduct of life, would make authority its almost absolute guide, the tendency in the opposite ones is to treat the same subjects as if training, capacity, and leisure to examine and judge were the average condition of mankind. It has always struck us that this is eminently the characteristic of Locke's[3] able treatise "On the Conduct of the Understanding." He writes as if he was writing of a world of thinkers, or at least where all might be thinkers but for their own fault; he hardly allows it to escape him that he is aware how very different the actual world is, and must be, at least for a long time to come; and how absolutely inapplicable his rules are—admirable as they are where they apply—to what is possible or conceivable, in the use of the understanding, in the majority of mankind. And the same feeling revives on reading the arguments of one who is not unworthy to be Locke's successor. His supposition, like Locke's, in one part at least of his argument for intellectual liberty is, that the comparatively intellectual and reasoning people, for the conflict of whose opinions he lays down conditions, may be taken as practically identical with the mass of society. But is the supposition sufficiently near to the truth for a general theory to rest upon, which recognizes no distinction between the parts of society where reasoning may go on, without limit as to its subjects, upon grounds approximately respectable and with the prospect of fruit, and parts where it cannot? It seems to us as inconceivable that all men should think out their opinions, as that the world should ever improve if none did; as absurd to require even in theory, that all should

[3] John Locke (1632–1704), English philosopher.

know enough, and have time and intelligence enough to stand on their own ground, as to bind those who can to foregone conclusions. And if so, what is to become of those whose independent reason and judgment will not serve them to find their place in the world? The wise and thoughtful may claim liberty for themselves, but what liberty are the mass to have among themselves, and what is liberty to do for them? We said that Mr. Mill presupposes, in one part of his argument, that the thinkers represent mankind, as they are to be regarded in a question of this kind; but his practical estimate of the majority is of a very different kind, and it lies at the foundation of his appeal for immunity from all accountableness to their judgment on behalf of those who do use their reason. "That miscellaneous collection of a few wise and many foolish individuals called the public," how are they to get on in the strife of opinions which they cannot master, and among reasons about which they are totally incapable of judging? In one of the most striking passages in his book, Mr. Mill tells us that human affairs would be almost desperate, but for the fact that errors are corrigible.[4] Well, but they would be almost desperate, if the mass of people, the ninety-nine out of the hundred, had nothing else that they could legitimately trust to, but the opinions they could think out for themselves, and the truths which they could see with their own eyes; unless common men might hope that they are not quite deceived in their ideas of truth and good, in their sense, however fallible, and however they come by it, of right and wrong, and had some sure instinct for teachers and rules of life, which at the time, at least, were found to respond to these ideas. Things would no doubt be desperate without the correction of errors, without remedy and medicine. But to live only on the correction of errors, to live only on medicine, is desperate too. And if the argumentative worth of their reasonings is all that men, as a body, have to trust to, they are in a bad case indeed: for of the imperfection of these if of anything, reason is a competent judge, and its witness is decisive against them.

If liberty be claimed for those who can use it by having the power to think for themselves, we should have thought that at this moment they have it in most ample measure, as far as is compatible with their living at all in a society of most various and complicated relations; and that they have it in a daily-increasing degree. If the same conditions of liberty, extending to the very foundations of belief and morality, are required to pervade the whole body of society, and to be realized among the masses of common men, it seems to us that this is as impossible as it is undesirable. By that liberty is understood, in Mr. Mill's book, not merely absence of the restraints of law, but much more, the absence of the restraints, more subtle but as efficacious,

[4] Here Church quotes, in a footnote, the passage from Mill's second chapter, on pp. 62–3, starting with "When we consider" and ending with "gone through a similar process."

of social opinion. Society in the mass, the society of active life and intercourse, the society of those who have little time for thought, must take many things, and many things of the utmost importance, for granted, and take them for granted as the exclusive truth. Men in general cannot be expected to be, at the same time, examining things and admitting the possibility of their being false and wrong, and acting upon them. How many, indeed, of those whose training is of a higher kind, can face the fact of a principle being open to question, and yet act earnestly upon it as if it were true? To preserve this true balance between thought and choice, is the fruit of the highest education of the whole man, in the highest sense of the word. And common men want beliefs, principles, rules of action, and supports of life, as well as those who can think them out for themselves; and where are common men to get them, except from the common stock, which has its warrant from the society in which they live? Unless they are to pass their lives drifting to and fro on a sea of doubt among the conflicts of opinion and argument, helpless navigators and hopeless of ever acquiring the art, they must stick on to something: they may, no doubt, choose to stick on to a stronger mind; but if they may do this, they may at least as legitimately stick on to the current beliefs and ideas sanctioned by public and general agreement around them. And, on the other hand, these current beliefs and ideas which society sanctions, it does not sanction at random. It takes for or against certain views, because, at the time, the evidence seems on the whole to preponderate that way, to those who have power to win the confidence of society, to those who seem to it the wise and good; because it thinks, according to its light, that the ideas are, not merely useful, but sound and the best, and believes itself faithful to the truth disclosed to it in accepting and maintaining them. But what society accepts in this way, it must accept with an exclusiveness, a peremptory universality, which is out of place in the schools of inquiry and independent thought. It is impossible that it can be otherwise. Whatever be the opinion come to, the weight of society adopting it—which, it is to be observed, is different in moral authority from the mere weight of numbers—invests it with the finality of a law, deferred to implicitly as a rule of action by those who seek support from it, hostile to those who oppose it. Society must come to some agreement, must have some general belief for the mass of its members, about chastity: whichever way it decides—and decide it must—it must inevitably press on a disagreeing minority. If it is in favour of chastity, it must take a practical tone which restrains liberty in those who do not adhere to its ruling views, and which they will call intolerant: if it is indifferent about it, those who go along with society will resent and proscribe, and punish with the penalties which flow from the disapproval and contempt of society, opinions of a severer and less indulgent tendency. In either case—

rightly or wrongly as we may think—from the very nature of a social standard, than which the mass of ordinary men in the ordinary course of life can have no other, there must be that assumption of being right, and that moral pressure to maintain and enforce what is so assumed, and to repel the invasion or corruption of it, which would be absurd and out of place, as soon as men feel themselves qualified, and bring themselves to consent, to raise the question from the beginning, and debate it as a matter of simple argument. Abridgment of liberty is the natural and necessary consequence of the prevalence round us of strong practical opinions; and unless there are strong practical opinions, opinions which merit the name of deep and earnest convictions, it is hard to see how society can go on.

Of course, society may be wrong, or may take wrong modes of imposing its opinions and enforcing its social principles. It may be corrupt or misled; and it may be oppressive. Its beliefs and usages are shaped and consolidated not only by the wise and good, but by the foolish, and yet even more, by the half-wise and the half-good. Everybody knows how often society has wanted reform and renovation before, and may well believe that it may need it in his own time: and, doubtless, when men, singly or in crowds, have made up their minds decisively and feel strongly, they are apt to persecute. But there is a natural counterpoise for this stringency of social authority, a natural remedy for its stagnation or degeneracy, a natural antagonist to its overzeal. It is the liberty, intellectual and moral, not of all, whether they can use it or not, but of those who *can* use it: not a chimerical and impossible liberty, proposed in theory to those who, if they would, cannot by the nature of things live in society and really use it, but a liberty, proportionate to and coextensive with each man's power to examine, to judge, to form his own opinions. That which is the salt of society, that which is the source of all improvement in it, and the antidote to the stiffness and hardness which grow out of belief and usage left too long to themselves, is the play and collision of minds, thinking their own thoughts and standing on ground of their own choosing or making. Society has been kept alive, and saved when on the brink of perishing, by an independence and originality, which were the opposites to its own habits of thinking in masses, and of taking for granted the authoritative and traditional. For such thinkers liberty may be claimed—claimed in as full measure as Mr. Mill makes the claim. As little as we can see what the preaching of such liberty as the paramount idea of society at large, could do, except make its present confusions worse confounded, so strongly do we feel the force of Mr. Mill's arguments for liberty among those who have earned their right to it. We cannot see any great harm in society keeping down with a pretty strong hand much that pretends to be original and independent. It may, doubtless, make great mistakes; but it has also a strong good sense, more often right than not, which detects this very cheap and very common form of imposture and conceit; and nobody ought to complain if society is hard, and hard in proportion to the consequences of the question, on one who starts a novelty which he cannot make a good fight for, or who opens a question which he is manifestly incompetent to handle. But when men show that they know what they are talking about, their right to such freedom as is consistent with the freedom of others seems unquestionable. Let those use it, at all risks, who can show a title to do so. If men and society were perfect, if all men were equally able to think for themselves, this freedom would be coextensive with society; of course it will spread and penetrate into society, in proportion as men learn to know and think for themselves. But it is from the way in which those who can, and those who cannot, think, are mixed and jumbled together in the world as we know it, that the difficulty consists in stating and adjusting this question of liberty fairly—fairly to the individual and to society, fairly to the established and invaded, and to the invading and tentative opinions; justly to the indefinitely varying degrees of aptitude and qualification for independent thought, uninvidiously to that vast mass of serious, conscientious, and active conviction, which calm judgment must pronounce in the main unreasoning, though by no means necessarily destitute of the support of reason.

We should have thought, however, that in this country, thinkers *are* their own masters, at least to a much greater extent than Mr. Mill seems to admit. The thinkers are their own masters on their own ground. They may think and say what they please, as thinkers; and not only so, but, in spite of prejudice and clamour, they are sure of a hearing from those whose judgment is most worth appealing to, and is ultimately of the most weight with society. There is nothing that we know of to prevent in England any man of seriousness, straightforwardness, and average courage, from proposing for consideration any theory on any subject in the range of human thought and we may be pretty certain that if he says what is worth attending to, there will be people, people whose attention is worth having, who will attend to it....

In attempting, then, to simplify and generalize the doctrine of liberty, and to lay down a principle which should decide without difficulty the "endless jar" between society and individual liberty, and cut away with a clean sweep the usurpations of the former, Mr. Mill seems to us to have given too little weight to considerations which make the application of his principles far from simple. The points which chiefly strike us as overlooked by him are two. First, the way in which the mass of the people must depend more or less on society for their opinions. In urging and claiming liberty you must suppose power; and though he himself certainly does not suppose it, as a matter of fact, in the minds of people at large, his argument does.

That supposes a state of things where people of the same average capacity and training are going through life, each for himself, without needing guidance or help besides his own; and where society does not want for itself settled principles, acknowledged standards, and a pervading spirit. The reality is far otherwise. He allows that his theory of liberty, as it is not applicable to children, so it is only but very partially applicable to many previous states of society, which have been only too happy if they had "an Akbar or a Charlemagne" to give them that guidance which they could not give to themselves. Things are greatly different now, of course; but the change, however estimated, is only one of degree. There are many, doubtless, who can judge for themselves; many more who do not, but who might and ought to do so; and the relaxing of authority is, in fact, gradually going on, in proportion as men become more and more qualified to judge for themselves. But the time is certainly not come yet, nor does it seem within view, when the many can cease to lean upon each other, or upon society, for their knowledge and principles, as the few can. And till that time comes, it seems useless to talk of abrogating or ignoring an authority which practically justifies and enforces itself. The second point is, that the interests of society and of others seem to us far too closely interwoven and entangled with those of individuals to allow of that clean division which Mr. Mill's theory requires. The limits of individual liberty are, he says, from society, self-preservation; from other individuals, what concerns themselves. Suppose the rule is admitted in words, though we do not think that this is the only or the best way of expressing the truth, what endless questions open, about what "self-preservation" in society means and involves, and as to how the concerns of one individual are affected by what another is and does. Surely these limits are not so clear at first sight as to be capable of being made the basis of a ready and sweeping test between liberty and encroachment. It makes a difference to society and to others what opinions a man holds, just as truly as it makes a difference to him what amount of liberty society allows him. Society is deeply interested in what men believe, and in what rules they go by; and if society may legitimately aim at creating and fostering a national character, a common spirit; if society may, as Mr. Mill says it ought to, cultivate a certain cast of character, that is favour one and discourage its opposite; if society may *educate*;—the principle seems to us conceded, that it may take measures to make people, within large limits, it may be, yet in some real sense, good, both for themselves, and, because its own interests are involved in what they are, for its own preservation and well-being. In each case of conflict between the individual and society, the question as to the effect and tendencies of the liberty claimed will raise a debate, and, as far as we see, must in each case be decided on its merits, and with reference, it may be, to many cross and complicated interests. Doubtless society may draw to itself what does not belong to it; but the individual may quite easily judge in his own cause partially, and refuse to see how deeply what he alleges to concern only himself concerns others also. What *does* concern the individual only? is the very question to be answered in a discussion on liberty.

All that he says about the importance of individuality, and the necessity of guarding jealously its limits, so as to leave room for it to put forth its energies and grow, is forcible and important. We may differ from him as to the extent to which individuality is, as he alleges, stifled and crushed among us. He underrates, as it seems to us, the degree to which individuality of any value has a fair chance to assert itself; and he does not attend sufficiently to the fact, that the forced and stimulated individuality of mediocrities would simply be a pest and nuisance, without any countervailing advantage. But estimates and measures of these matters of fact in our contemporaries are doubtless precarious things; custom, and laziness of mind, and dull sluggish compliance, and the fear of man, and servility to our circle or our party, and the insolence of vulgar and coarse opinion, are great powers among us still; and even if Mr. Mill's statements are one-sided and scornful, we may listen with advantage to his warnings against the insidious weight of what is established and customary, his sympathy with the fear, "lest one good custom should corrupt the world,"[5] and his indignant protests against the tyranny of opinion, blindly intrusive, meddlesome, and intolerant, overbearing the individual preferences of the weak, unforgiving to the manliness and courage of the independent. We may hesitate about the dignity as well as the truth of such unqualified assertions as that "individual spontaneity is hardly recognized by the common modes of thinking, as having any intrinsic worth, or deserving any regard on its own account;" "that spontaneity forms no part of the ideal of the majority of moral and social reformers, but is rather looked upon with jealousy, as a troublesome and perhaps rebellious obstruction to the general acceptance of what these reformers in their own judgment think would be best for mankind;" that there is a general unwillingness to admit "that to possess impulses of our own and of any strength is anything but a peril and a snare;" that "it does not occur to people now to have any inclinations, except for what is customary;" that the popular "standard, express or tacit, is to desire nothing strongly," and the popular "ideal of character is to be without any marked character;" that even the intelligent part of the public have to be made to see—what, we should have thought, was almost one of the truisms of the day—"that it is good that

---

[5] See Tennyson, "The Passing of Arthur" (*Idylls of the King*): "The old order changeth, yielding place to new,/And God fulfils himself in many ways,/Lest one good custom should corrupt the world." (ll.408–10).

there should be differences, even though not for the better, even though, as it may appear to them, some should be for the worse." Surely these generalizations, to be true, require large abatement. But this does not make the statement of the general principle less impressive....But when Mr. Mill applies to particular instances his discriminating test—what concerns the individual, to liberty, what concerns society, to authority, to be enforced either by law or opinion—when he points out cases of what "may be called moral police, encroaching on the most unquestionable liberty of the individual," the absence or the smallness of interest which society has in the matter in question seems to us far too lightly assumed, and certainly not to be so clear as to leave no room for argument. The illustrations from the Mahometan feeling about pork, and the exclusiveness of religious opinion in Spain would have been better away. It seems hardly in place in a discussion like this, to take the short and easy method of seeing no difference between the "moral police" of barbarous and half-civilized people, and that of those of more advanced and thoughtful ones; of people who have, to some extent at any rate, admitted that questioning and testing of their principles which Mr. Mill is recommending, and of those who have not admitted it at all. *We* can see that Mahometan proscription of pork and Spanish intolerance are unreasonable, on their own merits, even if Turks and Spaniards cannot: and it seems affected modesty to think our opinion on the matter no better than theirs. And to say that we should have no common ground but that of liberty, in discussing the question with them, is no more than may be said of most discussions with people more ignorant than ourselves. Dr. Livingstone[6] found it impossible to gain an argumentative victory over the South African rain-doctor on the question of "medicines" making rain. Fairer and better instances are "Sabbatarian legislation," the Maine Liquor Law, and the public feeling with respect to Mormonism. With respect to Sunday legislation and the Maine Liquor Law, we agree with Mr. Mill; entirely as to the latter, and to a great extent as to the former; and though we cannot say the same about his view of Mormonism, his remarks on it deserve attention. But on all these points, whether we agree with his conclusions, or not, it appears to us that the debate arises just on the very allegation which Mr. Mill takes as his starting-point—the purely "self-regarding" character of what is interfered with. The interests of society are inextricably interlaced with what in these cases concerns the individual; his course acts upon and materially influences the general character and spirit of society—whether well or ill, or, if either well or ill, whether to such an extent as to warrant the action of society upon him, is just the difficult question, upon which opposite probabilities appear,

---

[6] David Livingstone (1813–73), Scottish medical missionary and explorer in Central Africa. Church alludes to Livingstone's *Conversation on Rain-making* in *Missionary Travels* (1857).

and on which we require to find their balance. They must each be decided on their own merits, when all the interests involved have been fairly taken into account. But in this part of the subject we seem to miss the vigorous handling with which in the earlier part of the book objections are taken up and discussed....

We cannot entirely pass over a grave subject, which must be met with in an inquiry of this kind. With broad statements like those of Mr. Mill's Essay, on the exclusive claims of liberty, there always presents itself, as their inseparable correlative and anxious attendant, their bearing on the possibility of a religion. There would be nothing specially difficult in the question, if the world were made up of philosophers, or if only the religion of those who can examine and think were concerned. But religion is for the poor and weak. Religion must be a joint thing and a thing of faith. Men must believe together, and believe without doubt; be united in a common hope, and be united in full dependence on it, for those sympathies and harmonies to be developed among them by which they are supported themselves, and support one another, in the darkness and disappointments of life, on a trust which goes beyond it. No one can look at the documents of Christianity and doubt that this religion was meant to produce the same ordinarily unquestioning faith as that, for example, of our family affections: and without that entire faith it cannot be the religion which we read of in the New Testament. If there is not faith, it may be philosophy, but not religion; and if there is faith, then, at some period or other, doubt of its truth must be cast behind. How such a state of mind is possible, either in the individual, who, on the ground of the fallibility of man and the infinite revolutions of opinion, keeps himself on continual guard against the too certain persuasion of what he holds, or in society, in which it is the normal and perpetual condition, that every conviction and belief is for ever held to be on its trial, and where public opinion, neutral about conclusions, discourages nothing but slackness of debate and the disposition to feel too positive, is a question—we are very far from saying, unanswerable, but which deserves an answer. Mr. Mill does not help us to one, or even as to whether one is to be hoped for. But throughout the discussion, we feel that it is, however latently, on uneven ground. *La partie n'est pas égale.*[7] Mr. Mill's feeling about Christianity, respectful as it is, and just as he means it to be, is not that of those who feel that anything for life and death, to them and to the world, is involved in its truth. Christians believe that Christianity is as certain as anything given to men can be, for the very reason which Mr. Mill gives for any practical certainty;—that it has been open to question and denial, and that as yet no one has adequately

[7] [*La partie n'est pas égale.*] They are not evenly matched.

produced on men at large the impression of its falsehood. They feel that hitherto nothing else has shown a *prima facie*[8] case to compete with it. Of course, if the faith of civilized nations, or of those who are the teachers of their kind or generation, is shaken in it; if people feel that as a whole, or in any of its particular doctrines, it can be effectually and seriously challenged, it, or parts of it, will fall by degrees into the class of open questions. But so far it has stood a long test, one of a practical nature, and not of the most gentle kind. It is impossible to abolish the interest felt for issues like those of religion, or their power over the mind; or to make it as little hazardous to peace to discuss God and Christ, as to discuss monarchy and republicanism. Those, then, who value Christianity cannot look with indifference on the hazard of its going out in civilized society. Their own personal grounds for believing in its truth are no guarantee against this. If truth, as Mr. Mill justly remarks, may be endangered by persecution, it may also be endangered, not, indeed, by fair and honest inquiry, but by reckless, unscrupulous, and incompetent inquiry—by a spirit of mockery, indifference, or affected freedom. The saying that truth has nothing to fear from unlimited liberty is just as much a "pleasant falsehood" as the dictum that it has nothing to fear from persecution. It *has not*, in the long run, any more than in the long run, from persecution. But it may be overborne at a particular time by accident placing intellect, as at another time, power, in the hands of its opponents: and they who rely absolutely on its intrinsic power forget that being able to argue and refute is, at any given time, a matter seemingly of chance, and that an argument which is a weak one in the hands of its present holders may prove a very different one in the hands of others. And that this danger is incident to any strong stimulus of a promiscuous and absolute liberty of thought throughout society, seems as evident, and as much attested by experience, as the danger of persecution from religious earnestness and enthusiasm. Mr. Mill makes no secret of his anxiety about the latter. Christians may be pardoned, if, feeling strongly the value of their religion, they are not without uneasiness as to the former.

There is one incidental comment of Mr. Mill's on Christianity which appears strange in a writer of his largeness of mind. We entirely assent to the truth, and not merely the truth, but the needfulness of his remark that "if Christians would teach infidels to be just to Christianity, they should themselves be just towards infidelity." But this very remark makes the grudging and stinted justice the more surprising, of his assertion that "the ideal of Christian morality (so-called) is negative rather than positive; passive rather than active; Innocence rather than Nobleness; Abstinence from Evil

---

[8] [*prima facie*] at first view.

rather than energetic Pursuit of Good; in its precepts (as has been well said) 'thou shalt not' predominates unduly over 'thou shalt.'" The assertion is the more remarkable as it is not necessary for his argument. He is answering a supposed objection to his statement that the truths that we have are commonly half-truths, requiring the supplement of other and seemingly opposite truths—an objection drawn from the allegation, that Christian morality at least is not a half-truth. It would be perfectly true to answer, that in a sense it is: that there is no evidence, that the New Testament was meant to enable us to do without the morality of nature and experience; and that in the absence of that evidence, it is no disparagement to the authority of the New Testament to say, that we are not likely to go right, if we try to do without that morality. This is no more than has been said over and over again by Christian writers. It has been acted on in the chief schools of Christian education from the beginning to the present day, where the types of natural greatness and the masters of natural wisdom have been studied with fearless and hearty frankness: and any attempt to narrow this plan, to exclude them from their influence on character and moral ideals to confine the sources of moral truth even to the most sacred of its authorities, has been condemned by the general sense of Christendom. Such an attempt, more than anything else, was the ruin of the Puritans; and it has been energetically repelled in our own day in the Roman Catholic Church of France. It is surely a common-place among most Christian teachers of any authority, that Christianity, as such, was intended to teach us what nature and the world could not teach us; but that there is much that we were meant to be and to do, which it does not, and was not intended to teach us, because we were meant to learn it elsewhere. Of course, even its teaching would be imperfect, if it has not that supplied to it which it presupposes. As regards our Lord's own words, Mr. Mill makes in effect this answer. But he goes on to draw a distinction—a just one, if fairly stated—between Christian morality as taught by Him, and that which has grown up into a system in the Christian Church. Of this latter the same remark holds good as of the former: it is a system which primarily has in view objects not of this world, which, doubtless, often really, and more often apparently, clashes with what is wise and great for this world, but which, in the hands of its best expounders, has always sounded in harmony with, and implied the co-existence of, whatever was excellent in this world. It also needs something besides itself to complete, it may be, to balance it. This was enough for Mr. Mill's argument. But he goes beyond it, and as it seems to us, out of his way, to urge his unfavourable estimate of Christian morality. And we must repeat we read it with ever-increasing surprise. Mr. Mill, strangely enough, seems to take Calvinism as the type of Christianity; and when he wants an example of Christian greatness, to compare with and set below the heathen greatness of Pericles, he chooses John Knox: yet even the characteristic features of the Christianity of John Knox, with its rugged and inflexible zeal that stirred up the world, do not tally with a supposed ideal which is "negative rather than positive—passive rather than active—Innocence rather than Nobleness—Abstinence from Evil rather than energetic Pursuit of Good." But Mr. Mill need not be told that there is a larger, more ancient, more human conception of Christian morality than that of so called Calvinism. Let us take this where we will, in its early or its later expressions. Whether sketched, assuredly with no narrow outline, by its greatest apostle—"Finally, my brethren, whatsoever things are true, whatsoever things are honest, whatsoever things are just, whatsoever things are lovely, if there be any virtue, and if there be any praise, think on these things"[9]—or exhibited even in the middle ages, in scholastic systems which incorporated with their theories, and co-ordinated with the "Graces" of the New Testament, the Virtues of Aristotle, and in poetry like that of the "Divina Commedia," which catches life from everything that is living and that is great in man—or, lastly, more calmly analyzed and enforced by preachers and moralists like Bossuet and Butler,[10]—it must have suffered a strange eclipse to the mental eye, which sees, as the predominating mark in it, a negative fear of evil, and cannot see in it, except in a subordinate degree, the appreciation and love and "energetic pursuit" of good. Such misapprehensions are among the most impressive mementos of the limited grasp of the human mind. That a man like Mr. Mill should have made such a statement; that he should express himself, "that what little recognition the idea of obligation to the public obtains in modern morality is derived from Greek and Roman sources, not from Christian"; and that "in the morality of private life, whatever exists of magnanimity, highmindedness, personal dignity, even the sense of honour, is derived from the purely human, not the religious part of our education, and never could have grown out of *a standard of ethics in which the only worth, properly recognized, is that of obedience*";—is only to be explained by remembering how great phenomena are often unrealized, even by the most powerful minds, when foreign to their usual ways of thought and life. It is an illustration, to be taken note of, and borne in mind when we are disposed to be uncharitable, of the real difficulties of fairness.

We close Mr. Mill's book, not without great admiration for much clearly and nobly said, but yet with disappointment. Nowhere has the obligation been more strongly urged on those who are responsible for truth in society, of giving a fair hearing to opposite opinions; nowhere the advantage more

[9] *Philippians* IV. 8.
[10] Jacques Bênigne Bossuet (1627–1704), French prelate and orator; Joseph Butler (1692–1752), English bishop, theologian, and moral philosopher.

forcibly set forth, to opinion and belief, of collision with real opposition. He has added one more to the varied testimonies which meet us on all sides, to the indispensable importance, in an age in which public opinion is so strong of individual character being proportionally free and strong, self-determined and self ruling. He recalls, and forces us to reflect upon, in comparison with what we see and are,—the old type of manly grandeur, independent, fearless, and great in purposes, attempts, and deeds. And the protest is not unseasonable, which he enters against what is likely to be in increasing measure the evil of modern society, the intrusiveness and impertinence, as well as the oppressiveness, of social interference and narrowmindedness. And it is a rebuke to our lazy ways of thinking; a challenge to those, who have minds fit for it, to use them in serious conflict with the difficulties of thought and life. But we cannot find in it the clear line drawn, which it was written to draw, between liberty and the claims of society. It seems to us that, after all, our philosophical view of liberty is but slightly improved; that we must still work out its problems by experience, and find their limits by mere rule of thumb, and by taking out the scales, as each case arises for settlement, first from one side and then from the other, till the balance hangs even, as we do when measuring sugar against pound weights.

The value of a philosophical doctrine depends on the completeness with which it meets various and opposite difficulties of the case. It is not enough, that it states clearly and impressively the facts of one side, or that it wraps up and contains in itself a vast amount of important truth. If it does not lay this out in order and unravel it distinctly, so that the limits of each expression of truth are truly and dearly given—so that we are not obliged to take the truth in a lump with a whole tangle of possible ambiguities and misunderstandings hanging around it, it so far fails in its claim and utility as a philosophical doctrine. Aphorisms, as Mr. Mill has said elsewhere, contain truth in this manner—unanalyzed, unlaid-out, undiscriminated, unqualified, unbalanced. But a philosophical theory professes to do just what aphorisms do not. It professes to take account of difficulties, to meet exceptions, to give full prominence and due meaning to counter-appearances, to reconcile seemingly inconsistent facts, so that we feel that they are reconciled, and their fair and real weight given to each. If it does not do this, it is so far unsatisfactory; and however alluring and captivating at first glance, it must ultimately fail of its purpose, because it will more and more be felt to be not really available for the handling of practical questions.

And we cannot but feel that, with much that is true and admirable, this is the case with Mr. Mill's Essay. It is vitiated by the principle on which, according to it, the jurisdiction of society is to be regulated. That principle seems to us to leave but one great side of human nature, which is as clearly

to be taken into account as the one on which Mr. Mill's theory lays stress,—
the way, namely, in which by natural and inevitable laws, we do take account
of the good of others, and feel ourselves bound to look after it and promote
it, even in cases where they are indifferent or hostile to it. By the only
conditions of human life and society with which we are as yet acquainted,
we are invested with influence over others, over one another, of which we
cannot divest ourselves, which we cannot help feeling, and cannot help using,
ill or well. Mr. Mill is the last man to take mere abstract views of society. He
must take things as he finds them, as they really exist—not as they would be
under other imaginable circumstances, or as it might be supposed that they
ought to be, under the supposition of man being a reasonable and responsible
being. If he had stated the limits between the two principles, which often
come into conflict,—the right of the individual to look after his own good,
and the right and duty of others and of society to do so too,—he would have
done good service; but to leave one out in theory is not to abolish it in
nature, and to make a theory with one only, omitting the other as having no
existence, is not to give us a sufficient philosophy. A theory of freedom,
without also a theory of mutual action and influence, is but a theory of part
of the social relations of men. He has told us a great deal about man, conceived
as moving among others alone as an individual: he has not told us about
man as a link in the network of society, necessarily acting on others, and
acted on by them. People who are content with a vigorous, one-sided
statement about liberty, may think that Mr. Mill has done enough. People
who think that there is another side to the matter, besides individual liberty,
will wish that it had been fairly dealt with by so powerful a mind, and will
be of opinion that there is something still to be said and cleared up on the
subject. We want those whose love of liberty is beyond suspicion to tell us
the limits and benefits of custom and control; as we want those who do not
undervalue authority to speak honestly and heartily of the claims and necessity
of liberty.

6. *Liberty, Equality, Fraternity* (London, 1873). By James Fitzjames Stephen.

[Stephen, a kind of conservative utilitarian, published a book-length critique of *On Liberty* in March 1873, and Mill read it before his death in May. He said to Alexander Bain that Stephen "does not know what he is arguing against; and is more likely to repel than to attract people." For some of the annotation in the following selections from the book I am indebted to R. J. White, whose edition of *Liberty, Equality, Fraternity* was published in 1967 by Cambridge University Press.]

1. The Doctrine of Liberty in General

THE object of this work is to examine the doctrines which are rather hinted at than expressed by the phrase "Liberty, Equality, Fraternity." This phrase has been the motto of more than one Republic. It is indeed something more than a motto. It is the creed of a religion, less definite than any one of the forms of Christianity, which are in part its rivals, in part its antagonists, and in part its associates, but not on that account the less powerful. It is, on the contrary, one of the most penetrating influences of the day. It shows itself now and then in definite forms, of which Positivism is the one best known to our generation, but its special manifestations give no adequate measure of its depth or width. It penetrates other creeds. It has often transformed Christianity into a system of optimism, which has in some cases retained and in others rejected Christian phraseology. It deeply influences politics and legislation. It has its solemn festivals, its sober adherents, its enthusiasts, its Anabaptists and Antinomians. The Religion of Humanity[1] is perhaps as good a name as could be found for it, if the expression is used in a wider sense than the narrow and technical one associated with it by Comte. It is one of the commonest beliefs of the day that the human race collectively has before it splendid destinies of various kinds, and that the road to them is to be found in the removal of all restraints on human conduct, in the recognition of a substantial equality between all human creatures, and in fraternity or general love. These doctrines are in very many cases held as a religious faith. They are regarded not merely as truths, but as truths for which those who believe in them are ready to do battle, and for the establishment of which they are prepared to sacrifice all merely personal ends.

---

[1] The name given to the "secular" religion of the English followers of the French philosopher Auguste Comte, founder of the aforementioned Positivist ideology.

Such, stated of course in the most general terms, is the religion of which I take "Liberty, Equality, Fraternity" to be the creed. I do not believe it.

I am not the advocate of Slavery, Caste, and Hatred, nor do I deny that a sense may be given to the words, Liberty, Equality, and Fraternity, in which they may be regarded as good. I wish to assert with respect to them two propositions.

First, that in the present day even those who use those words most rationally—that is to say, as the names of elements of social life which, like others, have their advantages and disadvantages according to time, place, and circumstance—have a great disposition to exaggerate their advantages and to deny the existence, or at any rate to underrate the importance, of their disadvantages.

Next, that whatever signification be attached to them, these words are ill-adapted to be the creed of a religion, that the things which they denote are not ends in themselves, and that when used collectively the words do not typify, however vaguely, any state of society which a reasonable man ought to regard with enthusiasm or self-devotion.

The truth of the first proposition as a mere general observation will not, in all probability, be disputed; but I attach to it a very much more specific meaning than is conveyed by a mere commonplace. I mean to assert that the most accredited current theories upon this subject, and those which have been elaborated with the greatest care, are unsound; and to give point to this, I say more specifically that the theories advanced upon the subject by Mr. John Mill in most of his later works are unsound. I have several reasons for referring specifically to him. In the first place, no writer of the present day has expressed himself upon these subjects with anything like the same amount either of system or of ability. In the second place, he is the only modern author who has handled the subject, with whom I agree sufficiently to differ from him profitably. Up to a certain point I should be proud to describe myself as his disciple, but there is a side of his teaching which is as repugnant as the rest of it is attractive to me, and this side has of late years become by far the most prominent. I do not say that the teaching of his works on Liberty, on Utilitarianism, and on the Subjection of Women is inconsistent with the teaching of his works on Logic and Political Economy; but I wish to show the grounds on which it is possible to agree with the greater part of the contents of the two works last mentioned, and even to maintain principles which they rather imply than assert, and at the same time to dissent in the strongest way from the view of human nature and human affairs which pervades the works first mentioned.

No better statement of the popular view—I might, perhaps, say of the religious dogma of liberty—is to be found than that which is contained in

Mr. Mill's essay on the subject. His works on Utilitarianism and the Subjection of Women afford excellent illustrations of the forms of the doctrines of equality and fraternity to which I object. Nothing is further from my wishes than to make a captious attack upon the writings of a great man to whom I am in every way deeply indebted; but in stating the grounds of one's dissent from wide-spread and influential opinions it is absolutely necessary to take some definite statement of those opinions as a starting point, and it is natural to take the ablest, the most reasonable, and the clearest.... [Here Stephen summarizes the introductory chapter of *On Liberty*.]

There is hardly anything in the whole essay which can properly be called proof as distinguished from enunciation or assertion of the general principles quoted. I think, however, that it will not be difficult to show that the principle stands in much need of proof. In order to make this clear it will be desirable in the first place to point out the meaning of the word liberty according to principles which I think are common to Mr. Mill and to myself. I do not think Mr. Mill would have disputed the following statement of the theory of human actions. All voluntary acts are caused by motives. All motives may be placed in one of two categories—hope and fear, pleasure and pain. Voluntary acts of which hope is the motive are said to be free. Voluntary acts of which fear is the motive are said to be done under compulsion, or omitted under restraint. A woman marries. This in every case is a voluntary action. If she regards the marriage with the ordinary feelings and acts from the ordinary motives, she is said to act freely. If she regards it as a necessity, to which she submits in order to avoid greater evil, she is said to act under compulsion and not freely.

If this is the true theory of liberty—and, though many persons would deny this, I think they would have been accepted by Mr. Mill—the propositions already stated will in a condensed form amount to this: "No one is ever justified in trying to affect any one's conduct by exciting his fears, except for the sake of self-protection"; or, making another substitution which he would also approve—"It can never promote the general happiness of mankind that the conduct of any persons should be affected by an appeal to their fears, except in the cases excepted."

Surely these are not assertions which can be regarded as self-evident, or even as otherwise than paradoxical. What is all morality, and what are all existing religions in so far as they aim at affecting human conduct, except an appeal either to hope or fear, and to fear far more commonly and far more emphatically than to hope? Criminal legislation proper may be regarded as an engine of prohibition unimportant in comparison with morals and the forms of morality sanctioned by theology. For one act from which one person is restrained by the fear of the law of the land, many persons are restrained from innumerable acts by the fear of the disapprobation of their neighbours, which is the moral sanction; or by the fear of punishment in a future state of existence, which is the religious sanction; or by the fear of their own disapprobation, which may be called the conscientious sanction, and may be regarded as a compound case of the other two. Now, in the innumerable majority of cases, disapprobation, or the moral sanction, has nothing whatever to do with self-protection. The religious sanction is by its nature independent of it. Whatever special forms it may assume, the fundamental condition of it is a being intolerant of evil in the highest degree, and inexorably determined to punish it wherever it exists, except upon certain terms. I do not say that this doctrine is true, but I do say that no one is entitled to assume it without proof to be essentially immoral and mischievous. Mr. Mill does not draw this inference, but I think his theory involves it, for I know not what can be a greater infringement of his theory of liberty, a more complete and formal contradiction to it, than the doctrine that there are a court and a judge in which, and before whom, every man must give an account of every work done in the body, whether self-regarding or not. According to Mr. Mill's theory, it ought to be a good plea in the day of judgment to say "I pleased myself and hurt nobody else." Whether or not there will ever be a day of judgment is not the question, but upon his principles the conception of a day of judgment is fundamentally immoral. A God who punished any one at all, except for the purpose of protecting others, would, upon his principles, be a tyrant trampling on liberty.

The application of the principle in question to the moral sanction would be just as subversive of all that people commonly regard as morality. The only moral system which would comply with the principle stated by Mr. Mill would be one capable of being summed up as follows: "Let every man please himself without hurting his neighbour"; and every moral system which aimed at more than this, either to obtain benefits for society at large other than protection against injury or to do good to the persons affected, would be wrong in principle. This would condemn every existing system of morals. Positive morality is nothing but a body of principles and rules more or less vaguely expressed, and more or less left to be understood, by which certain lines of conduct are forbidden under the penalty of general disapprobation and that quite irrespectively of self-protection. Mr. Mill himself admits this to a certain extent. In the early part of his fourth chapter he says that a man grossly deficient in the qualities which conduce to his own good is "necessarily and properly a subject of distaste, or in extreme cases even of contempt," and he enumerated various inconveniences to which this would expose such a person. He adds, however: "The inconveniences which are strictly inseparable from the unfavourable judgment of others are the only ones to which a person should ever be subjected for that portion of his conduct and character which concerns his own "good", but which does not affect the interests of others in their relation with him." This no doubt weakens the effect of the admission; but be this how it may, the fact still remains that morality is and must be a prohibitive system, one of the main objects of which is to impose upon every one a standard of conduct and of sentiment to which few persons would conform if it were not for the constraint thus put upon them. In nearly every instance the effects of such a system reach far beyond anything that can be described as the purposes of self-protection.

Mr. Mill's system is violated not only by every system of theology which concerns itself with morals, and by every known system of positive morality, but by the constitution of human nature itself. There is hardly a habit which men in general regard as good which is not acquired by a series of more or less painful and laborious acts. The condition of human life is such that we must of necessity be restrained and compelled by circumstances in nearly every action of our lives. Why, then, is liberty, defined as Mr. Mill defines it, to be regarded as so precious? What, after all, is done by the legislator or by the person who sets public opinion in motion to control conduct of which he disapproves—or, if the expression is preferred, which he dislikes—which is not done for us all at every instant of our lives by circumstances? The laws which punish murder or theft are substitutes for private vengeance, which, in the absence of law, would punish those crimes more severely, though in a less regular manner. If there were laws which punished incontinence, gluttony, or drunkenness, the same might be said of them. Mr. Mill admits in so many words that there are "inconveniences which are strictly inseparable from the unfavourable judgment of others." What is the distinction in principle between such inconveniences and similar ones organized, defined, and inflicted upon proof that the circumstances which call for their infliction exist? This organization, definition, and procedure make all the difference between the restraints which Mr. Mill would permit and the restraints to which he objects. I cannot see on what the distinction rests. I cannot understand why it must always be wrong to punish habitual drunkenness by fine, imprisonment, or deprivation of civil rights, and always be right to punish it by the infliction of those consequences which are "strictly inseparable from the unfavourable judgment of others." It may be said that these consequences follow, not because we think them desirable, but in the common order of nature. This answer only suggests the further question, whether nature is in this instance to be regarded as a friend or as an enemy? Every reasonable man would answer that the restraint which the fear of the disapprobation of others imposes on our conduct is the part of the constitution of nature which we could least afford to dispense with. But if this is so, why draw the line where Mr. Mill draws it? Why treat the penal consequences of disapprobation as things to be minimized and restrained within the narrowest limits? What "inconvenience," after all, is "strictly inseparable from the unfavourable judgment of others"? If society at large adopted fully Mr. Mill's theory of liberty, it would be easy to diminish very greatly the inconveniences in question. Strenuously preach and rigorously practise the doctrine that our neighbour's private character is nothing to us, and the number of unfavourable judgments formed, and therefore the number of inconveniences inflicted by them, can be reduced as much as we please, and the province of liberty can be enlarged in a corresponding ratio. Does any reasonable man wish for this? Could any one desire gross licentiousness, monstrous extravagance, ridiculous vanity, or the like, to be unnoticed, or, being known, to inflict no inconveniences which can possibly be avoided?

If, however, the restraints on immorality are the main safeguards of society against influences which might be fatal to it, why treat them as if they were bad? Why draw so strongly marked a line between social and legal penalties? Mr. Mill asserts the existence of the distinction in every form of speech. He makes his meaning perfectly clear. Yet from one end of his essay to the other I find no proof and no attempt to give the proper and appropriate proof of it. His doctrine could have been proved if it had been true. It was not proved because it was not true.

Each of these propositions may, I think, be established by referring to the commonest and most important cases of coercion for other purposes than those of self-protection. The most important of them are:

1. Coercion for the purpose of establishing and maintaining religions.
2. Coercion for the purpose of establishing and practically maintaining morality.
3. Coercion for the purpose of making alterations in existing forms of government or social institutions.

None of these can in the common use of language be described as cases of self-protection or of the prevention of harm to persons other than those coerced. Each is a case of coercion, for the sake of what the persons who exercise coercive power regard as the attainment of a good object, and each is accordingly condemned, and the first and second were no doubt intended to be condemned, by Mr. Mill's principle. Indeed, as he states it, the principle would go very much further. It would condemn, for instance, all taxation to which the party taxed did not consent, unless the money produced by it was laid out either upon military or upon police purposes or in the administration of justice; for these purposes only can be described as self-protective. To force an unwilling person to contribute to the support of the British Museum is as distinct a violation of Mr. Mill's principle as religious persecution. He does not, however, notice or insist upon this point, and I shall say no more of it than that it proves that his principle requires further limitations than he has thought it necessary to express.

Returning, then, to the three kinds of coercion mentioned, I say that it was Mr. Mill's business to show not merely that they had had bad effects—it would be as superfluous to show that surgical operations have bad effects—but that the bad effects arose from the coercion itself, irrespectively of the objects for which it was employed, and of the mistakes and excesses of those who employed it. He had to show not that surgery is painful, or that the loss of a limb is a calamity, or that surgeons are often unskilful or rash, but that surgery is an art bad in itself, which ought to be suppressed. This, I say, he has never attempted to show from the beginning of the book to the end of it. If he had, he would have found his task an impossible one. As regards coercion for the purpose of establishing and maintaining religions and systems of morality it would be waste of time to insist upon the principle that both religion and morals are good on the whole, notwithstanding the evils of various kinds which have been connected with them. Nor need I repeat what I have already said on the point that both religion and morality are and always must be essentially coercive systems. Taking these matters for granted, however, it will be desirable to consider somewhat more fully the nature of moral and religious coercion, and the manner in which they operate. If Mr. Mill's view of liberty had always been adopted and acted upon to its full extent—if it had been the view of the first Christians or of the first Mohammedans—everyone can see that there would have been no such thing as organised Christianity or Mohammedanism in the world. Even after such success as these and other religions have obtained, the morality of the vast mass of mankind is simply to do what they please up to the point at which custom puts a restraint upon them, arising from the fear of disapprobation. The custom of looking upon certain courses of conduct with aversion is the essence of morality, and the fact that this aversion may be felt by the very person whose conduct occasions it, and may be described as arising from the action of his own conscience, makes no difference which need be considered here. The important point is that such disapprobation could never have become customary unless it had been imposed upon mankind at large by persons who themselves felt it with exceptional energy, and who were in a position which enabled them to make other people adopt their principles and even their tastes and feelings.

Religion and morals, in a word, bear, even when they are at their calmest, the traces of having been established, as we know that in fact they were, by word of command. We have seen enough of the foundation of religions to know pretty well what is their usual course. A religion is first preached by a single person or a small body of persons. A certain number of disciples adopt it enthusiastically, and proceed to force their views upon the world by preaching, by persuasion, by the force of sympathy, until the new creed has become sufficiently influential and sufficiently well organised to exercise power both over its own members and beyond its own sphere. This power, in the case of a vigorous creed, assumes many forms. It may be military power, if the early converts are fighting men; it may be power derived from threats as to a future state—and this is the commonest and most distinctive form of religious power of which we have practical experience. It may be power derived from mere superior energy of will, or from organisations which those who possess that energy are able to set on foot by means of it. But, be the special form of religious power what it will, the principle is universally true that the growth of religions is in the nature of a conquest made by a small number of ardent believers over the lukewarmness, the indifference, and the conscious ignorance of the mass of mankind....

As for the third set of cases in which coercion is habitually employed—I mean coercion for the purpose of making alterations in existing forms of government and social institutions—it surely needs no argument to show that all the great political changes which have been the principal subject of European history for the last three centuries have been cases of coercion in the most severe form, although a large proportion of them have been described as struggles for liberty by those who were, in fact, the most vigorous wielders of power.

Mr. Mill and his disciples would be the last persons in the world to say that the political and social changes which have taken place in the world since the sixteenth century have not on the whole been eminently beneficial to mankind; but nothing can be clearer than that they were brought about by force, and in many instances by the force of a minority numerically small, applied to the conduct of an ignorant or very partially informed and for the most part indifferent majority. It would surely be as absurd to say that the Reformation or the French Revolution was brought about freely and not by coercion as to say that Charles I[2] walked freely to the block. Each of these and many other cases which might be mentioned were struggles for political power, efforts to bring about a change in the existing state of things, which for various reasons appeared desirable to people who were able to carry out their designs more or less successfully.

---

[2] Title of Charles Stuart (1600–1649). King of England from 1625 until beheading in 1649.

To say that force was justifiable in none of these cases would be a paradox which Mr. Mill would probably be the last person to maintain. To say that it was justifiable only in so far as it was necessary for self-protection would not explain the facts. Take such a case as the establishment of a new religion and the reduction of an old one to the position of a permitted form of private opinion. Life has gone on for ages upon the supposition of the truth of the old religion. Laws and institutions of various kinds are founded upon it. The great mass of the population of a country have no particular wish to disturb the existing state of things even though they may be ceasing to believe in the creed which it implies. Innovators arise who attack corruptions and preach new doctrine. They are punished. They resist, sides are formed, and the results follow with which history is filled. In what sense can it be said that the acts of violence which take place on such occasions are acts done in self-defence and in order to prevent harm? They are acts of aggression upon an established system which is regarded as bad, and with a view to the substitution of a different system which it is supposed will be better. If any one supposes that in regard to such transactions it is possible to draw a line between what ought to be done and what ought not; if any one will undertake to say how the French Revolution or the Reformation ought to have been conducted so as to avoid all violence on both sides and yet to arrive at the desired conclusion, he will be able to give us a universal political constitution and a universal code of laws. People in such positions as those of Charles V, Philip II, Henry VIII, Queen Elizabeth, Louis XVI, and many others, must take a side, and must back it vigorously against its antagonists, unless they mean to be devoured themselves.

The only way by which this can be reconciled with Mr. Mill's principle is by describing such violence as a case of self-protection. Now if the word "self-protection" is so construed as to include every act of violence done for the purpose of procuring improvements in the existing state of things it will follow that if men happen to be living under a political or social system with the principles or with the working of which they are not satisfied, they may fight out their difference, and the conqueror may determine the matter in dispute according to his own will, which reduces the principle to an absurdity. On the other hand, if no act of violence done for the purpose of improving the existing state of things is described as a case of self-protection, no such act is justifiable, unless it is necessary for the immediate protection of the agent. This again is an absurdity.

The truth is that the principle about self-protection and self-regarding acts is not one by which the right or wrong of revolutions can be measured, because the distinction upon which it depends is radically vicious. It assumes that some acts regard the agent only, and that some regard other people. In fact, by far the most important part of our conduct regards both ourselves and others, and revolutions are the clearest proof of this. Thus, Mr. Mill's principle cannot be applied to the very cases in which it is most needed. Indeed, it assumes the existence of an ideal state of things in which everyone has precisely the position which, with a view to the general happiness of the world, he ought to hold. If such a state of things existed there would be some plausibility in saying that no one ought to interfere with anyone else except for the sake of protecting himself against attack, by maintaining the existing state of things. But as no such state of things exists or ever yet existed in any age or country, the principle has at present no *locus standi*.[3]

Not only is an appeal to facts and experience opposed to Mr. Mill's principle, but his essay contains exceptions and qualifications which are really inconsistent with it. He says that his principle "is meant to apply to human beings only in the maturity of their faculties," and, he adds, "we may leave out of account those backward states of society in which the race itself may be considered in its nonage." Despotism, he says, "is a legitimate mode of government in dealing with barbarians, provided the end be their improvement, and the means justified by actually effecting that end. Liberty as a principle has no application to any state of things anterior to the time when mankind have become capable of being improved by free and equal discussion. Until then there is nothing for them but implicit obedience to an Akbar or a Charlemagne if they are so fortunate as to find one. But as soon as mankind have attained the capacity of being guided to their own improvement by conviction or persuasion (a period long since reached in all nations with whom we need here concern ourselves), compulsion is no longer admissible as a means to their own good, and is justifiable only for the security of others."

It seems to me that this qualification either reduces the doctrine qualified to an empty commonplace which no one would care to dispute, or makes an incredible assertion about the state of human society. No one, I suppose, ever denied either in theory or in practice that there is a sphere within which the tastes of people of mature age ought not to be interfered with, and within which differences must be regarded as natural and inevitable—in which better or worse means that which the individual prefers or dislikes. On the other hand, no one ever suggested that it was or could be good for anyone to be compelled to do what he did not like, unless the person compelling was not only stronger but wiser than the person compelled, at all events in reference to the matter to which the compulsion applied.

[3] [*locus standi*] recognized standing.

Either, then, the exception means only that superior wisdom is not in every case a reason why one man should control another—which is a mere commonplace—or else it means that in all the countries which we are accustomed to call civilised the mass of adults are so well acquainted with their own interests and so much disposed to pursue them that no compulsion or restraint put upon any of them by any others for the purpose of promoting their interests can really promote them.

No one can doubt the importance of this assertion, but where is the proof of it? Let us consider how it ought to have and would have been proved if it had been capable of proof. Mr. Mill might have specified the different classes of which some considerable nation—our own, for instance—is composed. Then he might have stated what are the objects which, if attained, would constitute the happiness of each of those classes. Then he might have shown that a knowledge of those interests, a knowledge of the means by which they must be attained, and a disposition to make use of the means proper to obtain them, was so generally diffused among each class that no compulsion put by the other classes upon any one class as a whole, or by any part of any class upon any other part of it, could increase the happiness of the persons compelled to such an extent as to overbalance the pain of the compulsion itself. Before he affirmed that in Western Europe and America the compulsion of adults for their own good is unjustifiable, Mr. Mill ought to have proved that there are among us no considerable differences in point of wisdom, or that if there are, the wiser part of the community does not wish for the welfare of the less wise.

It seems to me quite impossible to stop short of this principle if compulsion in the case of children and "backward" races is admitted to be justifiable; for, after all, maturity and civilisation are matters of degree. One person may be more mature at fifteen than another at thirty. A nation or a particular part of a nation may make such an advance in the arts of life in half a century that other nations, or other parts of the same nation, which were equally civilised at the beginning of the period, may be relatively barbarous at the end of it.

I do not overlook the qualification contained in the passages quoted above. It fixes the limit up to which compulsion is justifiable at the "time when mankind have become capable of being improved by free and equal discussion." This expression may imply that compulsion is always or never justifiable, according to the manner in which it is construed. I am not quite sure that I know what Mr. Mill means by "equal" discussion, but was there ever a time or place at which no men could be improved on any point by free discussion? The wildest savages, the most immature youths, capable of any sort of education, are capable of being improved by free discussion upon a great variety of subjects. Compulsion, therefore, in their own interests would, at least in relation to these subjects, be unjustifiable as regards them. If boys in a school can be convinced of the importance of industry, you must never punish them for idleness. Such an interpretation of the rule would practically exclude compulsion altogether.

A narrower interpretation would be as follows. There is a period, now generally reached all over Europe and America, at which discussion takes the place of compulsion, and in which people when they know what is good for them generally do it. When this period is reached, compulsion may be laid aside. To this I should say that no such period has as yet been reached anywhere, and that there is no prospect of its being reached anywhere within any assignable time.

Where, in the very most advanced and civilised communities, will you find any class of persons whose views or whose conduct on subjects on which they are interested are regulated even in the main by the results of free discussion? What proportion of human misconduct in any department in life is due to ignorance, and what to wickedness or weakness? Of ten thousand people who get drunk, is there one who could say with truth that he did so because he had been brought to think on full deliberation and after free discussion that it was wise to get drunk? Would not every one of the ten thousand, if he told the real truth, say in some dialect or other—"I got drunk because I was weak and a fool, because I could not resist the immediate pleasure for the sake of future and indefinite advantage"? If we look at the conduct of bodies of men as expressed in their laws and institutions, we shall find that, though compulsion and persuasion go hand in hand, from the most immature and the roughest ages and societies up to the most civilised, the lion's share of the results obtained is due to compulsion, and that discussion is at most an appeal to the motives by which the strong man is likely to be actuated in using his strength. Look at our own time and country, and mention any single great change which has been effected by mere discussion. Can a single case be mentioned in which the passions of men were interested where the change was not carried by force—that is to say, ultimately by the fear of revolution? Is it in any degree true that when the brains are out a question dies? Look at small matters which involve more or less of a principle, but do not affect many men's passions, and see how much reasoning has to do with their settlement. Such questions as the admission of Jews into Parliament[4] and the legalisation of marriage between brothers and sisters-in-law drag on and on after the argument has been

---

[4] The first Jewish Emancipation bill was debated in Parliament in 1830; Jews were not admitted to Parliament until 1858.

exhausted, till in course of time those who take one view or the other grow into a decided majority, and settle the matter their own way. Parliamentary government is simply a mild and disguised form of compulsion. We agree to try strength by counting heads instead of breaking heads, but the principle is exactly the same. It is not the wisest side which wins, but the one which for the time being shows its superior strength (of which no doubt wisdom is one element) by enlisting the largest amount of active sympathy in its support. The minority gives way not because it is convinced that it is wrong, but because it is convinced that it is a minority.

This again suggests an observation on a different part of the passage quoted from Mr. Mill. In rough states of society he admits of Charlemagnes and Akbars, if the world is so fortunate as to have them at hand. What reason is there to suppose that Charlemagnes or Akbars owe their power to enlightenment superior to that of the persons whom they coerce? They owe it to greater force of character and to the possession of power. What they did was to suppress anarchy—to substitute the vigorous rule of one Sovereign for the jarring pretensions of a crowd of petty rulers. No doubt powerful men are generally comparatively enlightened men, as were both Charlemagne and Akbar, for knowledge is a high form of power, as light implies intense force. But power in whatever form is the essential thing. Anarchy may be mischievous in civilised as well as in uncivilised life, and the only way out of it is by coercion. To direct that power aright is, I think, the principal object of political argument. The difference between a rough and a civilised society is not that force is used in the one case and persuasion in the other, but that force is (or ought to be) guided with greater care in the second case than in the first. President Lincoln attained his objects by the use of a degree of force which would have crushed Charlemagne and his paladins and peers like so many eggshells.

The correctness of the assertion that "in all nations with whom we need here concern ourselves," the period at which "mankind have become capable of being improved by free and equal discussion has long since arrived," may be estimated by reference to two familiar points:

1. Upon all the subjects which mainly interest men as men—religion, morals, government—mankind at large are in a state of ignorance which in favourable cases is just beginning to be conscious that it is ignorance. How far will free discussion carry such knowledge as we have on these subjects? The very most that can be hoped for—men being what they are—is to popularise, more or less, a certain set of commonplaces, which, by the condition of their existence, cannot possibly be more than half-truths. Discussion produces plenty of effects, no doubt. People hunger and thirst after theories to such a degree that whatever puts their own wishes into a

compact and intelligible form will obtain from them a degree of allegiance which may be called either touching or terrible. Look at the great popular movements which discussion has provoked, and consider what approach any one of them made to the real truth. Innumerable creeds, religious and political, have swept across the world, arguing, preaching, gesticulating, and fighting. Compare the amount of recognition which the worst of them has obtained and the devotion which it has called forth with the degree of really intelligent appreciation which has been awarded to science. Millions upon millions of men, women, and children believe in Mahommed to the point of regulating their whole life by his law. How many people have understood Adam Smith? Did anybody, except perhaps Mr. Buckle, ever feel any enthusiasm about him?...

2. Men are so constructed that whatever theory as to goodness and badness we choose to adopt, there are and always will be in the world an enormous mass of bad and indifferent people—people who deliberately do all sorts of things which they ought not to do, and leave undone all sorts of things which they ought to do. Estimate the proportion of men and women who are selfish, sensual, frivolous, idle, absolutely commonplace and wrapped up in the smallest of petty routines, and consider how far the freest of free discussion is likely to improve them. The only way by which it is practically possible to act upon them at all is by compulsion or restraint. Whether it is worth while to apply to them both or either I do not now inquire; I confine myself to saying that the utmost conceivable liberty which could be bestowed upon them would not in the least degree tend to improve them. It would be as wise to say to the water of a stagnant marsh, "Why in the world do not you run into the sea? you are perfectly free. There is not a single hydraulic work within a mile of you. There are no pumps to suck you up, no defined channel down which you are compelled to run, no harsh banks and mounds to confine you to any particular course, no dams and no flood-gates; and yet there you lie, putrefying and breeding fever, frogs, and gnats, just as if you were a mere slave!" The water might probably answer, if it knew how, "If you want me to turn mills and carry boats, you must dig proper channels and provide proper waterworks for me."

2. On the Liberty of Thought and Discussion

Though, as I pointed out in my last chapter, Mr. Mill rather asserts than proves his doctrines about liberty, the second chapter of his essay on the Liberty of Thought and Discussion, and the third chapter on Individuality as one of the Elements of Well-being may be regarded as arguments to prove certain parts or applications of the general principle asserted in his introduction; and as such I will consider them. I object rather to Mr. Mill's theory than to his practical conclusions. I hope to show hereafter how far the practical difference between us extends. The objection which I make to most of his statements on the subject is, that in order to justify in practice what might be justified on narrow and special grounds, he lays down a theory incorrect in itself and tending to confirm views which might become practically mischievous....

The chapter [on Liberty of Thought and Discussion] in question is, I think, one of the most eloquent to be found in its author's writings, and it contains, as is not unfrequently the case with him, illustrations which are even more valuable for what they suggest than for what they say.

These illustrations are no doubt the part of this chapter which made the deepest impression when it was first published, and which have been most vividly remembered by its readers. I think that for the sake of them most readers forget the logical framework in which they were set, and read the chapter as a plea for greater freedom of discussion on moral and theological subjects. If Mr. Mill had limited himself to the proposition that in our own time and country it is highly important that the great questions of morals and theology should be discussed openly and with complete freedom from all legal restraints, I should agree with him. But the impression which the whole chapter leaves upon me is that for the sake of establishing this limited practical consequence, Mr. Mill has stated a theory which is very far indeed from the truth, and which, if generally accepted, might hereafter become a serious embarrassment to rational legislation.

His first reason in favour of unlimited freedom of opinion on all subjects is this: "If any opinion is compelled to silence, that opinion may, for aught we can certainly tell, be true. To deny this is to assume our own infallibility."

He states fairly and fully the obvious objection to this—that "there is no greater presumption of infallibility in forbidding the propagation of error than in any other thing which is done by public authority on its own judgment and responsibility." In other words, the assumption is not that the persecutor is infallible, but that in this particular case he is right. To this objection he replies as follows: "There is the greatest difference between presuming an opinion to be true because, with every opportunity for contesting it, it has not been refuted, and assuming its truth for the purpose of not permitting its refutation. Complete liberty of contradicting our opinion is the very condition which justifies us in assuming its truth for purposes of action; and on no other terms can a being with human faculties have any rational assurance of being right."

This reply does not appear to me satisfactory. It is not very easy to disentangle the argument on which it rests, and to put it into a perfectly distinct shape, but I think it will be found on examination to involve the following propositions:

1. No one can have a rational assurance of the truth of any opinion whatever, unless he is infallible, or unless all persons are absolutely free to contradict it.
2. Whoever prevents the expression of any opinion asserts by that act that he has a rational assurance of the falsehood of that opinion.
3. At the same time he destroys one of the conditions of a rational assurance of the truth of the assertions which he makes, namely, the freedom of others to contradict him.
4. Therefore he claims infallibility, which is the only other ground on which such an assurance of the truth of those assertions can rest.

The first and second of these propositions appear to me to be incorrect. As to the first, I think that there are innumerable propositions on which a man may have a rational assurance that he is right whether others are or are not at liberty to contradict him, and that although he does not claim infallibility. Every proposition of which we are assured by our own senses, or by evidence which for all practical purposes is as strong as that of our own senses, falls under this head. There are plenty of reasons for not forbidding people to deny the existence of London Bridge and the river Thames, but the fear that the proof of those propositions would be weakened or that the person making the law would claim infallibility is not among the number.

A asserts the opinion that B is a thief. B sues A for libel. A justifies. The jury give a verdict for the plaintiff, with 1000 pounds damages. This is nearly equivalent to a law forbidding every one, under the penalty of a heavy fine, to express the opinion that in respect of the matters discussed B is a thief. Does this weaken the belief of the world at large in the opinion that in respect of those matters B is not a thief? According to Mr. Mill, no one can have a rational assurance upon the subject unless every one is absolutely free to contradict the orthodox opinion. Surely this cannot be so.

The solution seems to be this. The fact that people are forbidden to deny a proposition weakens the force of the inference in its favour to be drawn from their acquiescence in it; but the value of their acquiescence considered as evidence may be very small, and the weight of other evidence, independent of public opinion, may not only be overwhelming, but the circumstances of the case may be such as to be inconsistent with the supposition that any further evidence will ever be forthcoming. Again, an opinion may be silenced without any assertion on the part of the person who silences it that it is false. It may be suppressed because it is true, or because it is doubtful whether it is true or false, and because it is not considered desirable that it should be discussed. In these cases there is obviously no assumption of infallibility in suppressing it. The old maxim, "the greater the truth the greater the libel," has a true side to it, and when it applies it is obvious that an opinion is silenced without any assumption of infallibility. The opinion that a respectable man of mature years led an immoral life in his youth may be perfectly true, and yet the expression of that opinion may be a crime, if it is not for the public good that it should be expressed.

In cases in which it is obvious that no conclusion at all can be established beyond the reach of doubt, and that men must be contented with probabilities, it may be foolish to prevent discussion and prohibit the expression of any opinion but one, but no assumption of infallibility is involved in so doing. When Henry VIII and Queen Elizabeth silenced to a certain extent both Catholics and Puritans, and sought to confine religious controversy within limits fixed by law, they did not assume themselves to be infallible. What they thought—and it is by no means clear that they were wrong—was that unless religious controversy was kept within bounds there would be a civil war, and they muzzled the disputants accordingly.

There are, in short, two classes of cases to which, as it appears to me, Mr. Mill's argument does not apply—cases in which moral certainty is attainable on the evidence, and cases in which it is not attainable on the evidence.

Where moral certainty is attainable on the evidence the suppression of opinion involves no claim to infallibility, but at most a claim to be right in the particular case.

Where moral certainty is not attainable on the evidence the suppression of opinion involves no claim to infallibility, because it does not assert the falsehood of the opinion suppressed.

The three remaining arguments in favour of unlimited liberty of thought and discussion are:

1. That the silenced opinion may be partially true and that this partial truth can be brought out by discussion only.
2. That a true opinion when established is not believed to be true unless it is vigorously and earnestly contested.

3. That it comes to be held in a dead conventional way unless it is discussed.

These arguments go to show, not that the suppression of opinion can never be right, but that it may sometimes be wrong, which no one denies. None of them show—as the first argument would if it were well founded— that persecution in all cases proceeds on a theory involving distinct intellectual error. As to the first argument, it is obvious that if people are prepared to take the chance of persecuting a proposition which may be wholly true as if it were wholly false, they will be prepared to treat it in the same manner though it is only partially true. The second and third arguments, to which I shall have to return hereafter, apply exclusively to that small class of persons whose opinions depend principally upon the consciousness that they have reached them by intellectual processes correctly performed. The incalculable majority of mankind form their opinions in quite a different way, and are attached to them because they suit their temper and meet their wishes, and not because and in so far as they think themselves warranted by evidence in believing them to be true. The notorious result of unlimited freedom of thought and discussion is to produce general scepticism on many subjects in the vast majority of minds. If you want zealous belief, set people to fight. Few things give men such a keen perception of the importance of their own opinions and the vileness of the opinions of others as the fact that they have inflicted and suffered persecution for them. Unlimited freedom of opinion may be a very good thing, but it does not tend to zeal, or even to a distinct appreciation of the bearings of the opinions which are entertained. Nothing will give either but a deep interest in the subject to which those opinions relate, and this is so personal and deeply seated a matter that it is scarcely capable of being affected by external restraints, unless, indeed, it is irritated and so stimulated by them.

I pass over for the present the illustrations of this chapter, which, as I have already said, are by far the most important part of it; and I proceed to the chapter on Individuality as one of the Elements of Well-being.

The substance of the doctrine eloquently expounded in it is that freedom is essential to originality and individuality of character. It consists, however, almost entirely of eulogies upon individuality, to which Mr. Mill thinks the world is indifferent. He accordingly sets forth at length the advantage of having vigorous impulses and plenty of them, of trying experiments in life, of leaving every man of genius free, not indeed "to seize on the government of the world and make it do his bidding in spite of itself," but to "point out the way." This individuality and energy of character, he thinks, is dying out under various depressing influences. "The Calvinistic theory" regards "the crushing out the human faculties, capacities, and susceptibilities," as "no evil," inasmuch as "man needs no capacity but that of surrendering himself to the will of God, and if he uses any of his faculties for any other purpose but to do that supposed will more effectually he is better without them." Apart, however, from this, "society has now fairly got the better of individuality." All of us are enslaved to custom. "Energetic characters on any large scale are becoming merely traditional. There is now scarcely any outlet for energy in this country except business." "The only unfailing and permanent source of improvement is Liberty, since by it there are as many possible independent centres of improvement as there are individuals." Individuality, however, is at a discount with us, and we are on the way to a Chinese uniformity. Much of what I had to say on this subject has been anticipated by an article in "Fraser's Magazine".[5] It expands and illustrates with great vigour the following propositions, which appear to me to be unanswerable:

1. The growth of liberty in the sense of democracy tends to diminish, not to increase, originality and individuality. "Make all men equal so far as laws can make them equal, and what does that mean but that each unit is to be rendered hopelessly feeble in presence of an overwhelming majority?" The existence of such a state of society reduces individuals to impotence, and to tell them to be powerful, original, and independent is to mock them. It is like plucking a bird's feathers in order to put it on a level with beasts, and then telling it to fly.
2. "The hope that people are to be rendered more vigorous by simply removing restrictions seems to be as fallacious as the hope that a bush planted in an open field would naturally develope into a forest tree. It is the intrinsic force which requires strengthening, and it may even happen in some cases that force will produce all the more effect for not being allowed to scatter itself."
3. Though goodness is various, variety is not in itself good. "A nation in which everybody was sober would be a happier, better, and more progressive, though a less diversified, nation than one of which half the members were sober and the other half habitual drunkards."

I might borrow many other points from the excellent essay in question, but I prefer to deal with the matter in my own way, and I will therefore add some remarks in confirmation and illustration of the points for which I am indebted to the writer.

[5] This article, on "Social Macadamisation" (in the August 1872 issue of *Fraser's*) was written by Fitzjames Stephen's brother, Leslie Stephen, father of Virginia Woolf.

The great defect of Mr. Mill's later writings seems to me to be that he has formed too favourable an estimate of human nature. This displays itself in the chapter now under consideration by the tacit assumption which pervades every part of it that the removal of restraints usually tends to invigorate character. Surely the very opposite of this is the truth. Habitual exertion is the greatest of all invigorators of character, and restraint and coercion in one form or another is the great stimulus to exertion. If you wish to destroy originality and vigour of character, no way to do so is so sure as to put a high level of comfort easily within the reach of moderate and commonplace exertion. A life made up of danger, vicissitude, and exposure is the sort of life which produces originality and resource. A soldier or sailor on active service lives in an atmosphere of coercion by the elements, by enemies, by disease, by the discipline to which he is subjected. Is he usually a tamer and less original person than a comfortable London shopkeeper or a man with just such an income as enables him to do exactly as he likes? A young man who is educated and so kept under close and continuous discipline till he is twenty-two or twenty-three years of age will generally have a much more vigorous and more original character than one who is left entirely to his own devices at an age when his mind and his tastes are unformed. Almost every human being requires more or less coercion and restraint as astringents to give him the maximum of power which he is capable of attaining. The maximum attainable in particular cases depends upon something altogether independent of social arrangements—namely, the nature of the human being himself who is subjected to them; and what this is or how it is to be affected are questions which no one has yet answered....

There is one more point in this curious chapter which I must notice in conclusion. Nothing can exceed Mr. Mill's enthusiasm for individual greatness. The mass, he says, in all countries constitute collective mediocrity. They never think at all, and never rise above mediocrity, "except in so far as the sovereign many have let themselves be guided and influenced (which in their best times they always have done) by the counsels and influence of a more highly gifted or instructed one or few. The initiation of all wise or noble things comes and must come from individuals; generally at first from some one individual." The natural inference would be that these individuals are the born rulers of the world, and that the world should acknowledge and obey them as such. Mr. Mill will not admit this. All that the man of genius can claim is "freedom to point out the way. The power of compelling others into it is not only inconsistent with the freedom and development of all the rest, but corrupting to the strong man himself." This would be perfectly true if the compulsion consisted in a simple exertion of blind force, like striking a nail with a hammer; but who ever acted so on others to any extent worth mentioning? The way in which the man of genius rules is by persuading an efficient minority to coerce an indifferent and self-indulgent majority, which is quite a different process.... Mr. Mill worships mere variety, and confounds the proposition that variety is good with the proposition that goodness is various....

If this advice [to encourage eccentricity] were followed, we should have as many little oddities in manner and behaviour as we have people who wish to pass for men of genius. Eccentricity is far more often a mark of weakness than a mark of strength. Weakness wishes, as a rule, to attract attention by trifling distinctions, and strength wishes to avoid it. Originality consists in thinking for yourself, not in thinking differently from other people.

7. *Fortnightly Review* 20 (August 1873), 234–56. By John Morley.

[John Morley (1838–1923), disciple of Mill, was a liberal journalist and author, the editor of *Fortnightly Review* and *Macmillan's Magazine*, and also a politician, chief secretary for Ireland and secretary of state for India. Much of Morley's essay is a defense of *On Liberty* against the strictures of Stephen's book of 1873. Also included here, in the footnotes, are several of Stephen's rejoinders to Morley's criticisms of him; these appeared in the second edition (1874) of *Liberty, Equality, Fraternity*.]

Mr. Mill's Doctrine of Liberty

MR. MILL'S memorable plea for social liberty was little more than an enlargement, though a very important enlargement, of the principles of the still more famous Speech for Liberty of Unlicensed Printing with which Milton ennobled English literature two centuries before.[1] Milton contended for free publication of opinion mainly on these grounds: First, that the opposite system implied the "grace of infallibility and incorruptibleness" in the licensers. Second, that the prohibition of bold books led to mental indolence and stagnant formalism both in teachers and congregations, producing the "laziness of a licensing church." Third, that it "hinders and retards the importation of our richest merchandise, truth", for the commission of the licenser enjoins him to let nothing pass which is not vulgarly received already, and "if it come to prohibiting, there is not aught more likely to be prohibited than truth itself, whose first appearance to our eyes, bleared and dimmed with prejudice and custom, is more unsightly and implausible than many errors, even as the person is of many a great man slight and contemptible to see to." Fourth, that freedom is in itself an ingredient of true virtue, and "they are not skilful considerers of human things who imagine to remove sin by removing the matter of sin; that virtue therefore, which is but a youngling in the contemplation of evil, and knows not the utmost that vice promises to her followers, and rejects it, is but a blank virtue, not a pure; her virtue is but an excremental virtue, which was the reason why our sage and serious poet Spenser, whom I dare be known to think a better teacher than Scotus or Aquinas,[2] describing true temperance under the form of Guion, brings

---

[1] John Milton (1608–74), *Areopagitica* (1644).
[2] Edmund Spenser (1552?–99), published Books I–VI of *The Faerie Queene*, referred to here, in 1596. Duns Scotus (1265?–1308), Scottish philosopher and theologian. Saint Thomas Aquinas (1225–74), Italian Dominican monk, philosopher, and theologian.

him in with his Palmer through the cave of Mammon and the tower of earthly bliss, that he might see and know and yet abstain."…

If people believe that the book of social or moral knowledge is now completed, that we have turned over the last page and heard the last word, much of the foundation of Mr. Mill's doctrine would disappear. But those who hold this can hardly have much to congratulate themselves upon. If it were so, and if governments were to accept the principle that the only limits to the enforcement of the moral standard of the majority are the narrow expediencies of each special case, without reference to any deep and comprehensive principle covering all the largest social considerations, why then the society to which we ought to look with most admiration and envy is the Eastern Empire during the ninth and tenth centuries, when the Byzantine system of a thorough subordination of the spiritual power had fully consolidated itself.

Mr. Stephen's recent examination of Mr. Mill's doctrine does not seem to contribute much to its rectification. Many passages in that examination read as if the author had not by any means grasped the principle which he repudiates in so operose a manner. The dialectic has an imposing air of strictness and cogency, yet it continually lands you in the fallacy of Irrelevancy. Mr. Stephen labours certain propositions which Mr. Mill never denied, such as that society ought to have a moral standard and ought to act upon it. He proves the contradictory of assertions which his adversary never made, as when he cites judicial instances which imply the recognition of morality by the law.[3] He wishes to prove that social coercion would in many cases tend to make men virtuous. He does so by proving that the absence of coercion does not tend in such cases to make men virtuous. Of course the latter proposition is no more equivalent to the former, than the demonstration of the inefficacy of one way of treating disease is equal to a demonstration of the efficacy of some other way.[4] A short glance at some of Mr. Stephen's propositions will be a convenient mode of setting Mr. Mill's doctrine in a clearer light.

1. "Before he affirmed that in Western Europe and America the compulsion of adults for their own good is unjustifiable, Mr. Mill ought to have proved

---

[3] Rejoinder by Stephen: "Mr Morley says…: 'Mr Stephen…proves the contradictory of assertions which his adversary never made, as when he cites judicial instances which imply the recognition of morality by the law.' I think Mr Morley misunderstands my argument, which nevertheless appears to me very plain. It is simply this: I say laws can and do promote virtue and diminish vice by coercion in the cases and in the ways specified, and their interference does more good than harm. The contradictory of this proposition would be that in the cases specified legal interference does more harm than good. Surely if Mr Mill's general principle is true, this must follow from it. Therefore in denying it I deny a necessary inference from the principle which I attack."

that there are among us no considerable differences in point of wisdom, or that if there are, the wiser part of the community does not wish for the welfare of the less wise." Why so? Mr. Mill's very proposition is that though there is a wiser part, and though the wiser part may wish well to the less wise, yet even then the disadvantages of having a wise course forced upon the members of civilised societies exceed the disadvantages of following an unwise course freely. Mr. Stephen's allegation of the points which Mr. Mill should have proved, rests on the assumption of the very matter at issue—namely, whether freedom is not in itself so valuable an element in social life (in civilised communities), that for the sake of it we should be content to let the unwiser part have their own way in what concerns themselves only.[5]

2. "Look at our own time and country, and mention any single great change which has been effected by mere discussion. Can a single case be mentioned in which the passions of men were interested where the change was not carried by fear—that is to say ultimately by the fear of revolution?" It may be said, parenthetically, first, that it was free discussion which converted the force, and brought it over to the side of the change; say Free Trade, or the Reform of Parliament, or the Irish Land Act. And secondly, that there is all the difference between the fear of a revolution and a revolution actual, and this is a powerful argument in favour of the unlimited discussion which Mr. Mill vindicates, and of the social system that favours it. But, apart from this, have these great changes been made by force in the sphere which Mr. Mill set apart from the operation of force? Was the imposition of the corn-duties a purely self-regarding act? Did the duties hurt nobody but

[4] Rejoinder by Stephen: "Mr Morley says of me, 'Mr Stephen wishes to prove that social coercion would in many cases tend to make men virtuous. He does so by proving that the absence of coercion does not tend in such cases to make men virtuous. Of course, the latter proposition is no more equivalent to the former than the demonstration of the inefficacy of one way of treating disease is equal to, or demonstrative of the efficacy of some other way.' [In fact] I argue that all organized religions, all moral systems, and all political institutions, are so many forms of coercion for purposes extending beyond self-protection, and that they have done great good. Of course, if Mr Mill or his disciples can show that religion, law, and morals have in fact done more harm than good they answer me; but surely the burden of proof is on them. I say first (positively), the fact that law, morals, and religion are beneficial proves that coercion is beneficial; secondly (negatively), experience shows that in many cases the absence of coercion is not beneficial; and Mr Morley charges me with proving the first proposition by the second. Each is, in fact, proved independently...."

[5] Rejoinder by Stephen: "Mr Morley quotes only a part of my argument, which is this: 'You admit that children and human beings in "backward states of society" may be coerced for their own good. You would let Charlemagne coerce the Saxons, and Akbar the Hindoos. Why then may not educated men coerce the ignorant? What is there in the character of a very commonplace ignorant peasant or petty shopkeeper in these days which makes him a less fit subject for coercion on Mr Mill's principle than the Hindoo, nobles and princes who were coerced by Akbar?'"

the imposers? Was the exclusion of householders under ten pounds rental from the electoral body a self-regarding act? If not, Mr. Stephen is only beating the air by this talk about force being the *ultima ratio*.[6] It is an organic part of Mr. Mill's doctrine that the whole social force may be exerted in matters which concern others than the doers. Then, Mr. Stephen retorts, "the principle cannot be applied to the very cases in which it is most needed— cases where men happen to be living under a political or social system with the principles or with the working of which they are not satisfied, and in which they may fight out their differences, the conqueror determining the matter in dispute according to his own will." Is this in the least degree true? Take the most memorable of these cases, the first French Revolution. Will Mr. Stephen seriously contend that the principle of leaving self-regarding acts alone could not have been applied to any parts of that transaction? Hardly so, if he reflects that the most monstrous acts of the Revolution were exactly due to the neglect of this very truth, that there is a province of thought and action—the self-regarding, namely—which ought to be free from social or legislative interference. It was precisely because the Jacobins, headed by Robespierre and Saint Just[7], borrowed the principles of Hobbes and Rousseau,[8] as Mr. Stephen does; it was precisely because they rode roughshod over such a principle as Mr. Mill's, interfered alike with self-regarding conviction and self-regarding act, and adopted Mr. Stephen's formula of the *à priori*[9] expediency of identifying the law-maker and the moralist, that the worst exploits and most fantastic aspirations which are associated with the French Revolution stained and perverted the movement. To say therefore that Mr. Mill's principle is incapable of application in the cases where it is most needed, or that "it assumes the existence of an ideal state of things in which every one has precisely the position which he ought to hold," is either to forget the most tremendous event in modern history, or else to show that you have never fully considered what Mr. Mill's principle is.[10]

---

[6] [*ultima ratio*] final argument.
[7] Maximilien Francois Marie Isidore de Robespierre (1758–94), French revolutionary leader; Louis Antoine Léon de Saint-Just (1767–94), French revolutionary leader.
[8] Thomas Hobbes (1588–1679), English philosopher; Jean-Jacques Rousseau (1712–78), French political philosopher.
[9] [*à priori*] reasoning from cause to effect; deductive.
[10] Rejoinder by Stephen: "Mr Morley seems to have thought that I meant to say that in a revolution every sort of intolerance and fanaticism was right. I meant only to show that Mr Mill's fundamental distinction about self-regarding acts is shown by the case of revolutions to be quite unequal to the weight which he lays upon it, though of course there are cases in which as a mere practical rule, it would be useful in revolutions as well as at other times."

3. "If the object aimed at is good, if the compulsion employed such as to attain it, and *if the good obtained overbalances the inconvenience of the compulsion, I do not understand how upon utilitarian principles the compulsion can be bad.* I may add that this way of stating the case shows that Mr. Mill's simple principle is really a paradox. It can be justified only by showing as a fact that, self-protection apart, no good object can be attained by any compulsion which is not in itself a greater evil than the absence of the object which the compulsion obtains." The words in italics are introduced in a way, and have a significance, which show that, strange as it may appear, Mr. Stephen failed from beginning to end of his criticism to see that the very aim and object of Mr. Mill's essay is to show on utilitarian principles that compulsion in a definite class of cases, the self-regarding parts of conduct namely, and in societies of a certain degree of development, is always bad. Mr. Stephen's third proviso in the above quotation could never be complied with in self-regarding acts, according to his adversary's doctrine, and that it could never be complied with, was the central object of Mr. Mill's reasoning. He did show, or thought he had shown, that "as a fact," the good obtained in self-regarding acts could not overbalance the general inconvenience of the compulsion. I do not see that Mr. Stephen has anywhere directly confronted this position in the only manner proper to confute it, namely, by an enumeration, first, of the advantages of compulsion in self-regarding acts, second, of its disadvantages, followed by an attempt to strike the balance between the sum of the advantages and the sum of the disadvantages. The last three lines of the above quotation involved a similar misunderstanding. What Mr. Mill had to show was, not that any good object attained by compulsion was "in itself" a greater evil than the absence of the object procured by the compulsion, but something quite different, namely this; that though compulsion may procure objects which are good, yet the general consequences of the compulsion more than counterbalance the special good. Thus, to take a well-known illustration; sobriety might perhaps be procured by some form of coercive legislation, but the evil inherent in such legislation, its enervating effect on character, its replacement of self-control, self-respect, and the rest, by a protective paternal will from without, would more than counterbalance the advantages of sobriety so gained. This may be a mistake. Mr. Mill may or may not prove his case. But where is the sense of calling such a position a paradox?

Hence Mr. Stephen's third and favourite test of the utility of coercion,— that it should not be employed at too great an expense—is a mere *ignoratio elenchi*[11] as against Mr. Mill, who held that in all self-regarding matters it

---

[11] [*ignoratio elenchi*] ignorance of the point in dispute; the fallacy of appearing to refute an opponent by arguing an unraised point.

was necessarily employed at too great an expense. This position Mr. Mill defended on strictly utilitarian principles....Mr. Stephen has missed one of the cardinal points in the whole contention, that "it is of importance not only what men do, but also what manner of men they are that do it." It is its robust and bracing influence on character which makes wise men prize freedom, and strive for the enlargement of its province. "They are not skilful considerers of human things," wrote Milton, "who imagine to remove sin by removing the matter of sin. Though ye take from a covetous man his treasure, he has yet one jewel left, ye cannot bereave him of his covetousness. Banish all objects of lust, shut up all youth into the severest discipline that can be exercised in any hermitage, ye cannot make them chaste that came not thither so. Suppose we could expel sin by this means; look how much we thus expel of sin, so much we expel of virtue. And were I the chooser, a dram of well-doing should be preferred before many times as much the forcible hindrance of evil-doing. For God sure esteems the growth and completing of one virtuous person more than the restraint of ten vicious."

The same omission to recognise that the positive quality of liberty is the essence of the doctrine which Mr. Stephen has hastily taken upon himself to disprove, is seen in such statements as that "Discussions about liberty are in truth discussions about a negation. Attempts to solve the problems of government and society by such discussions are like attempts to discover the nature of light and heat by inquiries into darkness and cold." This, by the way, is not so felicitous as Mr. Stephen's illustrations sometimes are, for assuredly he would be a very wretched kind of investigator who thought he could discover the laws of heat without reference to the conditions of cold, or the laws of light without reference to the conditions of darkness. But is it true that liberty is a negation? You may certainly say, if you choose, that freedom from import duties is a negation, but even then I am not aware that the comparative advantages of free trade and protection are incapable of being profitably discussed. Mr. Mill, however, held that liberty was much more than a negation; and that there is plenty of evidence in the various departments of the history of civilisation that freedom exerts a number of positively progressive influences. It was Mr. Stephen's business to refute this, if he could. That he has failed to do so, further than by a number of blunt assertions and reassertions to the contrary, is a proof either that he was not able to refute the most essential part of Mr. Mill's doctrine, or else that he did not perceive in what its essential part consisted. Metaphors about wasps in a garden, and imaginary dialogues with the waters of a stagnant marsh, and the like, really do not help us. Mr. Stephen had to prove two things. First he had to show that freedom from interference in the expression of opinion and in purely self-regarding acts, is not a good thing in its general consequences. Most people, he says, cannot be improved by free discussion. "I confine myself to saying that the utmost conceivable liberty would not in the least degree tend to improve them." But he should not have confined himself to saying this. He should have tried to demonstrate it, which I cannot see that he does. Second, Mr. Stephen had to show that though liberty cannot improve people, compulsion or restraint can. Instead of this, he takes for granted that because liberty would not improve people, therefore compulsion must. An assumption that begs the whole question at issue.

Mr. Carlyle, more tersely than Mr. Stephen, has boldly said, in one of the *Latter-Day Pamphlets*,[12] that most people are fools. Mr. Mill himself in the book which has occasioned the present controversy has said something of the same sort. The essay on Liberty is in fact one of the most aristocratic books ever written (I do not mean British aristocratic, "with the politest and gracefullest kind of woman to wife"). It is not Mr. Carlyle, but Mr. Mill, who speaks of "that miscellaneous collection of a few wise and many foolish individuals, called the public." "No government by a democracy or a numerous aristocracy ever did or could rise above mediocrity, except in so far as the sovereign Many have let themselves be guided by the counsel and influence of the more highly gifted and instructed One or Few. The initiation of all wise or noble things comes and must come from individuals; generally at first from some one individual." "On any matter not self-evident, there are ninety-nine persons totally incapable of judging of it, for one who is capable." In the face of passages like these it is rather absurd to say that "the great defect of Mr. Mill's later writings is that he has formed too favourable an estimate of human nature"; and it is particularly absurd in a writer who, two hundred pages further on in the very same book, assures us that it would be easy to show from Mr. Mill's later works, "what a low opinion he has of mankind at large." Which of the two contradictory assertions that he has made does Mr. Stephen elect to stand by?

But now mark the use which Mr. Mill makes of his proposition that ninety-nine men are incapable of judging a matter not self-evident, and only one man capable. For this reason, he argues, leave the utmost possible freedom of thought, expression, discussion, to the whole hundred, because on no other terms can you be quite sure that the judgment of the hundredth man, the one judgment you want, will be forthcoming or will have a chance of making itself effectively heard over the incapable judgments. Mr. Stephen says otherwise. He declares it to be an idle dream "to say that one man in a thousand really exercises much individual choice as to his religious or moral principles, and I doubt whether it is not an exaggeration to say that one man

---

[12] *Latter-Day Pamphlets* (1850).

in a million is capable of making any very material addition to what is already known or plausibly conjectured on these matters."*Argal*,[13] beware of accepting any nonsensical principle of liberty which shall leave this millionth man the best possible opening for making his material addition; by the whole spirit of your legislation, public opinion, and social sentiment, habitually discourage, freeze, browbeat, all that eccentricity which would be sure to strike all the rest of the million in the one man and his material addition. If Mr. Stephen's book does not mean this, it means nothing, and his contention with Mr. Mill's doctrine of liberty is only a joust of very cumbrous logomachy.

We can thus understand how Mr. Stephen comes to accuse Mr. Mill of worshipping mere variety and "confounding the proposition that variety is good with the proposition that goodness is various." Mr. Mill deliberately held that variety is good on the ground that it is the essential condition of the appearance and growth of those new ideas, new practices, new sentiments, some of which must contain the germs of all future improvements in the arts of existence. It shows an incapacity to understand the essence of the doctrine, to deal with it by such statements as that it involves "a worship of mere variety." It plainly does no such thing. Mr. Mill prizes variety, not at all as mere variety, but because it furnishes most chances of new forms of good presenting themselves and acquiring a permanent place. He prized that eccentricity which Mr. Stephen so heartily dislikes, because he perceived that all new truth and new ways of living, must from the nature of things always appear eccentric to persons accustomed to old opinions and old ways of living; because he saw that most of the personages to whom mankind owes its chief steps in moral and spiritual advance were looked upon by contemporaries as eccentrics, and very often cruelly ill treated by them (on Mr. Stephen's principles) for eccentricity, which was in truth the very deliverance of humanity from error or imperfection. Not all novelties are improvements, but all improvements are novel, and you can only, therefore, be sure of improvements by giving eccentricity a fair hearing, and free room for as much active manifestation as does no near, positive, recognisable, harm to other people.[14]

Mr. Stephen, however, has a very qualified faith in improvement. He seems to think that the only change in the world is the constant multiplication of the total number of its inhabitants. One of the most extraordinary pieces in his book is a very strained passage after the manner of Mr. Carlyle—only not every one can bend the bow of the great Ulysses—to the effect that the world is like a sort of Stilton cheese, filled with so many millions of

---

[13] [*Argal*] therefore. Used humorously to indicate a clumsy or absurd reasoning; alteration of Latin *ergo*, therefore.

indomitable cheese-mites. Apart from the lofty poetic quality and delicate picturesqueness of the trope, it carries its author too far. If men are cheese-mites, I do not see why, for example, able lawyers should strain every nerve, writing articles, reading papers, urging politicians, stimulating ministers, merely in order that a puny group of these cheese-mites, say as many as you could press up on a thumb-nail—to sustain the nobility of the image—may have their laws done up into a code. Mr. Carlyle was much more consistent. He told men they were shadows, and he pursued with loud bursts of not always musical laughter, Political Economy, and Bentham, and parliamentary Reform, and everything else that has made the England of to-day a better place for men or mites to live in than it was half a century ago. Mr. Stephen, to do him justice, gives us very little of this kind of talk. It would be the stultification of his own special ability if he did so. For law, equally with freedom, is only interesting and only worth a serious man's attention in the way of reform, in so far as the progress and the improvement which Mr. Stephen burlesques in the above passage are substantive realities. But his conception of the possibilities of improvement is a narrow one. He draws hard and fast lines in respect of each of the greater interests of men, and anything beyond them he brands as eccentric and chimerical. Mr. Stephen some years ago hurt the feelings of old fashioned metaphysicians by delineating the case of an imaginary world in which two straight lines should be universally supposed to include a space. It is a matter of regret that he has not an equally courageous and powerful imagination in the region of morals. If he had, he would have less trouble in sympathizing with the idea that the

---

[14] Rejoinder by Stephen: "This seems to me like saying 'genuine banknotes are so valuable that for their sake forged banknotes ought to be encouraged.' To regard mere variety as furnishing most chances of new forms of good presenting themselves and acquiring a permanent place is to assume that people cannot be trusted to judge any variety or alteration upon its merits. This appears to me altogether unjust. The truth appears to be that in this, as in other parts of his writings, Mr Mill assumed that the common standards of good and evil were so thoroughly wrong that if men exercised any discretion as to the varieties which they would encourage or discourage, they would do more harm than good, and that, therefore, in the present bad state of affairs the best thing to do was to encourage all varieties. This view is quite intelligible, though I do not agree with it."

"As to eccentricity, surely the common use of language confines the word to affected oddity of behaviour. No one, I should suppose, would have called Mr Mill 'eccentric' for his peculiar views about women. If he had worn a strange dress, or kept different hours from every one else, or indulged in any other apparently unreasonable whim, he would have been eccentric. The eccentricity which, as Mr Morley says, I 'heartily dislike,' is merely affectation. It would, I think, be hard to show that the great reformers of the world have been persecuted for 'eccentricity.' They were persecuted because their doctrines were disliked, rightly or wrongly as the case might be. The difference between Mr Mill's views and mine is that he instinctively assumes that whatever is is wrong. I say, try each case on its own merits."

limits of human improvement, though they exist in every direction, have as yet not only not been reached, but are not even viable. And if he had appreciated this idea he would have seen deeper into Mr. Mill's principle than to detect, in one of the conditions attending it, nothing beyond a worship of mere variety.

And after all, even if it were so, is he warranted in taking for granted that worship of variety is less creditable or in any way more singular than worship of unity? Whatever the value of progress may be, says Mr. Stephen, "unity in religious belief would further it." But we really cannot be expected to take Mr. Stephen's authority for this. Such a proposition is one part of the great question at issue. I am not aware that the Byzantine empire, where there eventually existed a more complete unity of belief than has ever existed in any other part of Christendom, was the scene of any remarkable furtherance of progress in consequence. Or take the great theocracies, ancient Egypt, Islam under the Caliphs, India under Buddhists or Brahmins. What element of progress did this unity give? Is not unity of religious belief the very note of stationary societies? It is no doubt true that unity in religious belief as in other things will slowly draw nearer, as the result of the gradual acceptance by an increasing number of men of common methods of observing and interpreting experience. As Mr. Mill says —"As mankind improve, the number of doctrines which are no longer disputed or doubted will be constantly on the increase; and the well-being of mankind may almost be measured by the number and gravity of the truths which have reached the point of not being contested." But all the consequences of this quasi-unity may not prove to be beneficial, or favourable to progress, nor is it at all clear, as Mr. Stephen takes for granted, that unity of religious belief would further progress, unless you replaced the discussions to which such unity had put an end, by some other equally dividing subject of equal interest to an equal number of people.[15] In Mr. Stephen's opinion it would be impossible ever to find any other such subject, for he lays down the proposition which, I confess, strikes me as truly extravagant that, "If we were all of one mind, and that upon reasonable grounds, about the nature of men, and their relation to the world or worlds in which they live, [this is equivalent to previous expressions about "the attainment of religious truth"], we should be able *at once and with but little difficulty* to solve all the great moral and political questions which at present distract and divide the world."

[15] Rejoinder by Stephen: "This is exactly in Mr Mill's vein, and I must own that the nervous fear that a time may possibly come when there will be nothing left to argue about appears to me about as reasonable as the 'thought of the exhaustibility of musical combinations of the seven tones and semitones which make up the octave,' by which Mr Mill tells us (Autobiography) he was 'seriously tormented' at one time of his life."

4. A good deal of rather bustling ponderosity is devoted to proving that the actual laws in many points do assume the existence of a standard of moral good and evil, and that this proceeding is diametrically opposed to Mr. Mill's fundamental principles. To this one would say, first, that the actual existence of laws of any given kind is wholly irrelevant to Mr. Mill's contention, which is, that it would be better if laws of such a kind did not exist. Second, Mr. Mill never says, nor is it at all essential to his doctrine to hold, that a government ought not to have "a standard of moral good and evil, which the public at large have an interest in maintaining and in many cases enforcing." He only set apart a certain class of cases to which the right or duty of enforcement of the current standard does not extend—the self-regarding cases.[16] Mr. Stephen would not have been any wider of the mark if he had devoted an equal number of pages to demonstrating against Mr. Mill that not only society, but an individual, ought to have a standard of good and evil, which he is to maintain through good report and ill report. Mr. Mill no more denied this of a government than he denied it of an individual. All he said was—"It is a mistake to enforce your standard on me, if my non-recognition of it does no harm to any one but myself. Clearly there is a number of matters—lying, unchastity, and so forth—in which there is no attempt to enforce the recognised standard of good and evil. I extend this class of neglected breaches of the current laws of morals, so as to include all self-regarding matters whatever." Consequently, the statement that the assumption of a standard of moral good and evil which the public at large have an interest in many cases in enforcing, is diametrically opposed to Mr. Mill's fundamental principle, involves a misunderstanding of that principle; and such a statement ignores the plain fact that this principle does emphatically recognise the right of the state to enforce that part of its moral code which touches such acts as are not self-regarding.

[16] Rejoinder by Stephen: "As to the first point, surely it is not irrelevant to show that Mr Mill is at issue with the practical conclusions to which most nations have been led by experience. Those to whom I address myself may be disposed to doubt whether a principle which condemns so many of the institutions under which they live can be right.

"As to the second point, Mr Mill says in express words: 'Society, as society, has no right to decide anything to be wrong which concerns only the individual.' This I think is equivalent to denying that society ought to have a moral standard, for by a moral standard I understand a judgment that certain acts are wrong, whoever they concern. Whether they concern the agent only or others as well, is and must be an accident. Mr Morley, however, thinks that Mr Mill's opinion was that society may and ought to have a moral standard, but ought not to enforce it in the case of self-regarding acts. I say, and attempt throughout the whole of this chapter to prove, that as regards the 'moral coercion of public opinion,' this is neither possible nor desirable, and that as regards legal coercion, the question whether it is possible and desirable depends upon considerations drawn from the nature of law, civil and criminal. Whether I am right or wrong I cannot see that I have not understood Mr Mill, or that I have not contradicted him."

A similar neglect to master the real position taken by Mr. Mill is shown in Mr. Stephen's remarks about Pilate, and his parallel of the case of a British officer confronted by a revolutionary teacher in India. "If it is said that Pilate ought to have respected the principle of religious liberty as propounded by Mr. Mill, the answer is that if he had done so, he would have run the risk of setting the whole province in a blaze." Then in such a case Mr. Mill expressly lays down the limitation proper to the matter, in a passage to which Mr. Stephen appears not to have paid attention. "No one pretends," says Mr. Mill, "that actions should be as free as opinions. On the contrary, even opinions lose their immunity when the circumstances in which they are expressed are such as to constitute a positive instigation to some mischievous act."[17]

5. Let us take a concrete case with which Mr. Stephen furnishes us. "A set of young noblemen of great fortune and hereditary influence, the representatives of ancient names, the natural leaders of the society of large districts, pass their whole time and employ all their means in gross debauchery. Such people are far more injurious to society than common pickpockets, but Mr. Mill says that if any one having the opportunity of making them ashamed of themselves uses it in order to coerce them into decency, he sins against liberty, unless their example does assignable harm to specific people. It might be right to say, 'You the Duke of A. by extravagantly keeping four mistresses, set an example which induced your friend F. to elope with Mrs. G. and you are a great blackguard for your pains, and all the more because you are a duke.' It could never be right to say, 'You, the Duke of A. are scandalously immoral and ought to be made to smart for it, though the law cannot touch you.'"

[17] Rejoinder by Stephen: "Mr Morley says upon this that I do not understand Mr Mill. 'Mr Mill expressly lays down the limitation proper to the matter in a passage to which Mr Stephen appears not to have paid attention. "Even opinions lose their immunity when the circumstances in which they are expressed are such as to constitute a positive instigation to the mischievous act."' I think it is Mr Morley, in this case, who misunderstands my argument, or rather does not think it worth while to understand it. The passage quoted from Mr Mill is in substance only a way of saying that you may throw the abetment of a crime into the form of the expression of an opinion. No doubt you may do so. You may also throw it into the form of the statement of a fact, as was done by the courtier of Ahasuerus, who, when Haman got into disgrace, casually observed, "Behold, also, the gallows which Haman has set up." My argument upon Pilate's case is that the mere preaching of a religion which relates principally to matters of belief and self-regarding acts may, under circumstances, tend to disturb the existing social order. If in that case the representatives of the existing social order persecute the religion it appears to me that the question whether they are right or wrong depends on the comparative merits of the religion which is persecuted and the social order which persecutes. Whether Pilate was right in thinking that what took place in Judea threatened social order directly or indirectly we cannot tell, but it was his business by all means to protect social order. This is directly opposed to the whole of Mr Mill's chapter about the liberty of discussion."

But these two forms of remonstrance by no means exhaust the matter. An advocate of Mr. Mill's principle might say to the debauched duke one of three things: (*a*) "Your grace ought to be made to smart, only it is not worth while for the sake of making a poor creature like you smart, to invoke a principle which would endanger really fruitful experiments in living." (*b*) "We are much indebted to you for destroying your influence and character. Society will be more than compensated for the loss of your social services by the admirable deterrent effect which so hideous a spectacle as your grace, so conspicuous as your high station makes you, will exert over other dukes and men, in spite of your friend F., who imitates you. You are the Helot among dukes." (*c*) "My duke, codifiers and others would like to make you smart by law. We less peremptory heads perceive that you do smart. You smart by being the poor gross creature you are." Any of these rebukes would lie in the mouths of those who accepted Mr. Mill's principle, while the single rebuke which Mr. Stephen has imputed to such persons is the least adequate of the four, and is certainly not the rebuke to be found in the Essay on Liberty.[18]

Take another case put by Mr. Stephen:—

"A number of persons form themselves into an association for the purpose of countenancing each other in the practice of seducing women, and giving the widest possible extension to the theory that adultery is a good thing. They carry out their objects by organizing a system for the publication and circulation of lascivious novels and pamphlets calculated to inflame the passions of the young and inexperienced. The law of England would treat this as a crime. It would call such books obscene libels, and a combination for such a purpose a conspiracy. Mr. Mill would not only regard this as wrong, but he would regard it as an act of persecution if the newspapers were to excite public indignation against the parties concerned by language going one step beyond the calmest discussion of such an experiment in living."

I venture to propound two questions to Mr. Stephen. Is the practice of seducing women a self-regarding practice? And is the circulation of pamphlets calculated to inflame the passions of the young an act that hurts nobody but the circulator? The answer to these questions shows the illustration to be

---

[18] Rejoinder by Stephen: "Mr Morley says: 'But these two forms of remonstrance by no means exhaust the number. An advocate of Mr Mill's principle might say to the debauched duke one of three things' (which he goes on to specify). Once more Mr Morley totally misunderstands me. The object of the illustration is to expose the futility of Mr Mill's distinction between the cases in which you may and the cases in which you may not find fault with a man for vice, which is that you may do so when his vice inflicts specific injury on a definite person, and not otherwise. Thus the gist of the charge against the Duke of A would be that his example hurt F. To use the language of special pleading, the declaration would be demurrable unless it averred special damage. This, I say, is futile. It deserves notice that Mr Morley has not a word to say on the argument of which this illustration is a very subordinate part."

utterly pointless. It shows the assertion that on Mr. Mill's principles police interference would be wrong and public anger would be of the nature of persecution, to be a prodigious piece of misrepresentation. There was in the last century a famous case exactly in point, that of Wilkes and the Franciscans of Medmenham Abbey. These debauchees were as gross and scandalous a set of profligates as ever banded together. But they conformed to the conditions laid down in the doctrine of liberty, and no one thought of interfering with them. The law in this respect was conformable to Mr. Mill's principle. The exception to this non-interference shows the true side of this principle, and confirms the popular acceptance of it, under the circumstances described in Mr. Stephen's imaginary and, for the purposes of the discussion, quite inapposite case. Wilkes printed at his private press a few copies of the *Essay on Woman*, a ribald poem. The government contrived by corrupting a compositor to obtain a copy of it, it was ordered that Wilkes should be prosecuted for publishing a blasphemous libel, and he was convicted by the Court of King's Bench. This conviction has always been held a miscarriage of law, because there was no real publication. Mr. Mill's doctrine condemns the prosecution of Wilkes for the *Essay on Woman*, as all public opinion since has condemned it. A man has a right to keep poisons in his closet, it has been finely said, though he has no right publicly to distribute them for cordials—which is exactly Mr. Mill's position. Does Mr. Stephen hold that Wilkes was justifiably punished for this improperly imputed crime? If not, where is the force of his illustration?[19]

6. At the bottom of all Mr. Stephen's argumentation lies a fundamental reluctance to admit that there are such things as self-regarding acts at all. This reluctance implies a perfectly tenable proposition, a proposition which has been maintained by nearly all religious bodies in the world's history in their non-latitudinarian stages. Comte denied the existence of such a division among acts, and made care of health, cleanliness, sobriety, and the rest, into social obligations.[20] Mr. Stephen does not exactly deny either the possibility or the expediency of recognising the distinction between acts that affect only the doer and acts that affect the rest of society; but if he does not deny this, neither does he admit it, nor treat admission of it as all important to the controversy. Yet that, I submit, ought to have been the field of his discussion on Mr. Mill's doctrine, for it is from that that the other differences really spring. In default of this larger principle, he is constantly obliged to fall back on illustrations of the consequences which might, and very probably would, happen to other people from conduct that seems fairly definable as self-regarding. There is one objection obviously to be made to these illustrations. The connection between the act and its influence on others is so remote, using the word in a legal sense, though quite certain, distinct,

and traceable, that you can only take the act out of the self-regarding category, by a process which virtually denies the existence of any such category. You must set a limit to this "indirect and at a distance argument," as Locke called a similar plea, and the setting of this limit is the natural supplement to Mr. Mill's "simple procedure." Set it where you will, it must, to be a limit at all, come a long way short of Mr. Stephen's notion of self-protection.

In fact Mr. Stephen has failed to state in a definite and intelligible way his conception of the analysis of conduct on which the whole doctrine of

---

[19] Rejoinder by Stephen: "Upon this Mr Morley says: 'I venture to propound two questions to Mr Stephen. (1) Is the practice of seducing women a self-regarding practice? (2) Is the *circulation* of pamphlets calculated to inflame the passions of the young an act which hurts nobody but the circulator?'"

"I reply that each of these questions must, on Mr Mill's principles (though not on mine), be answered in the affirmative. As to the first, according to Mr Mill, the seduction of a woman, force and fraud apart, is distinctly a self-regarding act. The man's act regards the man, and the woman's act regards the woman. In passages already quoted Mr Mill distinctly justifies the toleration of fornication on the ground that society as society has no business to decide anything to be wrong which concerns only the individual. He doubts whether this extends to the case of a pimp; but surely seduction is an even more personal matter than fornication. To question 2 (whether the circulation of pamphlets calculated to inflame the passions of the young is an act which hurts nobody but the circulator), I answer Yes, on Mr Mill's principles it is, though not on mine. The whole of his argument on the liberty of thought and discussion is directed to prove the proposition that the 'appropriate region of human liberty' includes 'absolute freedom of opinion and sentiment on all subjects, *practical* or speculative, scientific, moral, or theological'; and he adds, 'The liberty of expressing and publishing opinions may seem to fall under a different principle, since it belongs to that part of the conduct of an individual which concerns other people, but being almost of as much importance as the liberty of thought itself, and resting in great part on the same reasons, is practically inseparable from it.'"

"Having regard to these quotations, I continue the quotation from Mr Morley: 'The answer to these questions shows the illustration to be utterly pointless.' That is, he would answer each in the negative."

"Which of us has misrepresented Mr Mill, Mr Morley or I?"

"Mr Morley goes on to state the case of Wilkes and the Franciscans of Medmenham Abbey. 'These debauchees', he says, 'were as gross and scandalous a set of profligates as ever banded together. But they conformed to the conditions laid down in the doctrine of liberty, and no one thought of interfering with them.' He then refers to Wilkes's 'Essay on Women' and asks: 'Does Mr Stephen hold that Wilkes was justifiably punished for this improperly imputed crime? i.e. for composing an obscene libel which he published only to his private friends in his own house.' I reply that I see no objection whatever to the punishment either of the Franciscans of Medmenham or of Wilkes, except the practical objections pointed out....The only reason why such acts should go unpunished is, that no police or other public authority can be trusted with the power to intrude into private society, and to pry into private papers. It is like the case of the rule of evidence which protects from disclosure communications made during marriage between husbands and wives. The evil is that justice is sometimes defeated, the good that the confidence of married life is to some extent protected, and the good is held (I think rightly) to overbalance the harm."

[20] In the matter of health, Mr. Mill professed the same opinion. See his *Auguste Comte and Positivism*. (Morley's note.)

Liberty rests. To some persons that analysis as performed by Mr. Mill seems metaphysical and arbitrary. To distinguish the self-regarding from the other parts of conduct strikes them not only as unscientific, but as morally and socially mischievous. They insist that there is a social as well as a personal element in every human act, though in very different proportions, while there is no gain, they contend, and there may be much harm, in trying to mark off actions in which the personal element decisively preponderates, from actions of another sort. Mr. Mill did so distinguish actions, nor was his distinction either metaphysical or arbitrary in its source. As a matter of observation, and for the practical purposes of morality, there are kinds of action whose consequences do not go beyond the doer of them. No doubt, you may say that by engaging in these kinds in any given moment, the doer is neglecting the actions in which the social element preponderates, and therefore even acts that seem purely self-regarding have indirect and negative consequences to the rest of the world. But to allow considerations of this sort to prevent us from using a common-sense classification of acts by the proportion of personal element in them, is as unreasonable as if we allowed the doctrine of the conservation of physical force, or the evolution of one mode of force into another, to prevent us from classifying the affections of matter independently as light, heat, motion, and the rest. The division between self-regarding acts and others, then, rests on observation of their actual consequences. And why was Mr. Mill so anxious to erect self-regarding acts into a distant and important class, so important as to be carefully and diligently secured by a special principle of liberty? Because observation of the recorded experience of mankind teaches us that the recognition of this independent provision is essential to the richest expansion of human faculty. To narrow or to repudiate such a province, and to insist exclusively on the social bearing of each part of conduct, is to limit the play of motives, and to thwart the doctrine—which Mr. Stephen at any rate is not likely to disown— that "mankind obtain a greater sum of happiness when each pursues his own, under the rules and conditions required by the rest, than when each makes the good of the rest his only object." To narrow or to repudiate such a province is to tighten the power of the majority over the minority, and to augment the authority of whatever sacerdotal or legislative body may represent the majority. Whether the lawmakers are laymen in parliament, or priests of humanity exercising the spiritual power, it matters not. Mr. Stephen and Comte rest their respective aspirations on a common principle—the assertion of the social element in every part of conduct. If Comte had lived to read the essay on Liberty he would have attacked it on the same side, by denying the possibility of saying of any part of conduct that it is self-regarding. Only he would have denied it boldly, while Mr. Stephen denies it in a timorous manner—not unnatural, perhaps, in one who holds that self is the centre of all things, and that we have no motives that are not self-regarding.

7. We may now notice one or two of Mr. Stephen's *obiter dicta*.[21] (*a*) "No rational man can doubt that Christianity, taken as a whole and speaking broadly, has been a blessing to men." Personally I am of Mr. Stephen's opinion that Christianity has been a blessing to men, but I should think twice before feeling myself entitled on the strength of this conviction to deny the title of "rational man" to such persons as the learned and laborious Gibbon, the shrewd, versatile, humane Voltaire, the scientific D'Alembert, the philosophic Condorcet.[22] But would these eminent men have doubted what Mr. Stephen says no rational man can doubt, if they had seen the Revolution? Condorcet, at any rate, saw the Revolution, and it did not shake his conviction, and men like James Mill and Mr. Grote came after the Revolution, and both of them doubted, or went beyond doubting, the beneficence of Christianity. Mr. Stephen makes too much play with his rational man, and reasonable people. The phrase does not really come to much more than the majority of the males of a generation, engaged in the pleasing exercise of "that hidebound humour which they call their judgment." (*b*) "There are innumerable propositions on which a man may have a rational assurance that he is right, whether others are or are not at liberty to contradict him. Every proposition of which we are assured by our own senses falls under this head." Were not men assured by their own senses that the earth is a plain, and that the sun revolves round the earth?[23] It may be said that before Copernicus they had a rational assurance that they were right in this. The belief was not correct, but it was a rational assurance. Precisely; and people would have lived to this day with their erroneous rational assurance uncorrected, unless Copernicus had been at liberty to contradict them.[24] (*c*) "The cry for liberty in short is a general condemnation of the past." Not condemnation at all, in any accurate or serious sense. In buying a new coat I do not condemn the old one; on the

---

[21] [*obiter dicta*] incidental remarks.

[22] Edward Gibbon (1737–94), English historian; Voltaire, pen name of Francois Marie Arouet (1694–1778), French satirist and historian; Jean le Rond d'Alembert (1717–83), French mathematician and philosopher; Marie Jean Antoine Condorcet (1743–94), French mathematician, philosopher, politician.

[23] Rejoinder by Stephen: "No; men were not assured of any such thing. They were assured by their senses of the appearance of the sun in the morning in the East, at noon in the South, and in the evening in the West, and they are still assured of the same fact by the same means. Whether that appearance is to be accounted for by the motion of the sun or the motion of the earth was a question on which their senses could tell them nothing."

[24] Rejoinder by Stephen: "Do I say they would not? or that Copernicus's liberty was bad? Not at all. I say only that persecution does not of necessity involve a claim to infallibility, which Mr Mill asserts. Mr Morley never distinguishes between the denial of a proposition and the denial of an argument in its favour."

contrary, I look to it with gratitude for helpful service, though it is now worn out or has become too scanty for me. We do not believe that the principle of all things is water, or that number is the principle of matter; but the rejection of such notions is not equivalent to a condemnation of Thales and Pythagoras.[25] On the contrary, we are thoroughly appreciative of the services rendered by them and their now worn-out speculations in first setting the human intelligence to work in a certain direction. The catholic church has contributed immensely to the progress of civilisation; to believe that it has now become retrogressive and obscurantist is not to condemn its past, but its present. Many of the forces of the past are now spent, but to hold this is a very different thing from saying that they were never forces, or that as forces they did no good, and a very different thing from condemning them—unless Mr. Stephen insists on using condemnation in the same arbitrary and unprecedented senses which he assigns to coercion. Mr. Stephen lacks historical perspective; he does not practise the historic method; we see no flexibility in his premises or his conclusions, nor any reference of them to specific social stages. He is one of those absolute thinkers who bring to the problems of society the methods of geometry. The cry for liberty, he says, "has shattered to pieces most of the old forms in which discipline was a recognised and admitted good"—as if this were really the one cause, and as if the old forms had not been previously disorganized by internal decrepitude, the result of their association with one or two great groups of ideas which had been slowly robbed of their vitality by a large number of various forces. (*d*) "If Mr. Mill's view of liberty had always been adopted and acted on to its full extent—if it had been the view of the first Christians or of the first Mahommedans—every one can see that there would have been no such thing as organized Christianity or Mahommedanism in the world". To this one might reply by asking how we know that there might not have been something far better in their stead. We know what we get by effective intolerance, but we cannot ever know what possible benefactions we lose by it. (*e*) "Concede the first principle, that unfeigned belief in the Roman Catholic creed is indispensably necessary to salvation, or the first principle, that the whole Roman Catholic system is a pernicious falsehood and fraud, and it will be found impossible to stop short of the practical conclusions of the Inquisition and the Terror. Every real argument against their practical conclusions is an argument to show either that we cannot be sure as to the conditions of salvation, or that the Roman Catholic religion has redeeming points about it." Unless we agree to limit the meaning of "real" arguments to such as

[25] Thales (640?–546? BCE), Greek philosopher and geometrician; Pythagoras, Greek philosopher of the sixth century BCE.

would convince the author of these assertions, such a statement is wholly inadequate. You may belief that the Roman Catholic religion is a pernicious falsehood and fraud, and that it has no redeeming point about it, and still stop short of the Terror, and not only of the Terror but of any coercive interference whatever, in consequence of this consideration, namely that falsehoods and frauds in religion are not to be extirpated by massacre or any penalties of that kind. Why is not that a real argument?

Nor is this the only possible restraining consideration. I may be convinced that I could stamp out the given form of pernicious belief by persecution, but yet may be of opinion that for various reasons—such as the effect of persecution on the character of the persecutor, the colour and bias given to my own true creed by associating it with cruelty to a false one, and so forth—for these reasons the evils incident to violent repression would counterbalance the evils incident to the tolerance of a faith without a single redeeming point. Why is not that also a real argument? Mr. Stephen asks any one who doubts his position to try to frame an argument which could have been addressed with any chance of success to Philip II[26] against the persecution of the Protestants, or to Robespierre against the persecution of Catholicism. Well, the two arguments I have just offered might well have been addressed alike to Philip II and to Robespierre. The fact that they would have had no chance of success, which I admit, is just what explains the abhorrence with which the world regards their names. They are arguments resting on a balance of expediencies, as shown through the experience of mankind. But Robespierre was proof against such arguments. He believed with Rousseau and Mr. Stephen in the duty of putting down vice and error coercively. He shared Mr. Stephen's enthusiasm "for a powerful and energetic minority, sufficiently vigorous to impose their will on their neighbours, having made up their minds as to what is true," and so forth. Well, according to the doctrine of liberty, this energetic way of violently imposing your will on other people, by guillotine or act of parliament, is as futile as it is hateful, and not only a crime but a mistake. Like the boisterous paeans of literary men in honour of coercive energy, eagerness to resort to drastic remedies is the outcome of mere unscientific impatience.

EDITOR

[26] Philip II (1527–98), King of Spain from 1556 to 1598.

8. *Revue Des Deux Mondes* 22 (1859) 322–52. By Charles de Rémusat. Translated by Rebecca Frieda Alexander.

[Charles de Rémusat was a leading Orleanist in mid-nineteenth century France. Although he was exiled, along with Victor Hugo, by Louis-Napoleon Bonaparte after the *coup d'état* of 2 December 1851, he was politically to the right of Mill. This excerpt is from a lengthy review essay on the general subject of "Liberty" which includes discussion of *La Liberté*, by Jules Simon, and Mill's *On Liberty*.]

On Civil and Political Liberty

It is remarkable that, while a distinguished philosopher in our midst deals with liberty, a philosopher held in high esteem by his fellow citizens in England approaches the same subject. *On Liberty* is the title of the work published by Mr. Stuart Mill. Thus, whether it is absent or present, liberty is a cherished object of study and reflection for philosophy.

Mr. Mill's works are not well-known to us, but they have placed him in the top ranks in his country. He has great authority and has earned the respect even of those who do not submit to his views. Those who disagree with him are often counted among his admirers, if we judge from our own experience; for he is a vigorous and original spirit, endowed with a powerful talent for exposition and discussion. Originally, he was an economist, but he is one of those for whom political economy is linked to philosophy, and his *System of Logic* is a work one cannot neglect, even if it occupies itself little with the means of finding, proving, and establishing the truth.... His reason, superior to his principles, and his cleverness, equal to his reason, make him a formidable adversary and critic of those very schools which believe themselves best equipped to dispute his ideas. One can separate oneself from his ideas, but one must contend with him. One cannot read him without experiencing a lively, combative interest for the sort of struggle which is present in all his works, between the force of his spirit and what we must call the weakness of his fundamental doctrines. The often happy, always meritorious effort to which he gives himself in order to elevate these doctrines, to bolster them sometimes by solid reasoning, sometimes by ingenious paralogisms and by profound and just views [but also] theories one could hardly call profound and just, and the clever artifice of dialectic he succeeds in employing to discard or mitigate the unhappy consequences that he himself wants no more than his adversaries do; finally, a certain sincere sophistication and good intention which has the virtue of giving rise to the true from the false, and good from evil, certainly make Mr. Mill one of the most instructive and most engaging among those who, in our century, work to base politics on philosophy.

The question which inspired his latest work is that of knowing the limits of power which society must exercise over its members. This question is one of those which, for the past ten years, has most justly preoccupied serious thinkers, and it is one of the few for which the answer is most difficult. Mr. Mill did not shy away from a grave difficulty which had already escaped the most able masters of the liberal school: namely, that in seeking political liberty, one could not be certain of preserving individual liberty, if one believed that, to assure the rights of men, it sufficed to abolish ancient forms of despotism, and to provide through legislation and government a fair representation of opinion and national will. One can, in effect, arrive at the idea—and the French Revolution has furnished the proof all too well—that because one has given to all-powerfulness a popular origin, one opens up for a tyranny of one or many—what am I saying?—for the tyranny of the majority a vaster, easier field. According to the principle that one must come to the aid of the weakest, Mr. Mill has mainly concerned himself with the cause of the individual. He has remarked that, with personal liberty, freedom of thought and originality of spirit were in danger of perishing under the oppressive leveler of public opinion become sovereign. He believed he was seeing, under the influence of growing democracy in his country, the decline of energy of character and of the superiority of the talented; and it is in the fear of forefeiting humanity by leveling that he has undertaken the revision of the notion of liberty in favor of the individual, not only against power, but against society; not only against law but against opinion. This thought, honorable in principle, is not without justice in its application, and it is true that, even from the side of those who believe themselves most distant from doctrines of servitude, certain ideas arise which encourage nothing so much as the subjection of the personality to the community. It is so much more fortunate that Mr. Mill declares his antagonism to these insidious and baneful ideas, and that he joins the advanced ranks of the party which is called progressive, so that he never shows himself insensitive to the complaints of democracy, which he has even attempted, in his latest essays on political economy, to make a part of certain claims of socialism. Finally, Mr. Mill is one of a few thinkers in England who have appeared to defer to the doctrines of Mr. Auguste Comte—that is to say, to the doctrines which place the emancipation of humankind in the substitution of the polytechnic school for the clergy or aristocracy of the Middle Ages, and which, as a consequence, promise us not liberty so much as a change of despotism. Following these doctrines, humanity will fight only *for the choice of tyrants*. Mr. Mill is far from these enormities. Honorably, he protests against the consequences which have been imputed to some of his ideas, and rises up with the greatest force precisely against the excesses of the doctrine [i.e., democracy] which he has most often been accused of encouraging.

In this connection, we cannot but approve of the spirit in which his work is conceived, and one will note how much this spirit is in accord with that which inspired the work of Mr. Simon. The two writers are attached to one another in claiming, in the general name of liberty, the liberty of the individual, and this concurring of intentions and efforts of two philosophers so different in origin about the same doctrine is certainly striking proof of the importance of the purpose to which they are dedicated, and the gravity of the danger they wish to avert.

But while Mr. Simon is a student of Plato, Mr. Mill is a primitive disciple of Bentham. While his spirit opens itself to a crowd of considerations and ideas which Bentham kept far away from, and while he takes account of almost all of that which Bentham made strictly abstraction, he does not at all renounce the principle of his master, and he does not flee from the consequences of this principle. Thus, in a work destined to give prevalence in an absolute manner to a speculative idea about the prejudices, practices, and norms of society…he again declares himself a devoted partisan of the moral system of utility. "I regard utility," says he, "as the ultimate appeal on all ethical questions; but it must be utility in the largest sense, grounded on the permanent interests of man as a progressive being." It is by virtue of this idea, convinced by history that the greatest progress of humanity was the victory of liberty of the spirit over vulgar prejudice, that every new truth encounters as its main obstacles the routine and the commonplace, that he has concluded that, in the interest of humanity and full freedom of thought, one must maintain and be dedicated to this liberty in science, in religion, in politics, even in morals…. Paradox, peculiarity, even eccentricity, seem to him as respectable as the extreme consequences and sometimes legitimate forms of liberty of thought, and it is not until the moment where the use of this faculty deals a direct blow to the rights of others, when it hurts the liberty of a third party, that the intervention of society…is permitted because it is only then that such intervention has more certain advantages than possible inconveniences. We believe that, in application, this rule will with difficulty be observable, so exclusively is it laid down, and we adhere to several objections which the author of a remarkable article in the *National Review* addresses to Mr. Mill; but the rule is so often true, it is so evident that, in the greatest number of cases, the right of the third party is the limit of the right of the individual, and the claim of community intervention, ultimately the opposing doctrine, has covered the world with so many abuses of power that they are far from having totally disappeared, that we cannot quibble too much with Mr. Mill about the applications of his principle. We declare ourselves with him, in almost all the cases he sets forth, for the individual against power, that is to say, for individualism against socialism; but we will not know how to keep ourselves from saying that Mr. Simon could teach Mill how pure utility would be a fragile foundation on which to build the inviolability of absolute liberty for individual intelligence. It is in effect impossible to maintain that there will never be a case in which the eventual inconveniences of political or legal action by society will be much less great, less real, less certain, than the dangers of unlimited liberty of the thinking individual. The delay brought by a censure or prohibition to an unknown discovery which might not have taken place sometimes, even often, enters into the balance with the damage brought indirectly but effectively to society, that is to say, to all third parties, by the personal opinions or actions of one who seems, in going astray, not to compromise with anyone but himself. And in citing the most odious and least plausible of oppressions, one would not be able to affirm that liberty of thought in religious matters has never led to more evils and iniquities in a previously peaceful society than when unity is forcibly maintained by oppressive custom, or even by the unjust and easy domination of the state over conscience. From the point of view of utility, one cannot generalize about anything in this regard. If, notwithstanding these dangers, liberty of conscience must be respected, it is very simply because it is respectable, and not because it is useful; it is because it is sacred, and utility has no part in the sacred. I cannot therefore, despite the forceful argument used by Mr. Mill in his work, deny myself recognition of the notion of liberty that emerges more complete, stronger, purer, from the book of Mr. Simon. Like him, I like to think that in establishing liberty, a service has not been rendered, but a debt paid....

9. *My Past and Thoughts: The Memoirs of Alexander Herzen* (New York: Knopf, 1968) III, 1075–85. By Alexander Herzen.

[Alexander Herzen (1812–70) was a Russian revolutionary and writer. He left Russia in 1847, living first in Paris, then in England.]

John Stuart Mill and his Book on Liberty

B UT now there appears a book that goes far beyond anything I have said.... The book that I am speaking of was not written by Proudhon, nor even by Pierre Leroux[1] nor by any other angry socialist exile:—not at all: it was written by one of the most celebrated political economists, recently a member of the India Board, to whom Lord Stanley[2] three months ago offered a place in the government. This man enjoys enormous, well merited authority; in England the Tories read him with reluctance and the Whigs with anger; on the Continent he is read by the few people (specialists excepted) who read anything at all except newspapers and pamphlets.

The man is John Stuart Mill.

A month ago he published a strange book in defence of *liberty of thought, speech and the person*; I say "strange" for is it not strange that, where Milton wrote two centuries ago of the same thing, it should be necessary for a voice once more to be raised "on Liberty"? But men like Mill, you know, cannot write out of satisfaction: his whole book is imbued with a profound sadness, not fretful but virile, censorious, Tacitean. He has spoken up because evil has become worse. Milton defended freedom of speech against the attacks of authority, against violence, and all that was noble and vigorous was on his side. Mill's enemy is quite different: he is standing up for liberty not against an educated government but against *society*, against custom, against the deadening force of indifference, petty intolerance, against "mediocrity."

...This man, full of energy, long versed in affairs of state and theories deeply thought out, accustomed to regard the world calmly, like an Englishman and a thinker—this man at last could bear it no longer and, exposing himself to the wrath of the registrars of civilisation who live on the Neva and the bookmen with a Western education by the Moscow river, cried: "We are drowning!"

He was horrified by the constant deterioration of personalities, taste and style, by the inanity of men's interests and their absence of vigour; he looks closely, and sees clearly that everything is becoming shallow, commonplace,

---

[1] Pierre Joseph Proudhon (1809–65), French utopian socialist; Pierre Leroux (1798–1871), French philosopher, publicist, political figure.

[2] Edward Stanley (1799–1869), 14th Earl of Derby, British statesman.

shoddy, trite, more "respectable," perhaps, but more banal. He sees in England (what Tocqueville observed in France) that standard, indistinguishable types are being evolved and, gravely shaking his head, he says to his contemporaries: "Stop! Think again! Do you know where you are going? Look: *your soul is ebbing away.*"

But why does he try to wake the sleepers? What path, what way out has he devised for them? Like John the Baptist of old he threatens them with what is coming and summons them to repentance; people will hardly be got moving a second time with this renunciatory lever. Mill cries shame on his contemporaries as Tacitus[3] cried shame on his: he will not halt them by this means any more than Tacitus did. A few sad reproaches will not stem *the ebbing of the soul,* nor perhaps will any dam in the world. "Men of another stamp," he says, "*made England what it has been, and only men of another stamp can prevent its decline.*" But this deterioration of individuality, this want of temper, are only pathological facts, and admitting them is a very important step towards the way out; but it is not the way out. Mill upbraids the sick man and points to his sound ancestors: an odd sort of treatment, and hardly a magnanimous one.

Come: are we now to begin to reproach the lizard with the antediluvian ichthyosaurus? Is it the fault of one that it is little and the other was big? Mill, frightened by the moral worthlessness, the spiritual mediocrity of his environment, cried out passionately and sorrowfully, like the champions in our old tales: "Is there a man alive in the field?"

Wherefore did he summon him? To tell him that he was a degenerate descendant of mighty forebears, and consequently ought to try to make himself like them.

For what?—Silence.

Robert Owen[4], too, was calling upon people for seventy years running, and equally to no purpose; but he was summoning them *for something.* Whether this *something* was Utopia, fantasy or the truth is not our business now; what is important to us is that his summons had an object; but Mill, smothering his contemporaries in the grim, Rembrandtesque shadows of the time of Cromwell and the Puritans, wants shopkeepers who are everlastingly giving short weight and short measure to turn from some poetic necessity, by some spiritual gymnastics, into—heroes!...

Instead of suggesting any way out Mill suddenly observes: "In the development of peoples there is a limit, it seems, after which the peoples stand still, and *becomes a China.*"

---

[3] Publius Cornelius Tacitus, Roman historian and orator of the late first and early second centuries.
[4] Robert Owen (1771–1858), British industrialist and reformer who, with his son Robert Dale, established the community of New Harmony, Indiana, in 1825.

When does this happen?

It happens, he replies, when individualities begin to be effaced, to disappear among the masses; when everything is subjected to received customs, when the conception of good and evil is confused with the conception of conformity or non-conformity with what is accepted. The oppression of custom halts development, which properly consists in aspiration towards *what is better,* away from what is customary. The whole of history is made up of this struggle and, if the greater part of humanity has no history, this is because its life is utterly subjected to custom.

Now let us see how our author regards the present state of the educated world. He says that, in spite of the intellectual excellence of our times, everything is moving towards *mediocrity,* that faces are being lost in the crowd. This "conglomerated mediocrity" hates everything that is sharply defined, original, outstanding: it imposes a common level upon everyone. And, just as in an average section of people there is not much intelligence and not many desires, so the miscellaneous mediocrity, like a viscous bog, submerges, on the one hand, everything that desires to extricate itself and, on the other, forestalls the disorderliness of eccentric individuals by educating new generations in the same flaccid mediocrity. The moral basis of behaviour consists principally in living as other people do: "Woe to the man, and especially to the woman, who thinks of doing *what nobody does;* but woe also to those who do not do *what every one does."* For this sort of morality no intelligence nor any particular will-power is required: people occupy themselves with their own *affairs,* and now and again, by way of diversion, with some "philanthropic hobby," and they remain respectable but commonplace.

To this mean belong power and authority; the very government is powerful in proportion as it serves as the organ of the dominant mean and understands its instinct.

What sort of thing is this sovereign mean? "In America all whites belong to it; in England the ruling stratum is composed of the *middle class."*

Mill finds one difference between the lifeless inertia of oriental peoples and the modern *petit bourgeois* state; and in this, I think, is the bitterest drop in the whole goblet of wormwood that he offers. Instead of a sluggish, Asiatic quiescence, modern Europeans, he says, live in vain unrest, in senseless changes: "In getting rid of singularities we do not get rid of changes, so long as they are performed each time by *everyone.* We have cast away our fathers' individual, personal way of dressing, and are ready to change the cut of our clothes two or three times a year, but only so long as everybody changes it; and this is done not with an eye to beauty or convenience but for the sake of change itself."

If individuals cannot get free of this clogging slough, this befouling bog, then "Europe, despite its noble antecedents and its Christianity, *will become a China.*"

So we have come back and are facing the same question. On what principle are we to wake the sleeper? In the name of what shall the flabby personality, magnetised by trifles, be inspired, be made discontented with its present life of railways, telegraphs, newspapers and cheap goods?

Individuals do not step out of the ranks because there is not sufficient occasion. For whom, for what, or against whom are they to come forward? The absence of energetic men of action is not a cause but a consequence....

The world of which Mill speaks has not arrived at this state of complete repose. After all its revolutions and shocks it cannot precipitate its lees: there is a mass of muck at the top, and everything is turbid: there is not the cleanness of Chinese porcelain nor the whiteness of Dutch linen. There is much in it that is immature, misshapen, even sick, and in this connection there lies before it one more step forward on its own path. It must acquire not energetic personalities or eccentric passions, but the particular morality of its situation. For the Englishman to stop giving false weight, for the Frenchman to refuse to give assistance to every police-force, it is not only "respectability" that is required, but a stable mode of living.

Then, in Mill's words, England can turn into a China (an improved one, of course), retaining all her trade and all her freedom and perfecting her legislation, that is, easing it in proportion to the growth of obligatory custom, which deadens the will better than any law-courts or punishments; and France at the same time can launch herself into the beautiful, martial stream-bed of Persian life, which is enlarged with everything that an educated centralisation puts in the hands of authority, rewarding herself for the loss of all the rights of man with brilliant attacks on her neighbours and shackling other peoples to the fortunes of a centralised despotism...already the features of Zouaves[5] belong more to Asia than to Europe.

Forestalling ejaculations and maledictions I hasten to say that I am not speaking here of my desires, or even of my opinions. My task is the purely logical one of trying to *eliminate the brackets* from the formula in which Mill's result is expressed; from his individuality differentials to form the historical integral.

So the question cannot be whether it is polite to prophesy for England the fate of China (and it was not I who did this, but Mill himself), or in good taste to foretell that France will be a Persia; although in all fairness I do not know, either, how it comes that China and Persia may be insulted with

---

[5] Zouaves. French infantry unit, composed of Algerian recruits, characterized by colorful oriental uniforms and precision drilling.

impunity. The really important question, that Mill does not touch upon, is this: do there exist the sources of a new vigour to renovate the old blood? Are there sprouts and sound shoots to grow up through the dwindling grass? And what this question adds up to is whether a people will let itself be used once and for all to manure the soil for a new China and a new Persia, condemned inescapably to unskilled labour, to ignorance and hunger, accepting in return that one in ten thousand, as in a lottery, for an example, encouragement and appeasement to the rest, shall grow rich and turn from eaten to eater?

The problem will be solved by events: it cannot be solved theoretically. If the people is overcome, the new China and new Persia are inevitable. But if the people overcomes, what is unavoidable is a *social revolution....*

If the people in England is routed, as it was in Germany at the time of the Peasants' Wars and in France during the July days, then the China foretold by John Stuart Mill is not far off. The transition to it will take place imperceptibly; not a single right, as we have said, will be lost, not one freedom will be diminished: all that will be diminished is *the ability to make use of these rights and this freedom.*

10. Constantine N. Leontyev, "The Average European as an Ideal and Instrument of Universal Destruction." From *Russian Philosophy*, II, eds. James H. Edie, James P. Scanlan, and Mary B. Zeldin. Trans. William Shaeffer and George L. Kline. Chicago: Quadrangle Books, 1965.

[Constantine N. Leontyev (1831–91) was a Russian physician, journalist, writer, and diplomat. He wrote this essay between 1872 and 1874.]

The Average European as an Ideal and Instrument of Universal Destruction

JOHN STUART MILL…bases his hopes on the *peculiarity* and *diversity* of human nature, correctly supposing that the diversity and depth of human nature renders creations of the mind as well as human actions profound and powerful. His essay, "On Liberty," was written with precisely this end in view; it should not be called "On Liberty," but rather "On Diversity."

Mill called his work "On Liberty" either out of caution, supposing that this simpler and more ordinary title would be more appealing to routine minds, or else he was mistaken in considering complete *political* and complete freedom in *everyday life* a necessary condition for the diversified development of human nature. He identifies these freedoms with the removal of all possible restraints on the part of society and the state. Being an Englishman, he has no fear of the state; but he attacks the despotism of public opinion and the tendency of contemporary society to "make all men the same."

"Those whose opinions go by the name of public opinion," Mill says, "are not always the same sort of public: in America they are the whole *white* population; in England, chiefly the middle class. But they are always a mass, that is to say, collective mediocrity" (Leontyev's italics).

Is it possible for thinkers to be original and heterogeneous in their thought where the [sociopolitical] "ground" is already homogeneous and well established? Mill proved by his own example that it is not possible, for, while seeming to be extremely original as the negator of that part of progress which displeased him, namely the notion of an *intermingling simplification* of nations, classes, and individuals, he himself becomes very ordinary when he tries to offer something positive in the way of ideals. In his essay "Representative Government" he is a very ordinary constitutionalist.…He cannot bear the *idea* of autocracy; like Buckle, he defames the great age of Louis XIV. He has no patience with the democratic crudeness of younger nations such as America and Greece, whose representatives have not yet been choked by the public opinion of average gentlemen and therefore sometimes fight in the halls of congress. In other words, Mill accepts the most ordinary and proper *juste-milieu*.[1]

[1] [*juste-milieu*] just (or golden) mean.

11. *Southern Review* V (1869), 249–74.

[Essay review of *On Liberty* and other works. The *Southern Review* was an American journal published in Baltimore and edited by A. T. Bledsoe, an advocate of the slave system. Bledsoe seems to have written most of the articles in the journal.]

What is Liberty?

WE glorify the State, and we honor its laws. "The struggle between Liberty and Authority," says Mr. Mill, "is the most conspicuous feature in the portions of history with which we are earliest familiar, particularly that of Greece, Rome, and England." Now this struggle, this antagonism between Liberty and Order, is purely imaginary. Liberty and Order, like twin stars, lend mutual support to each other....But despotism is not Order, any more than license is Liberty....

Political despotism itself is desirable, when, in any case, it serves to promote the moral freedom of man, or the great object for which he exists upon earth. This is, indeed, conceded by the blindest devotees of Freedom: not even excepting Mr. Mill himself.[1] Accordingly, in his work *On Representative Government*, Mr. Mill says: "A people in a state of savage independence...is incapable of making any progress in civilization *until it has learnt to obey.*...A constitution in any degree popular,...would fail to enforce the first lesson which pupils, in this stage of their progress, require, [that is, the lesson of obedience]. Accordingly, the civilization of such tribes, when not the result of juxtaposition with others already civilized, is almost always the work of an *absolute ruler*, deriving his power either from religion or military prowess; very often from foreign arms." Thus, in the case of savage tribes, political despotism, the most absolute, is deemed indispensable to render them capable of the very first step in civilization, or social progress.

Nay, on the same page of the same work, personal servitude itself is recommended as the means of promoting the "freedom" of such tribes. "Uncivilized races," says he, "and the bravest and most energetic still more than the rest, are averse to continuous labor of an unexciting kind. Yet all real civilization is at this price; without such labor, neither can the mind be disciplined into the habits required by civilized society, nor the material world prepared to receive it. There needs a rare concurrence of circumstances,

---

[1] The writer here alludes not only to the passage he goes on to cite but also to the passage in the introductory chapter of *On Liberty* in which Mill says that "Despotism is a legitimate mode of government in dealing with barbarians, provided the end be their improvement, and the means justified by actually effecting that end."

and for that reason often a vast length of time, to reconcile such a people to industry, unless they are for a while compelled to it. *Hence even personal slavery*, by giving a commencement to industrial life, and enforcing it as the exclusive occupation of the most numerous portion of the community, may accelerate the transition to a *better freedom* than that of fighting and rapine." If, indeed, Mr. Mill had only known how deep, and solid, and permanent, is the foundation of his own apology for "personal slavery" in the nature of savage tribes, he could scarcely have been so fierce an advocate of the violent emancipation of the blacks of this country, or of the terrible crusade preached by the abolitionists for that purpose. Be this as it may, we have, at least, his own explicit admission, that slavery is, in certain cases, one of the means or methods of "freedom" itself....

Select Bibliography

1. About *On Liberty*

Friedman, Richard B. "A New Exploration of Mill's Essay *On Liberty.*" *Political Studies* 14 (1966), 281–304.

Frye, Northrop. "The Problem of Spiritual Authority in the Nineteenth Century." *Literary Views: Critical and Historical Essays.* ed., C.C. Camden. Chicago: University of Chicago Press, 1964. Reprinted in *Backgrounds to Victorian Literature.* ed., Richard A. Levine. San Francisco: Chandler, 1967, 120–36.

Gray, J. and G.W. Smith, eds., *On Liberty in Focus.* London: Routledge, 1991.

Gray, John. *Mill on Liberty: A Defence.* London: Routledge and Kegan Paul, 1983.

Himmelfarb, Gertrude. *On Liberty and Liberalism: The Case of John Stuart Mill.* New York: Knopf, 1974.

Pyle, Andrew, ed., *Liberty: Contemporary Responses to John Stuart Mill.* Bristol: Thoemmes Press, 1994.

Rees, J.C. *Mill and His Early Critics.* Leicester: University College, 1956.

Ryan, Alan, ed., *Mill: Texts, Commentaries.* New York: Norton, 1997.

Spitz, David, ed., *On Liberty.* New York: Norton, 1975.

Stephen, James Fitzjames. *Liberty, Equality, Fraternity.* ed., R.J. White. Cambridge: Cambridge University Press, 1967.

Ten, C.L. *Mill on Liberty.* Oxford: Clarendon, 1980.

Wishy, Bernard, ed., *Prefaces to Liberty: Selected Writings of John Stuart Mill.* Boston: Beacon Press, 1959.

Wollheim, Richard. "John Stuart Mill and the Limits of State Action." *Social Research* 40 (1973), 1–30.

2. General Studies of Mill's Life and Thought

Alexander, Edward. *Matthew Arnold and John Stuart Mill.* New York and London: Columbia University Press and Routledge & Kegan Paul, 1965.

Anschutz, R.P. *The Philosophy of J. S. Mill.* Oxford: Clarendon Press, 1953.

Bain, Alexander. *John Stuart Mill: A Criticism.* London: Longmans, Green, 1882.

Berlin, Isaiah. "John Stuart Mill and the Ends of Life." *Four Essays on Liberty.* London: Oxford University Press, 1969.

Britton, Karl. *John Stuart Mill.* Penguin: Baltimore and Harmondsworth, 1953.

Burrow, J.W. *Whigs and Liberals.* Oxford: Oxford University Press, 1988.

Collini, Stefan, David Winch, and John Burrow. *That Noble Science of Politics.* Cambridge: Cambridge University Press, 1983.

Cooper, Wendy, Kai Nielsen, and Steven Patten, eds., "New Essays on John Stuart Mill and Utilitarianism," *Canadian Journal of Philosophy,* supplementary volume 5, 1979.

Donner, Wendy. *The Liberal Self: John Stuart Mill's Moral and Political Philosophy.* Ithaca: Cornell University Press, 1991.

Hayek, F.A. *John Stuart Mill and Harriet Taylor: Their Friendship and Subsequent Marriage.* Chicago: University of Chicago Press, 1951.

Kinzer, Bruce L., Ann P. Robson, and John M. Robson. *A Moralist In and Out of Parliament: John Stuart Mill at Westminster, 1865–1868.* Toronto: University of Toronto Press, 1992.

Laine, Michael. *Bibliography of Works on John Stuart Mill.* Toronto: University of Toronto Press, 1982.

Lyons, David. *Rights, Welfare, and Mill's Moral Theory.* New York: Oxford University Press, 1994.

Morales, Maria H. *Perfect Equality: John Stuart Mill on Well-Constituted Communities.* Lanham, Maryland: Rowman & Littlefield, 1996.

Packe, Michael St. John. *The Life of John Stuart Mill.* New York: Macmillan, 1954.

Rees, J.C. "The Thesis of the Two Mills," *Political Studies* 25 (September 1977), 369–82.

Robson, John M. *The Improvement of Mankind: The Social and Political Thought of John Stuart Mill.* Toronto: University of Toronto Press, 1968.

Rose, Phyllis. *Parallel Lives: Five Victorian Marriages.* New York: Knopf, 1983.

Rossi, Alice. "Sentiment and Intellect," introduction to *Essays on Sex Equality by John Stuart Mill and Harriet Taylor.* Chicago: University of Chicago Press, 1970.

Ryan, Alan. *The Philosphy of John Stuart Mill.* New York: Humanities Press, 1988.

———. *The Philosophy of John Stuart Mill.* London: Macmillan, 1970.

Schneewind, J.B. *Mill: A Collection of Critical Essays.* Garden City: Anchor, 1969.

Sen, Amartya, and Bernard Williams. *Utilitarianism and Beyond.* Cambridge: Cambridge University Press, 1982.

Smart, Paul. *Mill and Marx: Individual Liberty and the Roads to Freedom.* New York: St. Martin's Press, 1991.

Stephen, Leslie. *The English Utilitarians.* Vol. III. London: Duckworth, 1900.

Thomas, William. *Mill.* Oxford: Oxford University Press, Past Masters series, 1985.